Y0-BUC-426

9-28-70

FELLINI

FELLINI

ANGELO SOLMI

Translated by Elizabeth Greenwood

NEW YORK
HUMANITIES PRESS

First published
in the United States of America 1968
by Humanities Press Inc.
303 Park Avenue South
New York, N.Y. 10010

Library of Congress Catalog Card No. 67-89255

Printed in Great Britain

To the Reader

The story of Federico Fellini does not necessarily confine itself to the picturesque events of his life; it reflects not only his films but also the poetic world he creates. The first part of the book, therefore, is a review of the key themes which Fellini has fused into his work. I have placed it before the biography proper and the analysis of his films, so that I should not be forced to deal with these themes in a fragmentary way and at the same time run the risk of repeating myself. If the more hasty reader is, however, tempted to omit the introductory critical essay, I would remind other readers that without it they will find it more difficult to understand, in all its complexity, the value of Fellini's work. However, I flatter myself that I have made some contribution towards the better understanding of a man who, in recent years, has carried the name of Italy into every corner of the world, and earned unreserved admiration. Since the revival of the cinema is largely due to him and to his expressive idiom, this book pays homage to his art.

Contents

PART ONE

FELLINI'S WORLD OF IDEAS

CHAPTER I

The Man Who Revitalized the Cinema

FEDERICO FELLINI is the most significant figure of the present-day cinema. Because the cinema has woven itself into our lives, to shape not only our culture but also our way of life, there is no doubt that Fellini has had—and continues to have—a decisive influence on the formation and on the development of various aspects of our social and ethical ideas.

To say, as some people do, that Fellini's work is only a part, however revealing, of contemporary Italian cinema involves the attempt to confine a problem which on the contrary slides in and out of the restrictive sphere of present-day reality. Fellini's films are distinguished by their universal quality, which places them far beyond clearly defined geographical and chronological frontiers. It is like claiming that the satirical humour of Charlie Chaplin's tragic world is peculiar to this or that current of American or European cinema rather than belonging to the whole of humanity. It is true that Fellini is not Chaplin (or rather that he is not yet a Chaplin), and yet a study of his work will reveal that he is the only artist who, in certain respects, resembles the famous creator of 'The Little Man'.

In recent years all true masters of the cinema, and they are few—among them Eisenstein, Dreyer, René Clair, besides Chaplin himself—have transcended the limitations of their medium and stand out as leaders and guides to a new way of seeing and feeling reality through the make-believe of the film. But most of them with their scientific rationalism are indifferent, if not openly opposed to Fellini's style and interests. Only with Chaplin has he found a mutual understanding and inspiration. Like Chaplin, Fellini is 'a creature of instinct, informed first by his senses and then by his reason, and with the gift of an extraordinary imagination', as one of biographers has written. As a result, he is irresistibly attracted by the events of his own life which, as we shall be able to see more clearly, colour his poetical world in the same way.

But Fellini's greatest triumph and significance as a phenomenon of our day is to have said something new and sincere in a time which is transitional not only for the cinema, but for all the arts; to have been a director and an artist in an era when drama had to choose between poetry and industry, between cultural progress or immobility and even regression. The general public does not know (and many well-informed people do not or pretend not to know), that the '50s were years of great difficulty for the world of the screen. It was a question of death or survival in the face of new influences in the world of entertainment—primarily of course television.

The cinema's dilemma was whether to become complementary to television, or a substitute for it, forced to adapt itself to ever increasing commercial demands, and to artificial and technical expedients such as large screens, considered ends in themselves. This dilemma, in a less dramatic way, not only faced the cinema, but also literature, music, theatre and painting. Those who resisted had to build up a new aesthetic, moral and intellectual autonomy, freed from the past, to affirm the right to live as artists. Above all it meant belief in their own work, abjuring an easy scepticism, in order to show that the cinema had not yet expressed all that it was capable of expressing but that it had a great future before it in which everything was possible. Fellini was one of these 'men of the resistance', who became innovators through their temperament or through necessity. Among others could be named Ingmar Bergman, Antonioni, Kurosawa, three isolated figures who, like Fellini, have exerted a wide influence. None of these, however, has the forceful, overriding personality of the director of *La strada*; their range lies within the cinema and for the cinema, although it is true to say that Antonioni and Bergman show in their latest films an indisputable tendency to throw open doors which had previously appeared to be closed.

The dangerous crisis of the 1950s may be seen in part as the gradual extinction of the vigorous forces which developed in the immediate post-war period. After the long spiritual oppression of the war all that was enthusiastic, sincere, confused, uncontrolled, good and bad in these forces exploded. It was a long carnival of experiments, which were not carried out in the peaceful laboratory of ideas, but in the open and before the public. A new reality had to be confronted and studied, with a new outlook. All that had been locked away inside man for so many years had to be expressed in the light of a vague humanity often portrayed in its most ingenuous form. Even the old idols of the cinema were overthrown under the cruel blows of 'critical revision'.

Italian neo-realism was born in this tumultuous but spontaneous atmosphere; containing as it did the seeds of an original and creative *Weltanschauung* not limited to Italy or to the cinema. Fellini himself, as we shall see, made an appreciable contribution to neo-realism, and for several years he remained one of its recognized and most closely watched leaders. But in the very origins of neo-realism lay the seeds of its decadence and decay. That occasional note which passed unnoticed at the beginning sounded increasingly loudly and was in the end discordant with the new aspects of the external world. Neo-realism was in danger of becoming its own prisoner, of turning current events into historical facts. This fatal trap was avoided by the most intelligent and sensitive men of the cinema, above all by Fellini, who took it upon himself to renew the worn-out machinery and set it in motion again. He saved it from falling into disuse by setting it in a completely different atmosphere, not reflecting the past, but projecting the future. This kind of 'conversion', not perhaps to begin with the result of a premeditated conviction, but only intuitive, deserves separate discussion, because it holds the key to an understanding of Fellini the artist.

CHAPTER 2

Fellini and Neo-realism

LEFT-WING CRITICS usually condemn Felini as a 'traitor to neo-realism'. Greater injustice could not be done to the director of *La dolce vita.* In fact Fellini has never denied neo-realism as a human experience; more, he has completed the movement by endowing it with the poetry that it lacked and by rejecting the transient element which was its very essence, its dry documentation of a reality already surpassed by events. Certainly it is not possible to call Fellini a neo-realist, but this is primarily because classical neo-realism no longer exists and no true artist can be immersed in a non-existent current or in one which has lost its impetus. Secondly, Fellini has created a new form of expression which has superimposed itself upon neo-realism and has taken from the latter only what was worth retaining. The definition of this movement is not very important although someone has suggested, before *La dolce vita*, 'poetical magic', or 'lyrical-fantastic realism', or again 'a film-chronicle' in the sense of a documentary of high journalistic quality (as people said about *La dolce vita*) or even naturalism of a 'Kierkegaardian type', as Aristarco maintains it to be. It is easy to find a name which is only a convenient label for the occasion but the essential unity of Fellini's work enables us to talk of 'Fellinian realism', because the necessarily vague connotation of these terms expresses the two extremes of the problem which is continually dominated by the director's unmistakable personality.

It is interesting to note how Fellini judges himself in relation to neo-realism. Fellini allowed Tullio Kezich to interview him for *Settimo giorno* in February, 1959 and the article has also been printed in Kezich's excellent book on *La dolce vita*. (Capelli edition.) We shall make frequent mention of it because it is one of the most interesting writings on the director. Fellini, then in the process of making his most mature film, was asked: 'Why has neo-realism lost some of its impact?' and he replied, 'Because since the war Italian cinema has been less and less able to mirror everyday life. It is necessary to become a poet, to cope with its flatness. One must be imaginative and have something to say; documentation is no longer enough. Furthermore, the cultural hinterland of neo-realism has empty spaces, and improvisation must fill them out.' 'Unintelligent, acid criticism' is also to be blamed for all this (Fellini never misses the chance to flail left-wing critics, when he can do so), because 'only the abominable ignorance of our film world could give birth to that absurdity called the neo-realist aesthetic'.

When Fellini talks about improvisation, as he does here, he is not referring to a technical method of working on the set (because as we shall see later he is one of the greatest improvisors), but to a way of conceiving new ideas, of building up and systematizing them according to an organic plan which takes human as well as stylistic factors into account.

In reply to another question: 'Can one still speak of a neo-realistic current in the Italian cinema?' Fellini said, 'The attitude of those who mourn the passing of neo-realism is anti-historical. Neo-realism, as a state of mind, may be considered as a formative experience. Non-conformism, a concern for truth, directness and sincerity are commendable feelings. But let us not put them into the hands of those who are slaves to an aesthetic principle.'

The director expressed himself even more critically in an interview in *Bianco e Nero* in July 1958, at the time when *La dolce vita* was merely in embryonic form, and the echo of *Le notti di Cabiria* could still be heard. 'I emphatically repudiate the cinema which shelters old myths and old formulas with the excuse that neo-realism has exhausted itself. We must go *beyond* neo-realism, but we cannot be ignorant of it. The neo-realistic vision is positive, deeply human and based upon logic and precision. The cinema can and must stand on its own feet: directors who fish around in literature are like tailors, stitching garments of film over novels which they would otherwise never have read. They are not true directors.' He concluded by reaffirming his idea that with regard to the new currents that were attempting to overtake neo-realism, 'Italian criticism has always arrived last. . . .'

These ideas, with the hint of internal contradiction typical of his character, have been the unshakeable foundations of Fellini's creative concepts for a long time: and the open refutation of every compromise and literary contamination which Fellini loathes, is revealing.

Significantly enough it is a literary man (who is also connected with the cinema), Pier Paolo Pasolini, who has attempted to interpret the link between Fellini and neo-realism. In a chapter of Lino del Fra's book on the film *Le notti di Cabiria*, a text to which we shall also have to refer, Pasolini takes as his starting-point the observation that in the preceding film, *La strada*, a 'real' and a stylized reality, poetry and expediency, exist side by side. He maintains that Fellini is not a conscious innovator of the neo-realist vogue; his originality is purely unconscious. However, Pasolini himself admits that 'Fellini plays a wonderful role, that of preserving neo-realism with its original faults' and he concludes by calling Fellini's realism 'infantile realism', typical in times of transition.

Let us disregard all verbal excess and have our reservations about a definition which seems vague when it is applied to such a down-to-earth man as Fellini. (Pasolini justifies it by saying that 'the reality Fellini portrays is that of a mysterious world, terrifyingly hostile and overwhelmingly tender, and Fellini's man is an equally mysterious being who develops amidst that horror and that tenderness'.) There is, however, some truth in Pasolini's interpretation, for unconscious innovation is characteristic of nearly all true artists, as opposed to those who fall into the somewhat arid world of the essayist and the outside observer, patiently classifying definite cultural trends. It is not true that Fellini's unconscious has taken so firm a hold of him that he has no idea where he wants to go. As we shall see, after every film, his creative activity has been troubled by doubts and reflections which have carried him first in one direction and then thrust him back on his tracks to an acute reappraisal, not only of himself but of his original task. His instinct may guide him more than his reason, but Fellini is well aware of the changes that have gradually imprinted themselves on his work, from thence reflecting on to neo-realism.

Some idea of the director's assured grip on this problem has already been given. Let us close discussion of the matter by repeating an interview with Gidea Bachmann who published it in *Film 1961* (Feltrinelli), under the title 'I am compelled to be sincere'. In it, more calmly and less polemically, Fellini comes to the point of the argument.

When he was asked, 'Do you think that your work is derived from (or at least has been influenced by) neo-realist directors with whom you have worked?' Fellini replied, 'I was one of the first to write scripts for neo-realist films and I think that all my work is of a decidedly neo-realist type, even if some people do not consider it to be so today. For me neo-realism is a way of living without prejudice and a means of liberating oneself completely from bias, in short, a way of facing reality without preconceived ideas.'

'The camera mirroring life or photographing it as it is?' 'No, it is a question of feeling reality, but we always need an interpretation of it. Left-wing criticism is wrong when it says that the only thing to be shown in films is what happens around us. The important thing is always to know *who* is seeing reality. Things must be condensed in order to impose their essence. For me neo-realism is looking at reality fairly and squarely, but at every type of reality, not only social, but also spiritual and metaphysical reality, all that man has within himself. For me neo-realism is not contained in what is manifest, but in the way in which it is manifest. It is simply a way of looking about oneself, free of the burden of convention or prejudice.

Certain people are still convinced that neo-realism only serves to show a particular kind of reality, social reality. But then that would merely be propaganda. Someone called me a traitor to the neo-realist cause and accused me of being too much of an individual. I, on the other hand, am convinced that the films I have made so far are in the stylistic tradition of the first neo-realist films.' In conclusion Fellini let fall this decisive observation: 'Every investigation a man makes about himself, about his relations with other people and about the mystery of life, is a spiritual investigation and—in the true sense of the word—a religious one. I suppose that this is my philosophy. This is neo-realism, as far as I am concerned, in its pure and original sense; a quest for the essential self, my own and others, along all the paths of life.'

Obviously the fundamental misunderstanding in the disagreement between Fellini and what he calls left-wing, Marxist-type, criticism is unlikely to be clarified. But the fault is not entirely that of left-wing critics, who continue to describe as 'neo-realism' the state of affairs that existed in the years between 1945 and 1950, whereas Fellini intends to overcome difficulties emphasizing the elements which are certainly not alien to the neo-realism of that period, but did not constitute its essential base. The truth is that too often the real problem is hidden in a spate of words: the supporters of a now extinct brand of neo-realism are slaves to the past and to unrepeatable formulae. (And thus we have the paradox that some Marxists are hopelessly conservative in art.) In the same way Fellini is unaware that his anxiety to discover in the old form some justification for his new language leads him to take up positions that are dialectically untenable.

The dominant factor in Fellini's concern with reality lies in his preoccupation with the individual, as opposed to the collective or social reality which was the basis of the old neo-realism. He himself said (in an interview with Dominique Dalouche in 1956), 'I have been criticized for portraying exceptions in *La strada*, in the characters of Zampanò and Gelsomina. But the story of a man who discovers himself is just as important and real as the story of a strike.' This is a spiritual, not a materialistic vision of the world. The reshaping of neo-realist formulae is especially well seen here where the individual, the man, the picture of the changeable and variable reality that surrounds us, are stressed.

This was the meaning of Fellini's revolutionary attitude in a debate in *Contemporaneo*, April–May, 1955, centred on *La strada*. It was an attitude that few people then understood for they had confused it with a simple attempt to reconcile the social preoccupations of neo-realism with the director's own subjective view, whilst Fellini intended to go much further than that. He said, 'A common bond links all the various neo-realist tendencies, and it is love of man, of his life and his surroundings. Neo-realism is the "common man's" movement, that is man and his realationships outside and beyond himself. These relationships become the nucleus for a complicated change in the pattern of living, an existence which becomes *co*-existence.' And another time Fellini defined the cinema as: 'The art in which man recognizes himself in the most direct way, the mirror in front of which we must have the courage to discover our souls.'

From this point of view, we are not too far away from the Pasolini definition, quoted above. If we substitute the word 'man', individual, for the term 'creature' we get the concept of 'individualistic realism' or its equivalent of 'subjective realism'. But even this, taking everything into consideration, is pure abstraction. What now matters is to examine, rather, Fellini's general conception of life in the light of his individuality and of his exclusive interest in man. His work cannot be fully understood without this investigation and above all it would be impossible to appreciate the real antithesis between the bias of objective realism and a director who, whilst using the neo-realistic aesthetic as a point of departure, has in reality reversed its terms.

CHAPTER 3

In Search of the Man

VARIOUS PORTRAITS have been drawn of Fellini in the light of his films, which are of some importance in his biography. People have seen him as a middle-class type, enamoured with family, a catholic bigot, a fanatical Jansenist, a poet of magic, a fatalistic pessimist, a sentimentalist, a romantic, a decadent lover of the baroque and even an illusionist. There is a grain of truth in all these definitions because Fellini's character is very complex. Perhaps the 'Cagliostro of the cinema' as some call him best describes him—and Cagliostro is in fact one of his favourite characters. Certainly the most striking characteristics in his films are those of a conjurer or a tight-rope walker. But these become superficial in a study of Fellini's world in detail. As the recurring themes in his art and the basis of his approach to the cinema come to light, we soon realize that Fellini is primarily an individualist and one who is afraid of isolation.

Some have condemned him for his individuality, which they see as a fault, a limitation. This is so inherent a characteristic in Fellini that it is difficult to picture him as being otherwise or to imagine his work being created without this unmistakable trait of individuality. As a fiery individualist, he does not believe in detachment, and is compelled to see everything subjectively. This is a conscious effort and he rejects *a priori* any experience which he suspects of moral disengagement or a tendency towards objectivity on his part or on the part of a character. For example, he loathes delving into a literary text for inspiration—too elaborate a procedure—re-makes of any kind, historical or costume films, and, in general, most ideas for films offered by other people. Fellini has faith only in himself as a subject and, because his self-knowledge is supreme he makes himself the heart of his poetic inspiration in film. But is this a defect in an artist? Literary history is full of examples of unbridled individualism and many can be quoted. Did not Flaubert say: '*Madame Bovary c'est moi*'? Again, Fellini may be compared with Chaplin, for they both have, amongst other things, a love of constant self-portrayal, reflecting their own lives in their films.

Talk of autobiography irritates Fellini now: 'Critics can think of nothing else to say,' he complains. He is right if he is referring to a unilateral interpretation of his films, which does not take into account other equally important aspects of his imaginative world. But one of the greatest influences in his films is undoubtedly autobiographical, and Fellini has acknowledged this several times in the past. Moreover, he unreservedly restated this position when he said to Bachmann, 'The point of departure in a film is usually something that happened to me, and appears to have a certain relation to the experiences of others. I usually try, first of all, to express the emotions aroused in me, personally, and then look for a strand of significant truth which might be of importance to men of like mind.'

Renzi and others have argued that haunting his own life and extracting from it motifs for his films betrays the absence of solid cultural foundations: in other words, unable to find the beginnings of a story elsewhere Fellini is obliged to draw upon 'the storehouse of his memory, which is his most valuable asset and which he manages with great skill'. (Kezich.) This over-hasty conclusion is not only contradicted by many classical examples—showing paradoxically that Dante was a poet who lacked subject-matter, but proves that culture and erudition alone have never made an artist. Even if Fellini were to multiply his cultural interests an infinite number of times, he would always delve into personal experience, into his own memories for the subject of his films. The director's use of personal experience (someone has called autobiography the poetry of memory), is a further proof of his individualism. This individualism is translated into love of man for man, seen as clearly-cut entity; belonging to himself, and resembling no other. This is what Fellini is seeking, so that he has been wittily called 'The Diogenes of the cinema'. (Massimo Mida.)

All his films, except perhaps *Lo Sceicco bianco*, are constantly in this key. In *I vitelloni*, not only Moraldo, the hero, but also Riccardo, Leopoldo and the others were the objects of this love, because every one of these characters was a synthesis of Fellini and his youthful experience re-enacted. In *La strada* Gelsomina and Zampanò are two lonely beings in search of affection and ultimately in search of themselves. They are separated by their inability to communicate, but are still well-defined particles of humanity, projections of Fellini himself and his awareness of the terrible anguish of isolation.

In *Il bidone* Zampanò develops naturally into Augusto, and he restates more dramatically, by means of his individuality, the solitude of a failure, the more guilty because more conscious. Fellini has identified himself several times with both Zampanò and Augusto. In the same way, little Cabiria does not arouse his artistic curiosity because she is one of a miserable social group; he singles her out from the crowd of prostitutes to highlight her state of mind, her final, inconsolable bitterness. Finally even in *La dolce vita* where the dramas of a strange human situation seem to have become an almost universal chorus, the hero Marcello is still the subject of research, he is Moraldo brought up in the atmosphere of Rome, eager to discover himself through a great variety of human experience. It must be carefully noted that the journalist Marcello is not typical of a class or category (journalists), for this does not really interest Fellini, but once again the director participates in a series of social phenomena like those reflected faithfully in the psychology of his characters.

Fellini is not fundamentally interested in the depiction of classes or categories as such, the method followed, sometimes with success, by Marxists and other artists. Even if his films do generally satirize a group or an event, as in *I vitelloni* and in *Lo Sceicco bianco*, serious consideration will lead to the discovery that Fellini never intended to discount the individual, indeed a final analysis will show that he concerned himself only with the individual. Fellini must, therefore, be in sympathy with his characters, otherwise he would be unable to make a film. Fellini calls this attraction 'enjoying oneself making a film', 'feeling for the characters and the situations'. On 17 September, 1953, I received a long letter from Fellini which is important because it is the most telling picture of him, as yet unspoiled by the inevitable effects of fame. In it he wrote.

'. . . Now *La strada* has finally taken shape. I shall begin it at the end of October, at some risk because the capital is small and uncertain. But I must begin, come what may. I know I am lucky and that something will happen. I don't want to set myself up as a misunderstood poet or artist, but the fact is that if I do not enjoy what I am doing, then I am incapable of working. The defence of my subject or of my films is only a selfish indulgence, so that I can create ideal working conditions for myself. I have no professional sense whatever and faced with a story I did not like, I really wouldn't know where to begin with the camera. I wouldn't even be able to get up in the morning. That's how it is.'

And later, before he made *La dolce vita* he repeated with emphasis.

'I have to be galvanized into action by faith and enthusiasm otherwise, for all the money in the world, I could never pester people at all hours of the day or night in their homes, like an S.S. man, and parade the streets shouting like a clown into a megaphone.'

What is more these are not empty words: every film of Fellini's has been like a valiantly-fought battle, because he refuses to compromise, even at the cost (at least until *La dolce vita*) of setbacks and loss of money. 'I may change my producer, but I never alter the plot,' he boasts, 'I like working my own way.' Consequently he rejected astronomical offers to make *Simon Bolivar* in Brazil, and refused to make the kind of Western that Wallis wanted him to make. ('So as not to be thought mad, I had to make excuses about my health.') For the same reason he declined an offer from Hollywood in the region, it is rumoured, of several hundred thousand dollars. He is one of the surviving knights of a nearly unattainable artistic ideal, but one which it is worth pursuing to the end; this too is part of his individualistic temperament.

Fellini's individualism, his gift of introspection means that above all in his films, he speaks of and to himself by showing many aspects of reality and of *la condition humaine*. Little by little the director tends towards egocentricity, even narcissism or an exaggerated love of himself. Yet none of this, from an aesthetic point of view, has anything to do with egoism. Egocentricity, a preoccupation with the self, being the centre of one's creative world, presenting it to others as an analogical paradigm to awaken memories is an old device and is nearly always artistically fruitful. One has only to think of Horace, for example, or in more recent times, Leopardi. Of course this must not become an end in itself and it must be allied to other poetic factors. Fellini is successful because he combines it with sincerity and imagination: these are his weapons against the danger of isolation.

CHAPTER 4

Fear of Isolation

FELLINI'S INNATE sincerity is his most important gift of character and inspires his films, which are all conceived in a climate of artistic integrity. This means that Fellini is not capable of complete fabrication, but only of the distortion allowed by one of the more elementary laws of art. There is a need here for clarification; Federico's acquaintances could misunderstand his artistic honesty by the outward frankness of his relationships with other people, and they might be puzzled to know how the director reconciles two apparently contradictory attitudes. In his everyday life Fellini has proved somewhat inconsistent. Someone has said that he is nothing more than a charming liar, and another has said that he is always romancing. Countless anecdotes and examples (which we shall refer to later), some probably exaggerated, have been cited as proof of this accusation. Yet they bear witness to an undeniable paradox in his behaviour and in his words. If he is challenged with this, Fellini replies with disarming candour, 'Well, all right, I am a liar, but I am an honest one. And how can you avoid calling a liar one whose job it is to tell stories?'

The truth is that the director is consistent and true to himself, and what most interests him is this sincerity, which becomes an integral part of his films, once he is convinced he has achieved it.

Fellini has often related several versions of one event, in particular those he has used as a basis for scenes in his films. Sometimes he has amused himself by padding out real episodes with imaginary ones and at other times he has inserted true facts into fictitious happenings. More often he has integrated and modified various representations of truth, ending up by losing sight of the real nucleus in the fictional superstructure. In all these cases, Fellini is obeying an obscure artistic impulse to distort reality; making use of that faculty continuously, even before the actual period of creation begins.

In this way, Fellini has combined hyperbole with paradox which, through rationalizing has led him to believe that everything is susceptible to cinematic transformation; it is not bare, squalid reality itself that attracts him, but the image that he has refashioned. Once this re-creating, often unconscious, has been accomplished, Fellini accepts it as the whole truth, artistically, and at this point achieves a sincerity no less valid for being based on largely altered material. In brief this is how he justifies his paradoxical statement that he is sincere even when he is lying; moreover, it does not imply an interest in invention for its own sake, of which at any event he would be incapable.

Fellini's conclusive statement in the interview with Bachmann should be considered in this connection. 'In film-making only the absolute truth counts. In everyday life I can be a deceiver and trickster, but not in films. One's film is like a naked man, nothing can be hidden. I am compelled to be sincere in my films.'

Fellini's artistic sincerity, inherent in his individualism, means that he can never conceal himself in his films, but is clearly revealed, through identification with the characters who are trying desperately to be honest with themselves. Marcello in *La dolce vita* speaks for Fellini when he says to Steiner: 'We need a clear, unequivocal means of expression which is devoid of cant and lies, and, above all, it must have integrity.' The author identifies himself completely with the characters, be it Marcello or Augusto of *Il bidone*, no matter what unattractive and unlikeable qualities spoil their personalities. The director's sincerity is not daunted by negative points of character and he continually feels the need to confess to others, whether he does so in the film or to a crowd of spectators.

Fellini is said to have an extrovert character whose honesty acts as a safety valve for giving vent to his feelings. Because of this, his greatest danger lies in being alone, unable to communicate and express himself, whilst the introvert finds it easy to be self-sufficient and has no need of other people. The tragedy of isolation and of failure to communicate haunts Fellini at every step. It pervades his films with all the explosive force of a vital problem.

In real life Fellini inspires affection. He feels the need to be a friend to all, he has a smile for everyone and calls them by their name: when a film is being made it is he, even in the moments of greatest tension, who builds up confidence and a sense of comradeship amongst the film workers. His slaps on the back are proverbial and his kisses and embraces are given not only to friends of long standing, but to mere acquaintances. One might think that Fellini knows and practises the art of pleasing and ingratiating himself as a simple diplomatic ruse; but there is no calculation behind his manner, which is entirely spontaneous. Those embraces are a physical reaction to the deep-seated fear of solitude, as is the need for self-confession which he transfers skilfully to his films.

Other great cinema artists with a very different cultural background share this feeling of the urgent need to understand one another and of the difficulty of discovering a common point of contact. For example, Kurosawa in *Rashomon* declared that 'men remain a mystery to each other'. Bergman is worried by a similar problem, as in the past it has troubled the most thoughtful poetic minds, preoccupied with man's destiny. ('Too much is secret in this despairing world, only he who makes men his brothers in anxiety will not stray,' wrote Giovanni Pascoli, another poet from the Romagna.) This leitmotif is already clearly sketched in *Luci del varietà* in which Fellini took his first steps as a director, and is fully expressed in *Il bidone*. One needs only to remember the husband's nocturnal stroll and his yearning to communicate, if only with a prostitute he meets by chance. It is thrown into greater relief in *I vitelloni* where it not only shapes the characters' personalities but constitutes the very atmosphere of part of the film. Where the drama of isolation begins to dominate—and even becomes obsessive—is in the trilogy beginning with *La strada*, continuing in *Il bidone* and culminating in *Le notti di Cabiria*.

In *La strada* Zampanò and Gelsomina are two lonely beings, linked by an invisible chain of incomprehension, which they are incapable of breaking because they cannot unlock their own souls. Their sad, poetical adventure has its origins in the fact that though they both feel affection and love for each other they never admit to it, and so remain apart and shut out in the cold of their loneliness. Even the 'Madman', the third key-character in the story is an isolated figure. At the end, after Gelsomina's death, Zampanò gives voice to his despair on the deserted beach; his is the cry of a man alone who is unconsciously aware of the tragic circle which encloses him, but which he cannot break, except by howling like a wounded animal.

In *Il bidone*, the outline of Zampanò's position is repeated; it is the old trickster Augusto who is the man alone, afraid of his isolation. He has been unable to surround himself with affection in his life and is condemned to look on the ruins of his squalid existence. Finally *Le notti di Cabiria* is peopled by solitary individuals, separated by a wall of repressed feelings, by dark, self-centred natures and unstable relationships. Cabiria herself is the first to feel uneasy at being alone and ingenuously plays along with the crooked accountant, who ruins her. Yet Cabiria's isolation is different from that of Gelsomina: the latter did not know how to communicate because, through not fault of her own, psychological barriers prevented her from passing through the door to the outside world. Cabiria, on the other hand, is aware of the possibilities offered her, she thirsts for affection, for a clean life. She never feels exiled without hope of redemption, despite the wall built up about her by society and by prejudice. Her faith remains tenacious and indestructible, to the very last. But it is just at the end when the girl, delivered from the diabolical murderer and turning sadly homewards, is surrounded and serenaded by a group of boys, that her loneliness is more intensely felt. The basic problem remains unsolved, although the film and Cabiria's smiling buoyancy, offer a vision of hope greater than in any other film of Fellini's.

Even *La dolce vita* is basically a story of isolation, although the central themes are different inasmuch as this is not a film limited to one theme. However, Marcello is dogged by the fear of failing to communicate; even when he thinks he has found a solution amidst the warmth of the Steiner household, he is disillusioned because it is precisely Steiner with his doctrinaire intellect who is the most alone of all and, terrified by his haunting visions, commits suicide. Lastly, in *Le tentazioni del dottor Antonio* (an episode in *Boccaccio '70*), the hero, a censor obsessed with sex, is an isolated figure cut off from others, unable to restrain himself from giving way to his madness.

The instinctive longing for human warmth, for affection, for someone to confide in, has led Fellini to express himself with particular success against nocturnal backgrounds and scenes. In *La dolce vita*, loneliness is keenly felt amidst the moving traffic and the buzz and chatter in the 'Society Café' in the Via Veneto; but it is all the more chilling in the deserted streets and squares, in the great silence of the countryside, broken by an occasional animal-like cry, as in the scene of Marcello's and Sylvia's flight. The motifs of a nocturnal walk and a deserted square (in which a baroque fountain often serves as an architectural element) recur repeatedly in nearly all the director's films: in *Luci del varietà*, *Lo Sceicco bianco*, *I vitelloni*, *La strada*, *Il bidone*. Sometimes the sound-track with a trumpet blast or the gradually fading steps of a man or animal is used to heighten the sense of isolation. And it is not merely, as has been thought, the twilight 'poetry of futility' which makes Fellini portray this.

Not for nothing has the director's sympathy for the unsociable, those unable to adapt themselves to other men and surrounding reality, led him to love the heroic anachronism of Don Quixote—perhaps the only historical character Fellini would be inclined to bring back to life on the screen.

CHAPTER 5

Magic and Religion

WE HAVE already seen that the peculiar nature of Fellini's integrity leads him instinctively and almost inevitably to exaggerate, distort and contradict. The paradox is only superficial: on the one hand he is unconsciously protecting his sincerity and on the other he is driving himself ever onwards towards self-confession. But above all, this enlargement of certain aspects of reality, the reason for their special choice and exaggerated proportions—which is why his films are so often called baroque—are the products of the director's extraordinary imagination. Fellini is unable to invent successfully without some kind of starting point: he uses his imagination solely to embroider events stored in his memory which in certain given conditions have gradually come to fruition. In fact, Fellini's inventiveness is not a flight from reality, but an artistic development and elaboration of a genuine human situation.

Consequently Fellini deviates from the script when, as often happens, he improvises on the set. A crucial point may come out of an addition to the script itself or from an observation made on the spot, which involves stressing more heavily certain aspects. This is also because Fellini observes attentively and in great detail: he misses nothing of what is going on about him even amidst the greatest uproar and confusion. Anyone who believes Fellini to be absent-minded and abstracted is mistaken. Amongst other things, the director differs from nearly all his colleagues in that he is extraordinarily punctual both in his work and in his private life; he never forgets an engagement—except deliberately—however minor it may be. This outlook is also the result of his interest in everything, by now a legend. This curiosity has nothing to do with tittle-tattle, to which he is indifferent, but it enables him to build up his films piece by piece. Some small detail will give the director an idea or will perfect an idea, which he knows how to insert at the right moment, in the right place. Gherardi, his designer in *Le notti di Cabiria* and *La dolce vita*, said: 'Fellini is like a large money-box; drop a phrase into him, you may think he doesn't notice it, yet he comes up with it months later.' It becomes what is known as a 'cinematic find' thanks to a certain twist, embellished by his imagination.

Fellini's imagination works above all in the field of the metaphysical. He is irresistibly attracted, and at the same time repelled by the thought of

Fate, the unknown and the miraculous. Love of the adventurous is a purely psychic factor in him and bears no relation to his physical world. In this respect Fellini is more rational and consistent than is commonly believed. He does not like travelling and only does so for social reasons, when he is sometimes forced to attend Festivals or go to distant cities for the premières of his films. Above all he loves to take refuge at home, safe in port as it were, with his wife and a small group of friends. Here is how he sums it up in an autobiographical letter:

'I like enormously to lie in bed reading with Giulietta near me. I chat to her, become drowsy, and turn off the light, getting up later and going into the kitchen, where Giulietta prepares exceptionally good nocturnal spaghetti.'

This liking for the unknown and the mysterious is completely intellectual, a thing of the mind, as can be seen from his reading. He prefers Kafka, Buzzati, the 'Orlando Furioso', and favours science fiction, pseudo-scientific or occult books. At home he has an extensive library of works on magic and astrology (particularly those by Eliphas Levi), and he knows many magicians and seers. When he was making *La dolce vita* he gave a small part to Marianna Leibl, who is a famous astrologist, graphologist and palmist in Roman circles. People say that 'the enchantress' as Fellini called her, was indispensable to him, holding long impassioned discussions on the subject. The director is superstitious (beware if he sees a black cat cross the road!) and talks authoritatively and seriously about horoscopes and zodiacal influences. He believes in dreams; many of them, for all their bizarre complexity, are integrated into scripts for short films.

The director's taste for the mysterious, disquieting world of the unknown, is also apparent in what appeals to him in other people's films. Fellini, like Chaplin, rarely goes to the cinema, because he says it bores him, unless cartoon films are being shown or 'futuristic films about men who land on the moon'. Significantly enough he appreciates Dreyer and Kurosawa.

In long, nocturnal motor-car rides round the outskirts of Rome and the deserted countryside, Fellini has discovered and developed a private, magical territory which has become important in his work. Strange sights always take his fancy: sometimes it is a big, lone white horse walking slowly along the roadside (and which may very well turn out to be non-existent), it may be a strange-looking cowshed or an ancient ruin. In his films Fellini has often remembered these wanderings, usually made in the company of a friend.

His apprehensive predilection for the unknown and mysterious, which he transmutes with his imagination, probably has the same origin as his fear of isolation. Solitude is also a form of the unknown, a kind of spiritual darkness which is irresistibly attractive to Fellini. Just as it is true that the problem of solitude plays a large part in his films, he has also introduced as a theme the unknown, in a legendary world bordering on the enchanted. That is why many critics speak of 'magical' or 'lyrical' realism as being the main characteristic of his poeticism. In this connection *La strada* is his most significant film, permeated as it is with this acute sensitivity, though traces of it may be found in all his films up to *La dolce vita* (where it is most evident in the 'séance' sequence) and *Le tentazioni del dottor Antonio* which is a long fantastic dream throughout.

La strada has been mainly viewed and interpreted as a fable. In certain respects the framework is indeed that of a fairy-tale, but in Fellini's work 'magic' means a sense of the supernatural and thus of religion, in the attempt to understand the less explicable phenomena, such as miracles.

We must now consider one of the most delicate and controversial aspects of Fellini's complex personality: what is the nature of his religious inspiration, which is closely linked as we have seen to his fantasy world? It is 'the discovery of another world, where the spirituality and warmth of human relationships fuse, together directly, in candour and innocence'. (Del Fra.) It is a kind of Chaplinesque paradise where 'the feeling of enlightened simplicity and its miraculous force' (identified with Gelsomina in *La strada*) led Fellini to become deeply interested in religion and the supernatural. This interest extends to the magnificent processions and other external aspects of the liturgy, and the outcries of a superstitious community when faced with a possible miracle, interpreted by simple innocents. All these tendencies were already developing in Fellini in whom, just as in Rossellini's 'Il Miracolo', there were glimmers of faith and supernatural perception.

Is Fellini, then, a religious man? What of his attitude towards Catholicism and towards Christianity in general? It is a question that has often been put to me and to Fellini, especially when he visits France and the Anglo-Saxon countries.

Although I know Fellini well, it is difficult to give an answer. In September, 1960, *La civiltà cattolica* published an article which we shall examine more particularly later in connection with *La dolce vita*. In this article Father Baragli examined the problem thoroughly. His most important point was that it was essential to distinguish private practice of religion from the religious element in an artist's work, since the former cannot always be deduced from the latter. Now Fellini is most certainly not a practising Catholic, but if, as *La civiltà cattolica* states, we understand by 'religious' the avowed relationship of man's dependence upon God, seeing in Him his beginning and his final destiny; if a religious man is 'he who uses that relationship as a standard for the theoretical values and practices of human existence and its influence on them', then it is impossible to see how Fellini can be described as anything other than religious. A steadfast faith in the transcendental, and an undeniable sense of the presence and necessity of a God who is pure love towards all human beings, are part of Fellini's inheritance, evident in his work. The danger of this position is its resemblance to a vague theism which could become unqualified pantheism. In concrete terms, however, Fellini clarifies his views with 'declarations of faith' such as this one Dominique Delouche noted down in an interview in 1956.

'I believe in Jesus Christ. He is not only the greatest figure in human history, but he continues to live on in the Being who sacrifices himself for his brother. I am ignorant of dogma and perhaps I am heretical without knowing it. My Christianity is crude. I think of prayer as an exercise that draws us nearer to the supernatural. I have tried it in the past: now I cannot pray except when I am sad and afraid; but one should be able to pray out of happiness!'

As he so openly admits the mediation of Christ, the director must be thought of as a Christian. More recently Fellini talked about catholicism and clarified his own attitude and that of his films towards the Church. He said to me:

'I have a feeling of filial devotion towards the Church, and I see her for what she means to Catholics in Italy—a great mother, indulgent and affectionate towards the sinner. I should never dream of purposely exiling myself or opposing myself to her, for she is inseparable from my personality as an Italian.'

Christianity and religious inspiration understood in this way, however, are only secondary motifs in the work of the creator of *La strada*. Lack of faith is the downfall of his characters, while hope of redemption and salvation are not denied the sincere and pure of heart. But this is implicit in a part of the old problem of spiritual solitude, of the need to know man, to understand and love him. When Fellini talks of his own work and compares it to neo-realism and says, 'Man is an enigma for me, but God is to be found at the centre of the successive layers of reality, and he is the key to all mysteries', he reasserts the link between his personal religious standpoint and the general need to investigate the close ties between one human being and another. 'This investigation,' observes Guiseppe Ferrara, 'which attempts to reach the roots of being, or in other words the point of contact between man and the Universe, between man and the Unknown, was previously one of neo-realism's aims and it was trying to resolve what Rossellini had attempted without success.'

So a single thread of logical thinking joins Fellini's personal conception of reality to the problem of solitude, to that of the world of magic and lastly to the problem of religion: four stages in the same mental process, whose final expression (as we shall see) is symbolism. But Fellini's interest in the problems of religion has a strictly limited context: it does not widen its considerations to the many aspects of Christian revelation and their relevance to the present day. It remains a vaguely ethical and subjective factor. Fellini admits this in a picturesque way when he says half seriously, half jokingly.

'One day I met an angel who stretched out his hand to me. I followed him, but after a short time I left him and went back. He stopped and waited at the same place for me. I see him again in difficult moments and he says to me, "Wait, wait", just like I do to everyone. I am afraid that when I call him one day, I shall not find him. It is the angel who has always awakened me from my spiritual torpor. When I was a boy he was the incarnation of an imaginary world, and then he became the symbol of a vital moral need.'

It is clear that Fellini is anything but unconcerned about religious problems. But he studies Catholicism for its cinematic appeal and more often only sees in it the chance to highlight and define any dramatic outward manifestations. Father Baragli rightly said, in the article quoted above, that Fellini 'tends to seize hold of religion and portray its superficial aspects on the screen, those that are spectacular, frenzied or superstitious'.

Every one of his films depicts to a greater or lesser extent, this type of religious spectacle: in *Lo Sceicco bianco* there are the Jubilee Year pilgrims and the audience with the Pope at St. Peter's. St. Peter's also reappears in *La dolce vita* in the scene with Sylvia, *I vitelloni* depicts the sacred objects shop, the stolen angel, the monk up the tree who refuses to purchase it and so on. The processions, Madonnas, nuns and priests above all are part of the method of depicting typical psychological reactions. As Baragli says religion takes on shadowy irrational tones. The psychological reactions later have greater importance when they are backed by the semi-hysterical exaltation indulged in by crowds. (The 'Divine Love' in *Cabiria* and the false miracle in *La dolce vita*.)

Although the director's work is rarely inspired by a religious theme, religious motivation can be detected. This is the case, for example, at the beginning of *La dolce vita* in which the big statue of Christ the Worker hanging from a helicopter flying above, is of genuine Christian conception and has symbolic value. Perhaps *La dolce vita* is religiously ambiguous, but as *La civiltà cattolica* maintains this particular scene is incomprehensible when it is considered out of the context of the director's ardent preoccupation with religion. Other examples of a vigorous Christian conception which is not purely decorative are to be seen in *La strada*, particularly at the end, in the story of the pebble, despite Baragli's complaint that the words are put into the mouth of the nightmarish 'Madman'.

Many uncertainties have resulted from the complex problems of the true religious meaning in Fellini's work. They are also due to the producer's upbringing and his spiritual formation. He was a pupil of Rossellini who is considered by many to be an overtly Catholic artist, and he counted and continues to have many priests and strict Catholics amongst his friends. *La strada* was in particular seen as moving towards religiously-committed cinema, which many Catholics believe to be sadly lacking. But the mystical significance of *La strada* was sometimes extended beyond the limit we have indicated and consequently Fellini unintentionally disappointed his supporters.

When Fellini made *Le notti di Cabiria*, he visited Cardinal Siri, Archbishop of Genoa, to gain his support for a film whose plot and setting had troubled the censors. *Le notti di Cabiria* was followed by *La dolce vita* and the same Catholic circles became increasingly vociferous in their criticism. Whilst Fellini, aided by the untiring efforts of Father Arpa of the Genoa *Columbianum* and the Jesuit fathers of the Centro San Fedele in Milan, made an effort to calm general disapproval of religious and moral points, other ecclesiastical officials formed a singularly vicious faction against the director and even denied him any spiritual feelings or good faith.

I witnessed this battle of ideas and heard Fellini calmly defend himself in front of his Catholic friends. Even at the most difficult moments, when tactically some concession might have been wise, Fellini admitted with unfailing honesty that his films held no hidden religious meaning. They had only vague transcendental aspirations, but a detailed examination of his clear moral purpose—love of one's neighbour, the need to know and help one another—is consistent with the teaching of the Catholic Church. But no more than this. Kezich has related how at the time of filming, someone questioned the interpretation of the notorious fake-miracle scene in *La dolce vita*. 'You'll have to consult the Cardinal again,' Fellini was told, referring to his consultation over *Le notti di Cabiria*. 'If necessary I'll go to the Pope too,' he replied quite seriously and with a clear conscience.

Magic and Religion

We must emphasize that the religious theme in Fellini's work is part of his magical world, and that he is greatly attracted by supernatural occurrences, such as miracles. The esoteric, unfathomable qualities of miracles fascinate him because they offer extraordinarily powerful dramatic possibilities which his cinematic instinct exploits to the full. But unlike Dreyer (and to a lesser extent Bresson), Fellini will probably not be carried away by religious inspiration to the extent of using it for a whole film. Indeed at this stage of his career he could not be expected to produce a new *Ordet* (*The Word*) or a new *Journal d'un curé de campagne* (*Diary of a Country Priest*).

CHAPTER 6

Symbolism and Morality

SOMETIMES FELLINI'S feeling for the mysterious becomes excessive, the fairy-tale world is bizarre, magic is ghastly and grotesque. Then the framework of the picture becomes strangely distorted, and Fellini is accused of exaggeration. Yet despite his love of blowing things up to a gigantic size, Fellini is generally too intuitive an artist to be unaware of the limits of his poetical world and rarely falls into excess. Even in his later films where everything is on a grotesque, gigantic plane, the director has used the material at his disposal without, as he might have been tempted to do, completely distorting reality.

French critics have interpreted and praised the baroque qualities of Fellini's world in a completely different way from Italian critics. They have attempted to define the lyricism of his films (he has been called a 'visionary of reality'), and to link Italian neo-realism to eighteenth-century melodrama and sixteenth-century baroque. Geneviève Agel's book *Les chemins de Fellini* in particular gives an interpretation of Fellini which is baroque and mythological. Mlle. Agel takes Eugenio d'Ors definition of 'baroque' as that which has an 'open' as opposed to a 'closed' form and having, moreover, a variety of forms. She sees Fellini's films, therefore, as fundamentally baroque: the 'animated, chaotic, lavish, bombastic creations of a dynamic imagination'. Baroque explains the superficial contradictions in an artist who has crossed the frontiers of reality, yet has remained a realist. Hautecoeur maintains that the baroque artist is at once a realist and a non-realist. Fellini's interest in religion and in magic is also embodied in the baroque; he is intolerant of a rationalized theology, tends towards mysticism and exalts the complete liberty of the spirit. When he was asked whom he would like to meet out of the past, he replied 'St. Francis and Cagliostro'. It was subsequently shown that the cult of St. Francis and of magic typify the religious outlook of a baroque artist.

Whilst this interpretation may contain some obscure truth it is largely based on misleading words and adjectives. (What does 'animated, chaotic, lavish and bombastic' mean?) To situate Fellini's films somewhere between the baroque and the classic is to oversimplify and reduce their complex character. These two terms have no place in the history of the cinema, and we must not lose sight of the medium in which Fellini has worked.

The symbolic ('mythological') interpretation of Fellini is fraught with even greater danger. Here too French critics—especially Mlle. Agel—have discovered that symbolism exists in every detail of his work and they have taken pleasure in discovering the 'object-obsession' relationship that is supposedly lurking in his films.

They have found it in the trees, beaches and snow-covered wastes of *La strada*, and the stony stretches of *Il bidone*. The wind is always blowing and the walls against which the characters lean have a special meaning. They believe that the two principal symbols are the fire and the sea. The sea symbolizes pacifying and redeeming water, and fire is the sign of moral disintegration, the latter being connected with Zampanò and the former with Gelsomina. This over-worked symbolic interpretation borders on absurdity when it maintains that the bucket of ('purifying') water which the 'Madman' throws in Zampanò's face at the beginning of the quarrel which will end in his death, is also subtly symbolic.

Delicately-woven theories of this kind openly condemn themselves, though recurring motifs do lend themselves to symbolic interpretation. The sea does appear in nearly all his films but it is merely part of the background. In some cases, as in *I vitelloni* it might be a secret call towards an impossible escape, in others its immensity soothes turbulent passions. Fellini usually incorporates the sea almost intuitively because of the memories associated with it and with his childhood in a typical coastal town.

If we accept the symbolic theory in principle, we must qualify it by saying that every film, in so far as it is made up of concrete images which may be translated into symbols, is symbolic. Fellini says precisely this when he is challenged with the problem. A fertile imagination produces a certain kind of symbolism, which may superficially appear the opposite of realism. But the cinema is not without artists who have combined the two tendencies: Dreyer, Stroheim, Carné, Antonioni, Bergman are examples.

While critics often discover and attribute symbolism *a posteriori*, an author will sometimes use it consciously. In fact, in specific cases, the events and characters in a work not only can but must have allegorical value; this is the surest sign of the universality of concepts. It all depends whether the symbol is used naturally and clearly or if it is used too insistently or artificially. Unnecessarily used, it will suffocate the original theme and reduce it to a mere abstraction. Even so it is still a question of balance and of the artist's good taste; two of Fellini's best qualities. A symbolist, therefore, can only be defined within such limits.

Gelsomina, Zampanò, Moraldo, Cabiria, Marcello and Steiner are clearly symbolic at certain moments, but as we have seen they nearly always remain anchored to a genuinely human situation, that allows them no escape except a practical one. For example, the end of *La dolce vita* is openly symbolic, when after the orgy, Marcello goes on to the beach with his friends and sees the fishermen gathered round the monstrous sea-creature, the symbol of evil. Shortly afterwards he catches sight of Paola in the distance; she waves to him but the wind snatches her words away, Marcello does not understand and makes no reply to the recall to purity, simplicity and a normal life. He returns to his corrupt friends of *La dolce vita*. This final anguish (which Fellini studied from different angles to give it its present moral meaning) is much less abstract than had it been expressed in words, and it conforms to the canon of simplicity to which the director constantly adheres. His patent symbolism, therefore, does not disturb the clarity of the story, but combines with it to give the whole its lyrical value. The same may be said of the very clear allegory in *Le tentazioni del dottor Antionio*. Fellini has always treated symbolism in this way as far as possible: when he has been unable to avoid its weaknesses (as in *Il bidone*) it is because an already weak situation poetically together with a thin moral theme have caused the symbol to predominate and prevail instead of acting as a catalyst.

Fellini's interest in symbolism clashes with the moral preoccupations of his work. Fellini's moral standpoint is clear: he is convinced that man can only be himself by communicating with others and that he can only conquer his anguish and desperation by establishing real, genuine relationships (not false ones like so many in our society) with his fellow men. It is a difficult struggle which sometimes proves impossible but it is a worth-while one: without it men condemn themselves to an inevitable spiritual death. 'I am completely absorbed by this problem, perhaps because I have not yet resolved it for myself,' Fellini once said: and for him it is the sorest wound of contemporary society because egoism and indifference have caused people to isolate themselves into so many sterile compartments, deaf to every call. When asked 'Which do you consider humanity's greatest asset?' Fellini has always unhesitatingly replied 'Love of one's neighbour,' 'And its greatest defect?' 'Its selfishness.'

In fact the artist pities the confused, battered masses of humanity and he urges them on towards greater brotherhood and understanding. In May, 1960 the French magazine *La table ronde* published an article in which Fellini confirmed these ideas. 'Some way of improving relationships between men must be found. If I were a politician I would hold meetings, or enrol in a party or go and dance barefoot in the open square. If I found a solution and were capable of expressing it convincingly and in good faith, I should naturally not be a storyteller.' Moreover, this is more or less the basis for Chaplin's ethics. Like Chaplin, but using satire and not comedy, Fellini exposes the defects of society, with the ulterior motive of purging its vices. Sometimes Fellini has characteristically exaggerated the picture, but it would be unjust to suppose (as some do), that he participates in or condones it. On the contrary he uses paradox and exaggeration to shock the emotions and through them to stimulate reaction and catharsis.

Fellini is not merely an observer and a spectator in his films; he is emotionally involved and critical because he shares his characters' anxiety and anguish and indeed all their feelings. He obeys the ever-valid Horatian maxim: '*Si vis me flere flendum est primum tibi.*' He is a moralist of no particular school, one who does not pretend to solve problems. He believes in a different world from the one in which he lives, based upon greater justice for the individual rather than for society as a whole; in which man has firmly established a new faith or the old one is re-established and strengthened by contemporary experience. This is the meaning of *La dolce vita* for example where lack of faith is quite clearly indicated as causing the ills of our society.

Fellini's sympathy and compassion go out towards those who have lost the fight for an ideal; Zampanò, Augusto, Marcello. He feels that he is a misfit as they are. He has a real love for simple creatures like Gelsomina, Cabiria, Paola, Marcello's father, in whom the moral conflict is quietened because their simple faith leads them nearer the positive fulfilment of their world.

Fellini's ethics are often combined with an ironical and satirical observation of society; but his is not the subtle, good-natured satire of René Clair, it is bitter, cutting and pessimistic. Though he does not always admit it Fellini is naturally inclined towards social satire. *Lo Sceicco bianco* and *I vitelloni* are the beginnings of this openly satirical story-telling. Some people see an irreparable break in style between these first films and later ones and call him two-faced. They claim that the satirical vein is the true one and regret he has abandoned it.

The fundamentally serious side of Fellini's nature does not conflict with the other side, but rather completes it. The prevalence of one in particular depends upon the influence of one of his two usual scenarists. Pirelli has a reflective, melancholy nature, whilst Flajano is more humorous. At the beginning of a film Fellini is influenced by both, but as shooting progresses he goes his own way. Something of their influence, however, remains.

Fellini's essential pessimism can be traced in this impulse for bitter satire. He shares this characteristic with Chaplin, and like him is rarely tempted by 'a happy ending'. He has explained this several times. 'A happy ending invites the audience to live in a cotton-wool, passive world, it makes them believe that some time, somewhere they will strike lucky having made no effort themselves. On the contrary, they must know that they are responsible for solving their own problems.' So his films never have a real conclusion, he does not alienate himself from the spectator whose life 'has no solution'. All the responsibility for a solution lies with the audience itself: 'If my films strike the right note we must begin to establish new improved relationships with our neighbours.' This is a somewhat ingenuous philosophy though it is founded in good faith. It explains the director's reluctance to give his characters a rosy future, and his doubt as to whether his message is being accepted.

He is a pessimist because he is assailed by fear of the unknown. He suspects that, in spite of all our efforts, the darkness of isolation will envelop us and the attempt to understand each other will have been in vain. Some people maintain that this outlook has its roots in Kierkegaard and in the existentialist philosophy of *angst*, despite Fellini's scant knowledge of the Danish philosopher and his disagreement with his conclusions.

On occasions, however, the director is hopeful of salvation and gives us a fleeting glimpse of some positive solution, as in the end of *Le notti di Cabiria*. But is the heroine's smile one of conscious hope or is it one of simple unawareness? (Fellini said, 'At the last moment I hadn't the courage to kill Cabiria'.) Hope more often belongs to the magic world of illusion and takes on a metaphysical quality (as in the illusionist sequence in *Cabiria*). It is not always denied the hero, provided he can escape the arid mentality which oppresses him as does Marcello at the end of *La dolce vita*, when he meets the redeeming purity of Paola. It may be a positive (but conditional) solution, although more often it is a negative one as in *La strada*, *Il bidone*, and *Le tentazioni del dottor Antonio*. Yet the solution is always consistent with Fellini's morality and does not entail, as has been maintained, an ingrained distrust of mankind.

Love has a special significance in this moral world, for the spirit becomes aware of another being. 'All our anguish and mistakes occur when there is no love,' says the director. Some critics say that for Fellini love only exists in a spiritual form, and outside this it is merely eroticism. This is true in the sense that human aspirations towards love, as it is understood by the director are too often frustrated by the debasement of love. This is why Fellini is greatly attracted by the prostitutes portrayed in his films. Whether they are guilty or innocent they exemplify this sad plight. But Fellini has no real sympathy with sexual erotic problems, as such, and they, in the same way as the social position of prostitutes, are of secondary importance in his films. Eroticism, to Fellini is finally disgusting and nauseating as in *La dolce vita.* Here Sylvia, played by Anita Ekberg, is the incarnation of primitive lust, 'the woman whom all men desire', but she is desperately in need of love, like Cabiria and Gelsomina.

Fellini has understood the two extreme positions of love and depicts sex because it is part of an insuppressible human need and has become a kind of modern myth. Yet he has not failed to control and use it as a simple theme within his complex creative pattern. This is confirmed in *Le tentazioni del dottor Antonio*, where eroticism figures largely. In this film Fellini sets out to condemn the moralist who limits his ethical behaviour to a mere question of sex, which triumphs over him in its turn. This larger-than-life Anita is not so much a sex symbol as, for him, an absurd sense of sin.

CHAPTER 7

Style: the Characters and Background

EVEN THE most hostile critics have recognized Fellini's originality. Fellini is no one's follower, not even of Rossellini, his master. (Some even say that it was the other way round.) He is only a neo-realist to the extent we have described. He is not a pupil of preceding or contemporary trends of the Italian or foreign cinema. It must be repeated that Fellini sees very few films besides his own, and any reference to other films is quite fortuitous or the result of some unconscious intervention of a third party. Fellini's cultural background is not wide enough to be of very great influence: on the contrary he has been criticized, even if mistakenly, for his so-called 'lack of culture'. It is useless to look for Fellini's cinematic and literary origins. Saying that he likes Walt Disney or Chaplin, Palazzeschi or Landolfi, Kafka or Ariosto, carries hardly any weight at all.

'My only source of inspiration lies in myself, in my own experience and in my instinct,' Fellini once admitted to me. This is the case with Charlie Chaplin, who was also frowned upon for his lack of cultural background and who was guided by an intuitive sense of the cinema and entertainment.

Fellini is an isolated figure of the screen: it all depends on whether his artistic experience will remain unchanged too, whether his films will open up a new road which others will tread, improve, modify, perfect or simply question. This is certainly a problem of the future, but it can already be said that Fellini's revolutionary innovations have re-echoed not only in Italy but also in France, where he has influenced many young directors. The vitality of his style will surely make him the founder of a school in the eyes of future generations.

We have spoken of style and must now try to reply to the question, 'What is it that makes Fellini's films so moving?' So far we have discussed mainly individual and moral problems: and it is true that in Fellini moral problems are identified with aesthetic problems. But as the acute cinema critic Chiarini has said in *Realismo e stile*: 'A work of art precedes the theory and the artist does not compile a book of formula or a grammar before he creates, for theory is always the *result* of works of art, which are not born out of abstract rationalized schemes.' Now style is the concrete expression of an idea or feeling that will arouse emotion; in the cinema it is part of a strictly cinematic language with its own characteristics. All great artists of the screen have a style of their own, which characterizes their films and makes them in the eyes of the public 'good' or 'less good'.

The fundamental unity of Fellini's work facilitates a definition of his style; conversely, it is true that Fellini's work is unified by a consistent style. In any case this unity must be stressed. The director's films are like the chapters in a book: we progress from *Luci del varietà*, which already shows the themes of individuality and loneliness amidst an atmosphere of magic 'realism', to *Lo Sceicco bianco* and *I vitelloni*, where the investigation is carried on in an ironic manner through a critical and autobiographical projection; from thence to *La strada*, *Il bidone*, *Le notti di Cabiria*, a classic trilogy in which Fellinian themes are deeply explored. Only *La dolce vita* would seem, at first sight, to be excluded from this book because it hits out at the development of exceptional individuality: but close examination will tell us that *La dolce vita* completes and elevates preceding themes, taking on a new form to avoid repetition. Kezich uses Fellini's own words: that his work could be considered a series of 'numbers' in a filmed review, a large weekly rotogravure on film. Fellini especially talks of *La dolce vita*, saying that the rotogravure process is already an expressive medium in the modern world: films are only an extension of this, a personal interpretation. However, the idea can easily be extended to the whole of Fellini's work, and even to *Le tentazioni del dottor Antonio*, a fashionably contemporary satire despite its ancient origins.

To return to the aesthetic problem, it must be noted that Fellini has always instinctively obeyed certain rules without which it has been proved difficult, if not impossible, to make a good film. His primary concern is to create his characters and atmosphere with the simplest expressive means.

What does creating a character mean? It means that the spiritual conflict must be visually represented in an immediate way, that even the characters of secondary figures are fully drawn. Thus he avoids the dangers of mere coloured sketches of a rustic 'character' and genial, facile, impressionistic psychology which are all too frequent in Italian post-war cinema. Fellini, like every other talented director, matches the image to the state of mind perfectly. This relationship is the secret of the 'storehouse of emotion' which is the film. His characters are always non-conformists and non-conformism is one of Fellini's most striking qualities. It makes his psychological analysis violent, cruel and pitiless.

Lo Sceicco bianco, and its investigation of the human mind corrupted by the forces of society, enabled the director to see the great possibilities of similar projects. Fellini outlines from the beginning with light, simple strokes the moral weakness of a provincial couple with their narrow outlook and their meanness. The Cavalli family, the strip story, the troupe at Fregene, make up a whole gallery of types some of whom are only partially and imperfectly drawn, but their mentality is quite clearly portrayed. In *I vitelloni* Fellini talks about himself in as many ways as there are characters and brings to life people in whom we can all see part of ourselves. But as Renzo Renzi has pointed out 'spivs' like Fellini's do not really exist. The nearest thing is a similar state of mind, one of distrust, unfulfilled ambitions and rebelliousness. Fellini has endowed many other genuine, spontaneous, human characters with this restless instability, where loneliness and boredom predominate. Yet each one is different from the other.

Fellini always views a situation from inside his characters. The actress Yvonne Fourneaux cleverly observed this while making *La dolce vita*, but the same may be said of all his films. In *La strada*, this 'seeing from the inside' is given great emphasis, so that Gelsomina, Zampanò and 'the Madman', even if they have a symbolic function, are primarily characters. And even here the spectator identifies himself with the character to a lesser or greater extent, an important factor in a work of art. Gelsomina is deprived, ingenuous and poor-spirited, but each one of us has an inner defencelessness which makes us pity Gelsomina as we would ourselves. Fellini is continuing Chaplin's great discovery that a poor, degraded, down-trodden man symbolizes the whole of humanity. Does not Zampanò's brutality lie hidden in the depths of our consciousness, together with his gloomy despair and thirst for revolt because he had never known love? In *Il bidone*, Fellini portrays a series of types: cynics, tricksters, small-time swindlers and their victims, a group of frescoes worthy of Caravaggio or Goya. But Augusto, Roberto and Picasso are intensified and gain depth in *Le notti di Cabiria*, where some situations have been anticipated. Cabiria is striking and moving. She is pathetically proud and hard to please, always intent upon salvaging the non-existent remnants of respectability. Her desperate efforts and dreams are shared by the audience, she emerges from the dimensions of the screen into everyone's hearts, in a spiritual communion that would, at first sight, have seemed impossible. In *Le notti di Cabiria* all the prostitute's friends are exceptionally convincing as individuals: the fat, placid Wanda, Matilda, Cabiria's enemy, and the extortionist protectors ruled over by Storpio—the one who goes to the Madonna of Divine Love to pray for the miracle. *Le notti di Cabiria* and *La dolce vita*, are the films where the richness and depth of the characters are most evident. There is the famous actor (Nazzari) who goes to Cabiria's house and in a single scene reveals his utter lack of morality; there is the humble illusionist who sells dreams in exchange for a bite to eat; there is the honey-tongued d'Onofrio about whom we know nothing but who, in a few judicious scenes, is drawn in all his vileness and evil purpose.

In *La dolce vita* the galaxy of characters becomes a real crowd and with amazing skill Fellini has been able to distinguish one from the other without error or confusion, so that, though forming a chorus, they all have solo parts. Some characters stand out from others, but this is not to say that the psychological interest is concentrated in them alone. Take certain secondary characters, Sylvia's fiancé, for example, or Alan Dijon's incredible 'fawn' (in the scene at 'Caracalla's'); or Fanny the fierce, stupid little dancer who gives Marcello's father back the illusion of youth for an hour; or the prince Mareschalchi, the last member of a noble family resigned to his fate, or the tragic reversal of the ending.

But true-to-life characters can only exist in suitable surroundings, which have been patiently built up. They must be rich in detail and nothing must be left to chance. There must be an absolute correspondence between image and subject-matter. It is not an exaggeration to say that Fellini's genius shows itself above all in the creation of an atmosphere of tension. In this field he surpasses Chaplin, Eisenstein, René Clair and Bergman: only Dreyer's best work can stand comparison. Whether it is in the open air (as in the 'spivs' walk along the beach) or within four walls where the action's visual force is so great that it attains explosive power, Fellini knows how to create atmosphere. So he produced the grotesque 'carnival' in *I vitelloni*, and the mad thieves' party in *Il bidone*, with the obsessive rhythm of jazz and the frenzied movements of the crazed dancers. And again he conjured up the parties, 'nights', and orgies of *La dolce vita*. Fellini seems to have a predilection for these parties which have been called 'the climax of isolation'. Then, paradoxically, spiritual solitude is more strongly felt, and the characters are divested of all their artificial poses to appear naked in the judgment of the audience. In such scenes he finds it easy to maintain a surprisingly realistic atmosphere in a hallucinatory suspense story by means of psychological differentiation and varying dramatic tones.

More frequently Fellini's atmosphere is created by the scenery, as in *La strada* or in certain parts of *Il bidone*. As Pietro Bianchi says, it is pure scenery in *La strada*; throughout the seasons it remains, majestic and indifferent to man's suffering and loneliness. The scenery becomes magical and human beings seem to be actors in a fairy-tale, as when Gelsomina suddenly sees three yokels on their way to the village festival, marching along the causeway to a happy, musical rhythm. The same rhythm becomes more stately and solemn when played later at the procession of the Madonna. The processions, pilgrimages, miracles—they are essential elements in Fellini's films and he makes them unforgettable. They pulsate with an uncorrupted faith, full of the fantasies and superstitions and wild outbursts of a thousand years of civilization. To see in these highly mystical spectacles purely baroque decoration and to miss the spiritual aspiration and spontaneity of a *pathos* that is remarkably impressive, is to understand only partially the spirit of Fellini's work.

He creates atmosphere by seeking to immerse the actors in it. When he was filming the final orgy of *La dolce vita* Kezich tells us that he used sarcastic and violent speech as he built up the dialogue for Marcello and the others and identified the actors with the characters. More than one of the actors thus addressed paled beneath Fellini's invective. It seems as though he was playing a kind of game of truth with them, attacking them in no uncertain terms. The dialogue could easily slip into coarseness and obscenity, but Fellini knows what he is doing. Without this language it would be impossible to recreate the atmosphere of the party.

This may be an extreme case but Fellini always builds up atmosphere in this way. Dreyer uses the same method: in the witch scene of *Vredens Dag* (*Day of Wrath*), he even tied Anna Svierkier, an elderly actress, to a staircase for several hours.

All actors who have worked with Fellini say he is a marvellous director with a real talent for improvised and spontaneous dramatic teaching, even with the most difficult actors. Del Fra, talking about *Le notti di Cabiria* says: 'The players often act without knowing what their character is like; they are guided by the director who roughs out a dialogue with them behind the camera, a dialogue which has little to do with the action but with which Fellini intends to provoke definite psychological reactions from them, in mimicry.' He too confirms that Fellini 'insults and cajoles them, talks about this and that, and the actors react to the insults by responding ironically to the director'. Often the technicians are treated in the same way.

Fellini's method of creating and directing the atmosphere is the antithesis of René Clair's cold Cartesianism, yet it is no more lacking in an innate sense of balance than the Frenchman's. Balance and harmony between the different parts and the full use of each actor's powers are characteristic of Fellini's films. The result is a continuous, evenly paced, visual and narrative rhythm which is steady and firm, never ragged and whose climaxes and anti-climaxes are intentionally arranged by Fellini. (*Il bidone* and to a certain extent the second half of *Le tentazioni del dottor Antonio* are exceptions.) The internal rhythm contrasts with the general rhythm and a counterpoint effect of an image within the image is obtained. Fellini is able to balance these rhythms, and where he does not there is a reason for the syncopation; the violent contrast shocks the spectator all the more. The director's masterpieces unite poetic and technical resources.

But without music something essential would be missing from these masterpieces. In Fellini's films music plays a greater part than in other directors' work: it is the ideal complement to his style. I once happened to watch *La strada* and *La dolce vita* without the musical sound-track and I realized I was watching completely different versions of the same films. In *La strada* especially music is the 'spiritual buttress' of the film.

Fellini has a very sensitive ear for music like many *romagnoli*, although he has received little formal musical education. (His favourite composer is Stravinsky.) He firmly believes that the atmosphere in different scenes must be 'musically' narrated, rather than heavily emphasized as usually happens; music must be able to induce a state of mind. His films, therefore, are always full of music: in *I vitelloni*, the musical sound-track lasts an hour and a quarter, and more than two hours in *La dolce vita*. Only *La strada* has less than forty minutes because it is a shorter film and the music is more concentrated.

Fellini chose Nino Rota to create the atmosphere of his films through the music. Rota is one of the most highly esteemed musicians of today and he is certainly the most gifted film composer. He has been in charge of all the sound-tracks of Fellini's films except *Luci del varietà* (Felice Lattuada), and the short film *Gli italiani si voltano* (*Italians Turn Round*), from the title *Agenzia matrimoniale* (*Marriage Bureau*) (Nascimbene). Rota proceeds in perfect harmony with Fellini and writes the music as the film is shown through a *moviola*. Sometimes director and composer carry the piano into a small room, place it beside the *moviola* and work together as Fellini gives the melodic theme which Rota develops. Rota rightly believes that music is 'a means of expression to be used within the film, to clarify the characters and the similarity between some situations, to make the link which is often unexpressed between events and actions'. Fellini expounds the same idea when he tells him every time 'not to compose music which is too good' or which has a life and value of its own. Rota uses very simple musical ideas which, according to the director's demands, may not be new compositions but excerpts from other works suited to the needs of the moment. The music in *Lo Sceicco bianco* is romantic, colourful and full of humour; in *I vitelloni* it reflects the slow cadence of the film and is based upon a pathetic and persuasive theme, which becomes in turn discordant, frenzied and despairing. The musical themes in *La strada*, reflecting Gelsomina's character, are absurd and enchanting; Rota uses a whole range of instruments from the violin to the trumpet. (*La strada* also contains the beautiful musical trick which transforms the lively tune played by the marching bandsmen into the slow, solemn music of the procession.) In *Il bidone* it is the 'music of silence' which is so effective (by contrast), whilst in *Cabiria* the music is popular, much of it dance music. The music in *La dolce vita* changes according to the surroundings and is dominated by a sentimental, melancholy tune. Music must also create a living atmosphere, and other tunes are based upon contemporary jazz compositions and eastern music, the latter perhaps to express the decadence and corruption of some situations and characters.

'Fellini aims at bold effects,' says Rota, 'and he gives greater prominence to the music than I would myself.' This is logical because the director knows very well to what extent the musical background strengthens and colours his style.

CHAPTER 8

Technique and Improvisation

FELLINI'S STYLE is the result of a technique which he has gradually mastered, but which he has not allowed to rule him. Naturally his technique goes hand in hand with certain determined aesthetic aims.

Even at the time of *La strada*, Fellini had practically no technical skill. He then wrote to me:

'I can't take pictures and I know nothing about such matters. Kindly old cameramen have tried several times in a fatherly way to explain how a camera works, how and why the film is exposed, but with the best will in the world I can't understand. It's the same with a car engine: they explain everything, I understand as they go along, but I forget the whole thing altogether and it all seems very mysterious. The essential thing is that I do know how to drive a car.'

So the essential thing for Fellini is that he does know how to direct and this largely explains his character.

After *La strada* the director made a virtue of necessity and acquired greater technical knowledge, whilst maintaining a defensive position. ('All technical rigidity must be avoided.') This does not mean that he takes no interest in it. 'I know many people think so,' says his cameraman Martelli (as Kezich reports), 'but they are talking rubbish.' Otello Martelli has been the cameraman in nearly all Fellini's films except *Lo Sceicco bianco*—where Gallea was the cameraman—and *Agenzia matrimoniale* which required little skill. Also in *Le notti di Cabiria* Aldo Tonti took Martelli's place for most of the film. However, Martelli knows most about this side of Fellini and he should be left to speak. 'We think the same way about camera work, but it is not easy to satisfy him. Fellini never goes in for limited shots. Lighting is always a problem. Sometimes he even makes the camera turn through 360 degrees. He is very demanding. When the film is being shown he is the first to notice if it is grained or has jumped or has special qualities. In *La dolce vita* he always wanted to use long shots—75 millimetres and even 150 close-up lenses for the nearest foreground. He wanted to use them in motion on trolleys. He wanted to get the actor completely in focus, but he didn't care about the focal depth. With 75 millimetres, panoramic views and long range action can be difficult, giving a blurred effect. I told Fellini about it from the beginning, but he replied, "What do I care?", and he was right. It gave the film a certain individuality, its vision is restricted, the picture is selective, the characters are clearly defined and there is a distortion of the people and the surroundings.'

Lino del Fra also talks interestingly about Fellini's technique in *Le notti di Cabiria*. 'Fellini's script-writing is instinctive, not worked-out or constructed. It is sometimes surprising and far removed from grammatical refinement. The plans look like a lot of notes, without any detail, sketched out and repeated several different ways. The trolley is continually used because a character must be followed closely, so that some detail, some background or expression may be shot at the same time. He films an incident several times, but never in the same way; the result is always new and different and he leaves the final selection until the film is mounted. It is here that the film is really staged.'

Thus mounting is a very important stage in Fellini's films. He is aided by someone few people know, someone who is modest, but indispensable: Leo Cattozzo. Without Cattozzo Fellini's films would not be as we know them. Cattozzo was a civil servant with a safe, promising career in front of him; he gave up everything to follow a secret ambition, much to the astonishment of his parents and friends.

Del Fra goes on to say how remaking the scenario in the mounting shows that Fellini is at one and the same time loyal and disloyal to the script. His first feelings of confidence in the characters he worked out at the beginning are shaken by sudden ideas that lead him to branch off on to a new tack, and change not only details but also whole parts of the projected film. All this is tied up with one of the most interesting aspects of Fellini's method: his technique of improvisation.

Many critics have devoted much time to Fellini's love of improvisation. Rossellini is also reputed to improvise on the set no less than Fellini. (At least he was considered to do so at the peak of his career; today he lays greater emphasis on staging.) But Rossellini's improvisation—what one might call 'arranging' the score in jazz terms—is very different from Fellini's; it obeys changing moods, with a kind of laziness that does not take pre-elaborated plans into consideration. Fellini's improvisation is rational and is subordinated to a minutely worked-out plan. It is dialectical, logical improvisation and allows the director to develop his gifts of imagination, which would otherwise remain dormant. It is certainly not due to physical or intellectual laziness, for improvisation of this kind involves a squandering of energy much greater than that involved in polishing every detail in pre-cast staging. Watching Fellini at work, seeing his energy and capacity for inventing a new character, a whole scene or even a dialogue in the midst of chaos is really astrounding. Every now and again he complains about the confusion and gives orders for the outsiders watching the shooting to leave him relatively in peace. Then he appears full of astonishment and regret at his own decision and he realizes that he cannot concentrate and find new ideas without the confusion and the crowd of watchers. He calls everyone back, hoping the noise will be louder than ever; it has been said that Fellini would be unable to finish a film without chaos. In less exaggerated terms, Fellini would not benefit from an atmosphere of calm and silence.

Kezich says that in *La dolce vita* Fellini showed his true worth as an improviser in the 'aristocracy' scene, and observes that this is one of Fellini's most valuable assets because it allows him to develop his themes. The director would feel safer if he could rely on a cast-iron plan.

'But how can you faithfully execute the written text,' aks Fellini, 'if you have a better idea? You go over the same problem for days and think you have solved it. Then on the set you realize the situation is different; there is a special atmosphere and the next scene you had planned won't do. And so a different solution to the problem comes to you, almost by itself, simple, logical and perfect. Why should you reject it? Why didn't you think of it before?'

In this way Fellini uses the surprise element and draws out the actors' spontaneity. It is certainly a system which few others besides Fellini have used to good effect, and which often involves greater production time and costs. Fellini is a serious, conscientious artist, who is scrupulous towards those who have had enough faith in him to back his films. He usually tries to work within the limits of time and finance which have been laid down. If he cannot keep to them he is troubled to the point of renouncing a whole scene, as happened in *La dolce vita* in the nautical picnic sequence at Ischia.

'Directing is for me a continual shuttle between certainty and uncertainty,' Fellini declares. 'Sometimes I break off production in the early hours of the morning. When I have decided on a place for shooting I drive round in the car all night and find another. When I find the production team already on the move, I turn it round again.'

Improvisation thus prevents one from reading the entire script of Fellini's films, in the certainty that the dialogues and various situations are identical to those in the film, unless it is a script reconstructed *a posteriori* after the showing of the film. However, although they have been changed (or perhaps because they have been changed), the original scripts upon which the director improvised make impressive reading. We shall be able to see how many, and what sort of changes, subjects and treatments scripts underwent in various films and this too will be a measure of Fellini's extraordinary inventiveness.

CHAPTER 9

Fellini and his Critics—Poetry or Poeticism?

FEDERICO FELLINI had some difficulty in making a name for himself, but even so he was well known at a relatively early age. *Luci del varietà* was barely noticed, *Lo Sceicco bianco* made a resounding splash, but by his third film, *I vitelloni*, Fellini had become someone to be noticed, both by the public and a large number of the critics. *La strada* showed him to be a fully-fledged artist, though at the same time it let loose a sarcastic stream of criticism from left-wing intellectuals. They thought, not altogether correctly, that the director was veering towards right-wing Catholicism and that on a strictly aesthetic plane, his individualism alienated him from social problems. Fellini's principal faults were, so to speak, not being 'one of them', and refusing obedience to dialectical materialism. Fellini has never had, and still has not, any interest in politics and is satisfied with taking a stand, from time to time, on particular problems as he thinks fit—little caring if this attitude struck out at jealously defended positions. So, for example, Fellini has expressed the same views about censorship as the Marxists, but this does not imply any tactical compromise with them. It is equally absurd to claim that Fellini shares the beliefs of Catholic Christian democrats, or worse, that he is a 'trimmer' as someone else has disparagingly said. Fellini has many good friends who are Catholics, but he basically remains a 'free-thinker' in the broadest sense of the word, and as such he is not politically committed as a liberal. Even under Fascism Fellini took no clearly defined stand: he merely studied and observed the phenomenon—for which he has been reproached by his critics.

It is a fact that *La strada* was adversely received by left-wing critics, but the film had an immediate success abroad, especially in France where critics praised it unreservedly. Fellini's reputation in Europe was founded and destined to grow from then onwards, even with *Il bidone* which was not well reviewed by the majority of the Italian press. *Le notti di Cabiria* reversed the opinion of the most intelligent left-wing critics (Chiarini for example) and the Italian papers gave *La dolce vita* their almost unanimous approval.

In France, Germany and Italy and other European countries, meanwhile, admiration for the director became absolutely fanatical after *Le notti di Cabiria*. Very soon publications about him increased enormously and today Fellini is the most talked-about, commented on and analysed man in the cinema. His reputation in these circles equals that of Chaplin, though Chaplin found fame much later in life. With *La dolce vita* the United States has opened its doors to Fellini, particularly in the most progressive cultural circles.

Yet, in Italy especially (no man a prophet in his own country), there are critics who have remained intransigent, hostile and ill-disposed towards Fellini. In a survey which includes many aspects of the director's work, it is right to record these criticisms. Some are unfounded but others should be examined more closely.

The attitude of certain left-wing critics towards Fellini is perfectly exemplified by Fabio Carpi's *Cinema italiano del dopoguerra,* which was written before *La dolce vita.* Though he has slight reservations in favour of *Le notti di Cabiria* he maintains that up to *Il bidone* Fellini is but a 'tainted poet' who 'substitutes the exceptional for the normal and the character for man: reality is for him merely the backcloth against which individual drama is played out'. This objection has already been answered, in that a subjective artist like Fellini is not content with a banal representation of flat reality—the supposed task of neo-realism. Often all this is only another way of putting the eternal question; to what extent is a general pattern an effective means of representing what all of us feel and are conscious of according to our own convictions?

Carpi goes on to say that Fellini is not so much autobiographical in the events as in the conflicts that arise within the characters themselves. In his first two films events were significant, but later in *La strada* and in *Il bidone* they are underplayed, lyricized to the extent of losing all links with reality and taking on a purely allegorical function. This is the echo of a more serious criticism of Fellini, that he uses symbolism excessively—especially, it is said, in *La dolce vita.*

In *Il bidone* and *La strada,* Carpi further maintains, 'pathology replaces psychology, the message replaces the story, and reality is broken down into its poetical components. Thus Fellini regresses towards the shapeless and deformed, towards a perverted moral eroticism.' Fellini's predilection for the grotesque is condemned, but it is the result of an excess, not of a lack of poetry. It is misleading to assign it to a 'desperate search for poetry' on Fellini's part, or to his 'poetic sensitivity in the most impure realms of reality,' either of which would upset the balance of his judgments. Yet Carpi goes on: 'Fellini has the strength but not the sensibility of the story teller; he lacks the patience to wait trustingly until the miracle of poetry comes by itself.' This observation that Fellini seeks out poetical ideas rather than waiting patiently for their advent, is not entirely without foundation, even if it emphasizes a defect infrequently found in Fellini's work. Only when he is not in the mood—which is rarely—does Fellini slip from poetry into poeticism, which is obviously another matter, or to transferring simple, vague, poetic notions on to the screen. 'Believing too much in the poetry of one's own ideas,' says Chiarini, 'can be a mistake' because 'ideas have no aesthetic value in themselves.'

Fellini has been accused of being 'literary', especially in 'the Madman' of *La strada*, in Picasso in *Il bidone* and this 'literariness' can lead to long-windedness. But this charge has never in practice been backed with concrete examples from specific sources, and is therefore nothing more than an accusation on suspicion—an accusation from which it would be hard for anyone to exclude himself. It is one thing to say that some characters or themes are weaker and ineffective, but quite another to ascribe to them some pretended motive, with a clear statement of his intentions. Moreover, Fellini has widely confirmed that he has no need to seek inspiration for his work outside himself.

It may well be that these are partly tenable critical arguments, and as reasonable as those that warn the director of the danger of repeating certain sequences, of the abuses of some narrative ideas and constantly recurring scenery, but it is going too far and becomes ridiculous to conclude from these that Fellini's work is the product of 'artistic mystification', for his poetry would become non-poetry or perverted poetry and would result in decadence.

Finally, Fellini is often accused of deliberately avoiding tragedy as in the much discussed endings of *La strada* and *Il bidone*. But here again we are splitting hairs. However one looks at these two endings they are only episodes which Fellini has more or less successfully directed. What is more important is that Fellini has been able to express a sense of tragedy with undoubted power. One only has to think of the second part of *La strada* or of *I vitelloni*, where the whole atmosphere is impregnated with a drama that borders on tragedy, but which never actually breaks out (for this reason it is all the more sharp and painful), or again think of *La dolce vita* with the terrible nightmare of the Casa Steiner.

Negative criticism such as this should not be disregarded in relation to the complex character of Fellini's work. When it has been made objectively and in good faith, it has always benefited rather than harmed the director, who has made improvements and eradicated faults. Perfection may never be achieved, but it should always be striven for with great determination. Fellini is too honest and too much of an artist not to exert his capabilities to the full.

CHAPTER 10

The Influence of Giulietta Masina

A SURVEY of Fellini's personality and of his poetic world would not be complete without considering his artistic relationship with Giulietta Masina, his wife and the interpreter of some of the key-figures in his films. Did Fellini create the characters his wife has played, give them their dimensions and then mould them on to the actress, or did the reverse happen: were they more or less consciously suggested to him by Giulietta Masina?

Guilietta Masina played Gelsomina in *La strada* and Cabiria in *Le notti di Cabiria* but in these films she has done more than play the heroine, she has inspired the whole film. In all her husband's other films she has either had minor roles or has not appeared at all as in *I vitelloni*, in the short film *Agenzia matrimoniale*, in *La dolce vita* and in *Le tentazioni del dottor Antonio.*

In *Luci del varietà* she played Melina, a strolling player deserted by her partner, but the real heroine was Carla del Poggio. In *Lo Sceicco bianco* Guilietta was a prostitute, who presented herself as her elder sister; it was a small part at the end of the film whose hero was Brunello Bovo. In *Il bidone* she was Iris, the sorrowful wife of Picasso the 'swindler'-painter. This film shows few traces of the sentimental and moral characteristics of Gelsomina and Cabiria which pervade the other films.

Before she was directed by her husband, Giulietta Masina played other itinerant characters, in Lattuada's *Senza pietà* (*Without Pity*) and in Comencini's *Persiane chuise* (*Behind Closed Shutters*); she has seldom avoided being type-cast, apart from the extraordinary part of Gelsomina. In recent years Masina has also worked under other directors but without much success because producers and directors have merely tried to duplicate the character of *La strada* in another form (*Fortunella*), or have been unable to use her undoubted mimic and dramatic gifts to the full as in *Nella città l'inferno* (*Caged*).

At the time of *La strada* it was firmly believed that Giulietta Masina had influenced her husband decisively in the character of Gelsomina. Today few people agree with this, as a result of a radical, hasty change of opinion, fashionable in the cinema world. But I think that Giulietta Masina really did 'condition' Fellini in *La strada*, to the extent of giving the character a form which the director had only dimly envisaged, if at all. The first version of *La strada*, made by Fellini and Pirelli in 1951, was more of a fable, the world of magic had greater preponderance; at the same time there was a more sinister and dramatic atmosphere. As Del Fra has observed, Gelsomina's idiocy was more marked and bordered on madness. (She talked to the trees, rocks and to the flute.) Flajano brought this fantastical interpretation 'down to earth'. But it was certainly Giulietta Masina, Fellini's constant companion, who gave the character feminine fastidiousness, a pride in the dignity of life and that cheerful patience typical of women, who reduce the drama of living to small-scale activities. Gelsomina, thanks to Giulietta, is firstly a woman, then a symbol; as a woman she is capable of analysis if not of synthesis, and she has a thousand little feminine ways, self-pity, vanity and, in her own way, a keen sense of comedy. *La strada*, born as tragedy, with no trace of humour, became a touching real-life story, with a vein of romantic candour. All this—though we shall never know exactly to what extent—has been due to Giulietta Masina and Fellini followed her, knowing her to be on the right path.

'Gelsomina,' Giulietta herself wrote in *Cinema* (August 1954), 'had fascinated and alarmed me for a long time. She is one of those people who never gives in and holds on to life by her finger-tips, so to speak. Her tenacious desire is not to be alone, to create a basis for simple, affectionate living. I tried to express, also, in her relationship with Zampanò, the exasperation and difficulty of communicating with others, which is disguised by an artificial gaiety, to cover up the embarrassment of feeling out of place. I also thought I should bring out the somewhat conventional sentimentality of Gelsomina. When she meets the Madman I tried to make her a little incoherent and excited, like a cork exploding from an over-full bottle.'

If *La strada* could never have been made without Masina, or at least would have been a completely different film without her emanation of feminine 'mystique', the same cannot be said for *Le notti di Cabiria*. In the first place, Fellini had developed and revised the character a long time beforehand. Cabiria's psychological outline and perspective have not really been changed. Giulietta Masina identifies herself with this character too, but it is not so complete and influential an identification as with Gelsomina. She showed as Cabiria her great talent as an actress, but Fellini had already given Cabiria her soul. Obviously, he took advantage of his previous experience in *La strada*: Cabiria has the same punctilio, the sense of middle-class respectability and desire for a normal life, but these qualities were not invented by the actress, she merely stressed them in her interpretation. It is possible, however absurd, to think of another heroine in the film. As

Fellini neatly says: in *La strada* he was influenced by Giulietta the woman, in *Cabiria* by Giulietta the actress.

Giulietta herself says in Del Fra's book, 'When I finished acting in *Lo Sceicco bianco*, I didn't know that Cabiria was waiting for me. Federico only told me about his new film at the beginning of Spring 1956. I couldn't help saying to myself "Another prostitute!" Gradually Cabiria and I got to know each other. But I wasn't searching her out, she was looking for me. Besides I have never tried to identify myself with a character.' A character exists, Giulietta declares, outside the actor, who lends him his fantasy, his intuition and his imagination. 'In their temporary possession of me, Gelsomina and Cabiria sloughed off a heap of unrepeatable emotions, which I had collected through everyday living and which they spent for me. Consequently I could never re-act their parts under any circumstances. I thought that Cabiria moved in a spiritual atmosphere akin to Gelsomina, but Cabiria is more instinctive, she becomes harder and more violent, the more deeply her hopes and expectations are buried.' Giulietta Masina concludes that Cabiria's character 'purifies her in a world of immoral people'. This is so, but this clarity in the depth of a character is a typical Fellinian theme, to which the actress has added a touch of nobility.

PART TWO

A LIFE IN 8½ FILMS

CHAPTER I

Fellini Crosses the Rubicon: from Rimini to Rome (1920–39)

DID FELLINI find his source of inspiration by chance or by a process of conscious selection? In other words is the modelling of such an elegant and complete construction as we have attempted to describe, accidental, or the product of a contrived plan whose roots are buried deep, innate and insuppressible? In the light of Fellini's contradictory nature such questions are permissible. Some people declare that this world is *tout court* the invention of critics and writers (such as Brunello Rondi and others), to which Fellini has skilfully conformed, intuitively realizing its advantages. In this case the real Fellini only appears in *Lo Sceicco bianco* and *I vitelloni*, and to a very minor extent in *Cabiria*.

However, such an artificial thesis clearly ignores the many and undoubted examples of the director's coherence in all his films; neither does it explain how Fellini, by borrowing and developing the nebulous theories of others, produced his best works. These were acclaimed most warmly by the very people who accused him of plagiarism during this period of so-called artistic osmosis. This could happen but it usually coincides with entanglement and decline. It would be more accurate to say that Fellini has found and clarified a world of inspiration that was already fertile and had been a part of him since childhood and adolescence. To shed some light on this delicate question we must examine Fellini's life and works in detail for we have only looked at them briefly and in relation to aesthetic and moral problems.

Federico Fellini was born in Rimini on 20 January, 1920. Everyone is in agreement about this, including the director and the State authorities. Then matters become confused because Fellini's childhood and youth have a special significance for him, almost 'cinematic', which has led him to 'stage' the first period of his life more and more, through a somewhat distorted lens.

Let us start from a letter which Fellini wrote me in September, 1953. 'My father is a traveller in groceries, preserves and confectionery; my mother is a good housewife who has had too much cause to worry over me. Rimini is the small town in *I vitelloni*, and the characters in the film are my friends, and Moraldo—who goes away at the end of the film—is partly myself. But on further reflection, a little of myself is also in the other characters, so recognizably that when my wife saw the film, she looked at me suspiciously with new eyes and declared with some alarm that some of the spivs' conversation in the film contained a certain number of my own expressions.

'Until I was seventeen nothing happened to me. I was a terrible student, hopeless at mathematics and barely mediocre at Italian. Then I left home. Just as in *I vitelloni* I didn't tell anyone. I stayed in Florence for six months working for Nerbini as a typographer. I sketched too and began to make up plots for science-fiction strips, the type of thing in which Gordon fights the inhabitants of Saturn. Then I fell in love with a large blonde who had a rich friend in Rome, and went off with her. She was certainly not an ideal woman, especially for a lad who was barely eighteen. But she was a real mother to me and very devoted. She owns a bar here in Rome now, and when she sees me she gets very excited, jumps up and down and doesn't know what to do next. I am always afraid she will kiss my hand.

'What did I do at first in Rome? I went round the cafés and restaurants and drew caricatures, plastering fashionable store windows with awful cartoon figures. I became an insurance man, but only for a few days, then I joined a variety company, touring Italy in the guise of the company's poet. I got to know nearly all the theatre and cinema stages in the peninsula. It was a wonderful period in my life and I could make ten films about it. I can say with confidence that my character and imagination clearly formed themselves during these third-class journeys between one small town and another. I am jealously proud of those memories. Then I returned to Rome and took a permanent job on *Marc' Aurelio*, with a monthly salary of 600 lire.'

So far this is Fellini's version and it is significant that he declared that 'until I was seventeen nothing special happened'. We, on the contrary, will prove that several things that had a decisive influence on his films did take place. But he has related them on different occasions and in a variety of ways, which creates a problem for whoever takes on the job of reconstructing his life and putting certain essential facts into perspective.

Fellini himself does not give much help in this reconstruction. Sometimes he cannot distinguish the truth from the distortion he has made of it. Some events, though they are told with many modifications, recur regularly in his conversations and establish a base for discrimination, albeit vaguely: other sources of information or subtle inductive methods must be used. For example, when Fellini says that the long letter he sent me in '53 is 'fairly reliable' because at that time the construction of his life-story had 'hardly begun', he must not be believed without some reservations, all the less so when he points out that Camilla Cederna's witty profile of him in *Expresso-Mese* of summer 1961 is one of the most faithful. 'At that time I didn't know Camilla Cederna,' he maintains. 'I was rather awed by her, so it is likely that I was more sincere than usual.' It is just as difficult to imagine Fellini being swayed by someone as it is easy to realize that Camilla Cederna's brilliant article is the quintessence of the director's legendary life. So 'Fellini's confessions', valuable and useful in many respects, should be treated with great caution, despite its subject's recommendations.

Let us begin by taking a closer look at the Fellini family. His mother, Ida Barbiani, who is still living, is Roman and so Fellini is only half *romagnolo*. His father, Urbano Fellini, was a genuine *romagnolo* who died in May, 1956, aged sixty-two. Papa Fellini was an upright man, dedicated to his family, but because of his profession he could not give as much time to them as he would have liked. He was a reliable man of a traditional middle-class type, with a certain touching simplicity. His character is faithfully reproduced in *La dolce vita*, in the famous scene where Marcello's father arrives in Rome to seek his son. It is a portrait which reflects Italian provincial sanity, its traditional common sense, modest desires and steadfast moral conscience. 'You're a man now. Just remember not to do anything stupid. . . . It's all very well to have a good time . . . we're none of us saints. . . . But marriage is a serious matter.' In the film the father is a wine and liquor trader, but in reality he was a commercial traveller in confectionery and preserves, as Fellini says, and was also the representative for a coffee firm: but this makes no difference. It is his mentality that is important, and Fellini wanted to reproduce it exactly in *La dolce vita*. When he goes into the night-club, for instance, the father casually asks the waiter, 'Were you here in '32?' a question which Fellini used because he remembered having heard it many times. 'Poor papa, perhaps he said it to give the impression of a man of the world,' the director comments.

Papa Fellini would have liked Federico to have become a lawyer one day and sometimes he grieved that his son's only aptitude at school seemed to be for drawing: but in the end he reconciled himself to the situation and became a devoted, silent admirer of Fellini's films. He died of a heart attack and never had a chance to see *Il bidone*. He was afraid that his physical condition and the criticism the film had aroused would excite him too much and he would become 'heated' in the inevitable discussions, held in a typical *romagnolo* way.

As a child Fellini was, his mother affectionately recalls, a 'big head'. Photographs of the time nearly always show him with his brother, Riccardo, who is thirteen months younger. They both have huge heads of hair, and very black eyes. A few years later in 1927 Maddalena, their sister, was born. She is now married to a paediatrician and is the only one living in Rimini with her mother, in the old house in Via Oberdan. Riccardo also lives in Rome and is married to a musician's daughter. He followed in his elder brother's footsteps and, having been fairly successful as an actor—he played Riccardo in *I vitelloni*—he is now attempting to direct a film of his own.

Like all boys of the twenties and thirties Fellini devoured Salgari and adventure books of all sorts. He dreamed about them and they helped him to develop his imagination. 'I still remember,' he says, 'the great impression an empty theatre made upon me: there between the curtains, on the dusty stage and amidst the empty seats I saw my true world, which was only waiting to be brought to life. That world was at one and the same time mysterious and fascinating.' The theatre in question was the *Politeama* in Rimini, which was shut for long periods. The back entrance looked out on to an open space, which Fellini's home also faced. The future director often slipped inside the theatre with his young friends, taking advantage of the absence of caretakers and the ease with which the back-stage door could be opened.

But if Federico was already dreaming of the world of entertainment, he was not an assiduous or precocious film-goer. Even later he saw few films and then only John Ford's *The Informer* impressed him. True, he had little money to spend on entertainment, but Fellini had found a way out with one of his ideas: he used his skill at drawing caricatures of popular stars, appearing in films showing at the *Fulgor* cinema. He exhibited them in the town shops to advertise the films, so gaining free admission to the local cinema, a privilege which he did not abuse. When he was ten or fifteen years old, only journalism, which the outsider sometimes considers a substitute for the golden world of entertainment, appealed to Fellini.

Fellini's primary education was partly with the Sisters of Saint Vincent and partly in an ecclesiastical college at Fano, run by the Carissimi fathers: the third and fourth years, which he spent as a boarder at a seaside town in the Marches, do not hold pleasant memories for him. 'It was a dull provincial college,' he says, 'miserable and squalid. We ate badly, were severely punished. When I got nought—which sometimes happened—I was pilloried and shown to all the classes, the "nought" drawn on a sheet of paper and pinned to my chest.' Camilla Cederna hints at a kind of mystical talent which Fellini manifested then, partly in all seriousness, partly in jest. She adds that one of his specialities as a boy, was to pretend to be the victim of sudden maladies in order to attract attention at all costs. Once

Fellini is reputed to have stained his forehead with a bottle of red ink, and to have thrown himself on the floor at the foot of the stairs at home, but he was exposed by his stern uncle Alboino, well-accustomed to his childish exhibitionism.

One thing is certain, that in the summer the visit to his grandmother's house in the country could not come too soon for young Fellini. His paternal grandmother lived at Gambettola on the Emilia road, between Cesena and Savignano, the home town of all the Fellini family. And there right in the heart of the Romagna, with the unmistakable outline of the 'azure vision of San Marino', Federico spent happy months. Nostalgic memories of them have never faded away but are used as the background to some of his films. Even today the director confesses: 'I would like to make a film about *romagnoli* peasants, and their superstitions, faults and common sense'—an ambition which he may never fulfil.

The controversial story of his first flight to follow the shabby equestrian circus owned by a clown called Pierino is placed at about this time. Renzo Renzi tells the story and adds that the flight lasted three days and that one of his father's friends saw the boy at Bellaria whilst he was taking part in a parade through the town leading a zebra. Fellini was nine years old. Camilla Cederna also tells this tale in greater detail, and says that the boy was seven years old, that the circus was encamped behind the gaol in Rimini. One summer afternoon his father had taken him to a matinée performance where he was dazzled by the show. Next morning the boy made an excuse to leave school, and went to the circus where he was accepted easily, with no questions. He was immediately told to fetch water, 'to sponge down a feverish zebra'. In the late afternoon an acquaintance recognized Federico and took him home on the cross-bar of his bicycle. This version has been given a new twist and is quite different from the previous ones, in which Fellini was twelve, even fifteen years old and had joined the circus alone, when it had already struck camp and was on the way to Cesena. Federico stayed over a month at the circus, still looking after the zebra, a motif which has the recurring insistence of a symbol. Meanwhile his worried parents notified the police who took Fellini back to Rimini.

Will the truth ever be known? When he is pressed the director does not deny his flight (which would be denying the foundations of his legend). He confirms the exact time: the summer of 1927, which makes him seven. He admits it was just an episode that may even have passed unnoticed at home. But going into details he adamantly states that he was found a few days later at Pesaro, which is a good deal farther away than in previous versions.

One can go beyond the problems of the true story and let imagination run riot, as some biographers have done, to link the memories of that far-off adventure to the striped dress worn by Gelsomina and 'the Madman' in *La strada* and even later by Cabiria at the beginning of the film where she is fished out of the river. This costume was personally designed by Fellini. But perhaps the whole investigation is a waste of effort as Fellini's mother emphatically denies the whole affair. 'Do you think my boy would have behaved like that? Running away at the age of seven to the gypsies? No, no, he could not have been out of the house for even half a day, without our noticing it.'

Whatever the truth of that story, it cannot be denied that as a boy Fellini was exceptionally attracted by the magic world of the circus. 'As soon as I saw the first show,' he tells me, with perhaps Pierino's modest troupe in mind, 'I was mesmerized. I didn't eat or sleep for days, I didn't even want to get up. Afterwards I didn't miss one performance, and even today when the notes of the opening parade are played, I feel a kind of electric shock, which sends shivers up my spine.' Fellini alludes to Fucik's famous *March of the Gladiators*, which he wanted to bring into *La dolce vita* at all costs, in the scene with Marcello's father in the night-club.

Meanwhile Fellini had graduated from the gymnasium not too badly, and was on the threshold of adolescence. At the Lycée he did fairly well in Italian but loathed mathematics. He adds that the only subject which really appealed to him was the history of art, which was traditionally relegated to second place. Fellini has often described what happened at the Lycée, during those three years, which were dominated by the rhetoric of the 'Empire' and where fourteen madcaps intolerant of all discipline romped around the classrooms. 'We were the despair of the teachers, especially of poor Don Bastianelli, the scripture teacher, whose life we certainly shortened. I feel guilty about it even today. There were two unfortunate girls in our class, who lived in terror of our pranks.'

It was then that Fellini fell in love for the first time. She was not his contemporary, but a playmate, two years younger than he, a girl whom he had known since childhood, because she lived in the house opposite, then in Via Dante. Young Fellini had not been troubled by sex problems, which torment so many adolescents. He says he experienced the 'revelation of woman' when he was only eight on the beach at Rimini. There a plump, dirty Amazon supplied her not too obvious charms to the fishermen when they came home in the boats. 'Saraghina', as she was called, lived in a kind of garret, and the story of her meeting with Fellini, told by Cederna, is so picturesque that it serves as a further, involuntary contribution to the

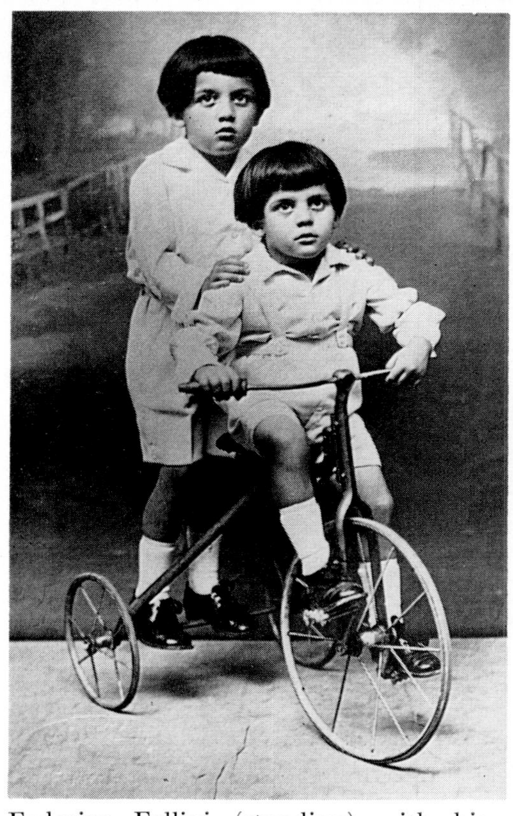

Federico Fellini (standing) with his brother Riccardo—June 1924.

1925.

First communion, 1929.

1930.

Brothers in uniform, 1933.

Fellini in 1940.

Federico (right) with two friends on the beach at Rimini—1937.

Fellini and Sergio Amidei, joint winners of the 1946 Oscar for the best film story (*Open City*).

Fellini legend. 'Three or four of us got together the necessary money, to induce the woman to lift up her petticoats,' says Fellini. 'I was charged with taking her the money.' Femininity was a species of monster, disquieting, legendary and alarming, a kind of Moby Dick to Fellini, something like the mythological monster at the end of *La dolce vita*.

But Fellini's young romantic love for Bianchina (she was then fourteen, a petite brunette) was a serious affair, which legend has treated gently without spoiling it, in spite of the usual distortions. Biographers usually couple Fellini's second flight with the idyll of Bianchina—this time as one of a pair going towards Bologna. Bologna was their goal but, it is said, the lovers took the wrong train and ended up in Ravenna with three lire in their pockets. Now, if some of the details about Fellini's youth are unverifiable, outside the source of the director's fantastic memory, the actual protagonists may be consulted about others. (We did so in this case.) Bianchina lives in Milan, where she is happily married with a grown-up son; she divides her time between writing short stories and being a housewife. Bianchina maintains a cordial, sisterly relationship with Fellini and unhesitatingly denied the story of the famous flight, either to Bologna or to Ravenna. She said, 'Do you really think that in those days, under the most rigid provincial moral code, two children like us—because we really were children—would dream of wandering about the countryside in a train? Our greatest escapades consisted of a few romantic walks outside the Porta d'Augusto, a few bicycle rides—with myself on the crossbar whilst Federico pedalled—around the outskirts of the town. And that was already a good deal, because Federico's mother, like my people, was difficult about these things.'

Bianchina says that their relationship was innocent, but long-lasting. They thought of themselves as engaged and she wore a little ring which Federico had given her, although his mother frowned upon the idyll. Fellini was a reserved and rather headstrong boy: one evening Bianchina caught him getting out of a window in the house and sliding down into the street, clinging on to two or three knotted sheets at the risk of breaking his neck. 'He loved to be elegant, in summer he always dressed in white or wore a close-fitting jacket over white trousers as was then the fashion.' (There is a photograph of him dressed like this amongst a group of his friends.) 'He came to meet me on the beach, but he never wore a bathing costume. We didn't go dancing, and I don't remember him taking me to the cinema once.'

Even then Fellini was a dreamer: he wanted to do marvellous things for her. ('We'll go to America, I'll buy you hundreds of beautiful dresses.') But everything remained in the world of fantasy. At last the idyll ended when the girl went to Milan, where she later married. But she lived on in Fellini's memory for a long time. Later he dedicated whole issues of his column to her in *Marc' Aurelio* and it was with her in mind that he was to introduce the radio character 'Pallina'.

Meanwhile in 1937, the world outside was restless and the future was threatening. Fellini and his friends without a thought in their heads, led the picaresque life of 'spivs'. In Rimini they formed a gang feared for its pranks, which often went beyond the usual students' ragging. It is superfluous to describe the atmosphere of the time in Rimini, for it has been so well depicted in *I vitelloni*. It was like so many Italian provincial towns of then and now, with this difference; that the youth of Rimini lived during the summer in the illusion of an exciting existence, when they came into contact with the season's carefree guests, who had flocked into the city to enjoy themselves. Then winter came in sad monotony, and reigned over the beach, the damp sand, the Kursaal, the bandstands, the cafés, roads and squares. In reaction they joined forces and formed gangs, whose members, goading each other on, sought some outlet for their energies with daring deeds of all kinds, especially at night.

At that time Fellini was tall, lean and already with a slight stoop. He was not physically very robust though no one remembers his being ill: it was merely due to his precocious and rapid growth. Rather than take a physical part in his friends' escapades, he was the guiding spirit behind them. Renzi recounts several of these episodes which are all more or less outlined in *I vitelloni*.

'We played practical jokes on the workmen just to get a slight thrill, after we had made sure we would not be attacked.' Once they went into a monastery at dawn and awoke the monks by turning the jet of water from the hydrant against the cell doors. At night they harassed the couples behind the boats on the shore. They spat on old pensioners' heads in public gardens and made egg flips from fifty eggs in a tub. Are all these escapades not always harmless? 'Well perhaps sometimes I did overdo it, always wanting to create my own legend,' Fellini admits. He does, however, affirm that the theft of the great clock in the Kursaal which he organized one evening, gave him the idea for the episode in which the angel is stolen in *I vitelloni*. 'It was a very heavy clock, and at first we hoped to sell it, but we couldn't find a buyer.'

In the meantime he had thought of exploiting his drawing talents and set up a small stall to sell caricatures (signed 'Fellas'), a smaller version of the one set up in Rome after the liberation. In the last summer he spent in Rimini he began touring the beach, making satirical sketches for good-natured ladies. He had also begun to contribute some cartoons in a small way to the *420*, a humorous magazine in Florence, edited by Nerbini. But he realized that these meagre resources were not enough. He was already thinking of leaving Rimini, tired of a life that amused, but also disgusted him. It was Moraldo's desire for escape (*I vitelloni*), whilst the two later moves, to Florence and Rome, are shown in *Lo Sceicco bianco* and another film project which was never actually screened called *Moraldo in città* (*Moraldo in the City*).

In autumn 1938 (sometimes Fellini talks about 1937 but he is certainly mistaken in the date), Fellini passed his exams at the Lycée after some difficulty and set off for Florence. He told his family he wanted to enrol at the University and he did in fact later enrol at the Law Faculty in Rome, but with the firm resolution never to attend lectures but to use his status as a student to postpone his military service *sine die*. On his own declaration he stayed six months in Florence as a typographer with Nerbini, working in the world of strip-cartoons which he portrayed in *Lo Sceicco bianco*.

The editor Nerbini was then printing *420*, a Tuscan magazine whose humour did not always appeal to the most delicate tastes. Young Fellini divided his time between correcting the proofs, acting as messenger boy and cartoonist, being paid three lire a drawing; he even submitted some caricatures to the elder brother of *420*, the *Marc' Aurelio*, which had a national distribution and was edited in Rome. It was, however, a precarious living: with better luck and continuous employment Fellini was able to dedicate himself to his first project as a script writer and director, not in the cinema, but in the realm of science fiction. Nerbini was also the editor of the *Avventuroso* which published American stories about Flash Gordon—who was a true precursor of science-fiction heroes—Mercuranians, Saturnians, Mandrake and Hawk Men. At that time a stern order had come from Rome not to buy anything from the transatlantic plutocrats and the editor, to get himself out of an embarrassing situation, put Fellini and the painter Giove Toppi in charge of Gordon's adventures with orders to make them a national Italian product. Even today the director's face brightens when he thinks of the amusement he derived from making up those cartoon strip stories, upon which he could lavish his imagination.

He declares he met Palazzeschi in Florence, who advised him to write poetry. But Fellini took care not to do so—his immediate ambition was, as we have said, to become a great journalist. 'I liked their overcoats and the way they wore their hats on the back of their heads. Journalists were the most fascinating people in the world for me.' But he felt the pull towards Rome: and in spring, 1939, Fellini set off to conquer the capital.

CHAPTER 2

The Conquest of Rome (1939–45)

FELLINI WENT to Rome in pursuit of a woman (a 'large blonde' according to Federico) who did not, however, have any further place in his life. This much is certain, that shortly afterwards the future director was reduced to living on his wits. He had told his family that he wanted to study jurisprudence, and his anxious mother had visited Rome and left under the impression that he was comfortably settled in a highly respectable rented room. But Fellini, goaded on by the demon of capriciousness, took to roaming the streets where there was such a lot to see and where he hoped to satisfy his irrepressible curiosity.

For three weeks he worked for the news section of *Il popolo di Roma* but he left, disappointed by the unexciting police and local court news he had to collect. He began to draw again and submitted his cartoons and short stories to newspapers (the *Marc' Aurelio* in particular); he sold caricatures in cafés and restaurants and decorated shop windows for publicity. His activities at this time find an echo in *Moraldo in città*: the hero persuades an unwilling tradesman to let him paint puppets on his shop window, but he cannot rub out the bad drawings and captions and runs away embarrassed by the ironic glances of the passers-by.

However, Fellini's talent was not wasted within the craftsman's limits for he later used it to draw nearly all the characters in his films and to give them a visible if not written image. Fellini begins the staging of his films with drawings, of his chief characters, accurate in every detail. Gelsomina and Cabiria took shape beneath the director's pencil—a precious aid to Fellini. With it he collaborates with the costume designers, architects and scenery makers, who are given a summary in sketches of what he wants. No discussion, however long, could ever replace the spontaneity of his drawings.

For a few months Federico assisted in compiling *Cinemagazzino*, edited and directed by a tailor. Fellini had made friends with the writer of the woman's column 'Letters from our readers' and enthusiastically read those extraordinary letters from moon-struck females, like those portrayed in *Lo Sceicco bianco*. Meanwhile he exercised the supreme Italian art of 'getting by'. One day a casual acquaintance, the prototype of the 'swindler', offered to sell him genuine diamonds at below cost price: they would have shared the proceeds. They were paste diamonds, but Fellini was unaware of this and thought that he would try to pass them off on certain cinema actors. So he went to Cinecittà where Valenti and Ferida were filming Blasetti's *Corona di ferro* (*The Iron Crown*). Fellini remembers the impression of magnitude and power the famous director made upon him with his jack-boots and riding whip; but he also remembers what a fool he looked when Valenti, in tartar costume, stepped from the coach whose wheels bristled with blades, took the diamond from his hand and ground it underfoot, laughing in his face. Another time Fellini claimed that his would-be buyer was Assia Noris, changing the whole scene except for the conclusion.

The instigator of all this, a highly-skilled trickster, took the blame with aplomb and the false gems were returned to him: he was called 'Lupaccio', the wolf, and the director based the character of Augusto in *Il bidone* on him. Augusto's arrest in the film (one of the most important scenes) is derived from something that actually happened to 'Lupaccio' and which Fellini claims to have witnessed. The same 'Lupaccio', moreover, had a small part in the film, in the famous 'crooks' party' and he allowed himself to be interviewed many times.

The meeting with Aldo Fabrizi, which in some respects was to be a decisive influence on the director of *La dolce vita*, took place shortly afterwards. Fabrizi, Federico maintains (as do his biographers), was playing in a second-rate curtain raiser at the Jovinelli, an old theatre where famous comedians had once played, but which was now very dilapidated. Fellini visited Fabrizi in his little room, saying he was a journalist (which was partly true) and they made a tour of the restaurants in Rome and found themselves in agreement about menus and a modest form of collaboration. Federico was to draw caricatures and sketches for the actor. They worked together so well that Fabrizi invited Fellini to accompany him on a tour of the provinces, with a company of travelling players which he directed. Fellini was to be the company's official 'poet', but in fact he became a general factotum: costumier, actor, secretary and scenery painter.

The company put on a revue called 'Sparks of Love' and took it up and down Italy for a few months (mostly in the south); it was, Fellini recalls, 'an insultingly bad show, and it was distressing to witness the enjoyment of the poor audience in the pit'.

His experience of makeshift, of miserable digs, of arriving at night and leaving at dawn, of skirmishes with the local big-wigs and with comedians, inspired *Luci del varietà* (and also the beginnings of *Vita da cani* (*It's a Dog's Life*), directed by Steno and Monicelli). There were eight dancers in the company, not all of whom were young or attractive: six of them in turn fell in love with the romantic young 'poet' and endless disagreements and noisy quarrels ensued. Fortunately the tour was coming to an end and when Fellini got back to Rome he fulfilled his old dream of getting a permanent post on the editorial staff of *Marc' Aurelio*.

So far, we have followed the director's own version of that extraordinary touring experience, which all his official biographers have reproduced, even in the books which have been published abroad. But Aldo Fabrizi, in a personal interview, gave an entirely contradictory version, seen from a slightly jaundiced point of view.

Fabrizi has always been aware of Fellini's tale of that famous tour, as for over ten years he has seen reports in the *Eco della Stampa* about his supposed adventure with Fellini. One day he met the director by chance and, smilingly, tried to touch upon the question. Federico then promised to put things right at the earliest possible moment at a press conference. Since it never took place Fabrizi sometimes finds himself in embarrassing, though amusing, situations. He does not want to deny Fellini's story and at the same time he cannot confirm it. So when two well-known radio newsmen from a foreign station insisted that he record the miserable strolling player's existence led by himself and Fellini, he tried to get out of the interview and invented every kind of previous engagement and in the last resort fled from his insistent followers. At last they grew tired and went away empty handed.

Aldo Fabrizi says he met Federico in the summer of 1939 when Fellini and Ruggero Maccari (now a famous scenario writer) were making a survey of the most famous people in the world of entertainment for *Cinemagazzino*. When they had interviewed Anna Magnani, Totò and others, they visited him in his dressing-room, which was not in the Jovinelli but at the Corso Cinema. At that time Fabrizi did not have his own supporting company, but was the star turn in a solo number and it seems that the programme was not too bad.

Fabrizi remembers having directed companies of his own only twice, once in a revue, the other time in straight plays, and these were ten years apart: in 1935, when the troupe was called 'Compagnia Nuovo Fiore', and in 1945, after the arrival of the Americans in Rome. He has never formed a company called 'Faville d'Amore' and he has never heard of it except in Fellini's postdated version.

One may rightly doubt whether Federico ever left Rome for long periods, at least before he became famous and the very picturesque 'artistic journeys' he made across Italy only refer to the one he made in 1945–46 with Rossellini.

It should be borne in mind that in the years 1939–42, the period we are considering now, Fabrizi was in daily contact with Fellini. But they did not see each other behind the scenes in provincial theatres but at the Bar Castellino in the Piazzo Venezia where artists used to meet and stay on until two or three in the morning. Fabrizi and Fellini (who at that time were living in the same quarter, outside the walls of San Giovanni) walked home together slowly, talking continuously. Aldo Fabrizi told Federico, who listened to him, fascinated, about his long periods of poverty and misfortune, both pathetic and comic, during his first years as an entertainer. Indeed Fabrizi got to know of the hard facts of life very quickly when, aged eleven, he was left with a mother and five sisters to support.

The popular comedian was pleased to let off steam to his educated, intelligent listener who was an exceptional audience, unlike the spectators in the pit. And he was really fond of Fellini, whom he asked to be godfather to his son Massimo at his first communion and at his confirmation. According to Fabrizi, some of the misfortunes he recounted to Fellini in discursive mood, with colourful sketches and satirical descriptions of various types, may have been useful to the director later in *Luci del varietà*, and he thinks that the famous scene in *I vitelloni* in which Sordi mocks the workers is a flash-back to those nocturnal Roman walks. But Fellini is uncompromising about this: the sequence was inspired by the dissolute youths of Rimini who were active in this kind of daring escapade. On the other hand Federico admits, and Fabrizi confirms this, that when he needed a few shillings he took a selection of his own witty stories along to the actor who inserted them into his monologues with his catch-phrase 'Do you mind?'

Now that we have heard Aldo Fabrizi's version, which seems to be more or less authentic, let us turn to those events in Fellini's career which can be verified or at least confirmed to a certain extent. His appointment on the *Marc' Aurelio* cannot be doubted and took place in the years 1939–40.

At that time the *Marc' Aurelio* was an *avant-garde* weekly (for a time it also appeared twice weekly): the lawyer Lupo owned it, De Bellis directed it and it was edited by persons whose names later became famous. Whilst it was less original than the *Bertoldo* of Milan, it had its own brand of comedy, especially popular with students. Who can forget 'The dandy who said to his friends', 'That guy Giggi—' and so on? As well as his caricatures, Fellini also contributed to various columns—'Third Year in the Lycée' (with souvenirs of his student escapades), 'City Lights' and 'Will you listen to me?' He also composed a series of short romantic-comic stories whose protagonists were a young married couple 'Cico' and 'Pallina' (Pallina, as we have already hinted, was originally a portrait of Bianchina).

Working for the *Marc' Aurelio*, Fellini was quite prosperous (600 lire a month) and he began to write scripts for the radio and to collaborate as a gag writer in Macario's first films *Il pirata sono io*, *Non me lo dire*, *Lo vedi come sei?* (*I'm the Pirate*; *Don't tell me*; *Do you know what you look like?*). Mattoli, the film director, happened to be short of ideas and one day he thought of turning to 'the boys on the *Marc' Aurelio*, who are always full of bright ideas', because he wanted them to strengthen the weaker scenes. He went to see the editor, and soon reached an agreement for collaboration. However, Fellini's real entry into the cinema was due to Aldo Fabrizi and this time both director and actor are in agreement. Fabrizi asked Fellini to touch up his plot for *Avanti, c'è posto* (*Come on, There's Room*), a film by Bonnard on which Zavattini had also collaborated. Following this Fellini did the staging for *Campo dei fiori* (*Field of Flowers*), again for Fabrizi (from an idea by Mario Girolami) and for *L'ultima carrozzella* (*The Last Roundabout*) which was originally Fabrizi's idea.

Fellini still remembers these plots and productions—amongst them *Documento Z3*, *Quarta pagina*, *Chi l'ha visto?* (*Document Z3*, *The Fourth Page*, *Who Has Seen Him?*). 'They weren't much,' he says, 'but they foreshadowed neo-realism with small scenes and social sketches depicted in a good-humoured fashion. In short, I think I had gone beyond the paraphernalia of white telephones and the mawkish situations of that era.' Just then his interest in the cinema had been re-awakened: he saw several films and he confesses his admiration for *Quai des brumes* (*Quay of Mists*) and *Alba tragica* by Carnè, as well as Duvivier's *Un carnet de bal* (*Christine*).

'If there is any indirect cinematic influence in my work for the screen up until *Roma, città aperta* (*Open City*) and *Paisà*, it is undoubtedly the influence of the French cinema which round about 1940 held sway over everyone, to some degree.'

Meanwhile war was imminent. Federico was the eternal student (though he attended no lectures) and was employed by the *Marc' Aurelio*, a magazine which was regarded with favour in higher circles (they had even tried to make it a bilingual weekly in Italian and German for distribution in Germany). Consequently he had been spared so far, but was soon to be disillusioned. One day Ettore Muti, the party secretary, went to inspect the editorial staff, and the principal writers of the paper were presented one by one. Fellini is inimitable when he recalls that grotesque ceremony: each man clicked his heels to attention and announced the name of his own column, which was not always in keeping with the Fascist rhetoric. There was for example 'Ugly Genoveffa' and also Fellini's 'Are you listening to me?' which besides lending itself to possible misinterpretation, was declaimed by a long, rakish, young man with a large head of ruffled hair and, moreover, dressed in civilian clothes. Muti stared at him puzzled and then said to him drily: 'Let me give you some advice. Get your hair cut, it is too low on your collar'.

Get your hair cut!—the director did not want 'trouble' and would not listen to reason, as the Fascist secretary had left without further comment. But there was more trouble to come for Fellini, after a letter written by him and signed 'Bianchina', addressed to a soldier at the front, had been published in the *Marc' Aurelio*. The mocking, paradoxical tone of the letter was not to the liking of the Minister of Popular Culture and the atmosphere around the happy-go-lucky editor became oppressive. Up till then, Fellini had got by with successive extensions of his convalescent's certificate which he had obtained from sympathetic friends or by means of a small bribe, with the excuse of a heart murmur. But one bitter winter's day—at the beginning of 1943—he went to the Celio military hospital for the usual renewal and realized that the medical staff had been completely changed. Moreover, German officers were watching at a distance, but with attention, the procedure of the visits. The only doctor who knew him rolled up his sleeves cautiously, behind the backs of the others, making desperate signs to warn him that he could do nothing. The result was that Fellini, in the twinkling of an eye, was declared fit, sent to his unit and told to join his regiment which, he recalls, was in Puglia.

As if he were in a dream, Federico found himself on the street with three documents in his hand signifying his condemnation. He was stupefied for a moment. Then in a fit of mad rage, he tore up the papers into tiny shreds. Immediately afterwards, he awoke to the realization of his mistake, and he hastened to make amends. On the advice of his friends he went to Forli, where other acquaintances condescended to give him a presentable military 'status' with the necessary documents. He went back to Bologna for another medical examination. His innate fatalism had already resigned him to his destiny when, just as he was about to undergo his examination, the siren went off and an air-raid burst upon the city. The military hospital was hit and Federico himself was slightly wounded as he slipped over, on what he does not know. He saved himself by a miracle, as he ran towards the station, which was also hit.

No more was said about military service: the records had been detroyed and there were other things to worry about. Soon afterwards came the landing in Sicily, then the collapse of Mussolini's régime and the fall of Rome.

When he returned to Rome Fellini experienced the second serious moral crisis of his life. He realized that life in the capital had not solved the problem of living: he was still the Rimini 'spiv', but on a different scale and his spiritual welfare was in a precarious state. Something was needed that would change his life: and exactly at that time Giulietta Masina appeared on the scene.

Federico's meeting with Giulietta Masina is of the utmost importance: without it perhaps he would not be the great artist he is today. Giulietta gave his life order and meaning: she taught him to appreciate simple things, she gave him faith and freed him from the image of the 'spiv' and 'cursed poet'; an image which Fellini secretly delighted in, but which would have led to nothing positive. Fellini often admits 'I was very lucky to find her. Giulietta is everything to me and I do not know what would have happened to me otherwise.'

It was June, 1943 and Fellini had thought of developing on the radio the two characters Cico and Pallina whom he had started in the *Marc' Aurelio*. The programme was sponsored by a perfume company, the 'Niba,' concern, 'the inspirers of Niba colognes, Dream of You, Awakening in the Woods, and Fire of Love'. A young actress who had made her name with the GUF drama company was asked to play the part of Pallina: she was Giulietta Masina. Giulietta was born in 1921 at San Giorgio di Piano near Bologna: she was thus a year younger than Federico and she also had a degree. She was an arts graduate from the University of Bologna and had written a thesis on archaeology, no less; without doubt, she is one of our best educated actresses.

One day Fellini saw a photograph of Giulietta in *Radiocorriere* and the interpreter of his sketches seemed to him so attractive that he decided to telephone her. He spoke to her in a slow, deep voice to create an impression and said, 'Hello Pallina, I'm Fellini'. 'And who is Fellini?' the girl replied. Fellini was put off balance. 'What do you mean, who is he? He's the author of the sketches in which you act.' 'Oh yes. Pleased to know you.' Then, after further useless attempts to impress her in which he talked about his sadness and his disgust at life, he said that before he decided to die he would like to meet her; and he invited her to lunch. They went to a smart restaurant and Giulietta remembers that she ate very little for fear that her shabbily-dressed escort would not be able to pay the bill. She listened to his catalogue of troubles (real or imaginary), and pretended to believe that the scars Fellini showed her on his wrists were due to a suicide attempt. They were in fact caused by a broken glass in a festive drinking session with his friends. She made him swear not to do anything stupid and promised in turn that she would see him again.

They became engaged and their engagement lasted exactly four months during the summer and the beginning of autumn 1943. When he went to Giulietta's aunt's house for the first time Fellini was struck by the stability and sanity of middle-class life, the typical northern common sense, and the austere apartment full of cuckoo clocks which seemed an inviolable refuge against the gathering clouds of war outside. One day he sent Giulietta two little goslings, alive, with cards saying 'Pallina' and 'Federico' tied round their necks. A brief note accompanied the gift: 'Pallina, will you marry me? I hope so.'

They were married on 30 October, 1943, regardless of the difficulties at the time. They did not even have to go out of the house because a priest lived in the same building and he made one room into a chapel and celebrated Mass there: here the two were married. A honeymoon was out of the question and Federico installed himself in Giulietta's aunt's flat until better times came. But shortly afterwards something happened that would have cost him dearly, but for his presence of mind. As usual Fellini contradicts himself as to the date: he has sometimes placed this occurrence the day before his wedding; other times he has maintained that it happened some months after; finally, he has decided to fix the date as being a week or two after his marriage. Apart from this discrepancy, it all happened approximately in this way.

One morning Fellini was crossing the Piazza di Spagna, when he noticed a movement around him, as if suddenly people were walking on eggs. 'I realised I had been caught in a trap more from the compassionate faces and sympathetic exclamations of the women to me than from what was really happening. Suddenly I found myself pushed into a corner by a boy in the uniform of the *Brigate Nere* who stuck a machine-gun in my back. He was almost a child and I couldn't believe he was serious.' Fellini was put into a lorry where there were some German soldiers and a group of other unfortunates captured in the same way. The lorry moved off whilst his luckless companions murmured in dismay: 'They are taking us to Germany, they are taking us to Germany!'

'I thought I'd had it,' says the director, 'and what I did later was more through instinct than reason. At a bend the lorry slowed almost to a halt and I saw two German officials standing on the pavement talking. I didn't lose time and I began to shout to them 'Fritz, my dearest Fritz!' and leaped down almost at the same time. The soldiers in the convoy were puzzled for a moment, all the more so when I boldly held out my hand to the nearest German officer, and embraced him, still calling loudly "Dearest Fritz". When I think about it now, it gives me the shivers. Nothing happened: whether the soldiers believed in the comedy, or whether they hesitated to shoot at someone who used the body of one of his superiors as a shield, the important thing is that there was no fatal burst of machine-gun fire and a few moments later I heard the rumble of the lorry as it drew away. Meanwhile, the two German officials pushed me away in annoyance and went off in pursuit of their own affairs. They had probably understood, but let the matter slip. I found myself alone in the Via Margutta, weak at the knees, my heart thumping, but safe.'

Sometimes Fellini likes to add that he fainted and came round in a chemist's shop, but even without this addition it can be concluded that—if the facts were as recorded—he had made a very successful escape.

Until the liberation of Rome, Fellini stayed at home as much as possible, living like all Romans at that time: awaiting the Americans. Giulietta was pregnant and in summer 1944 she gave birth to a little boy ('Federichino' Fellini calls him tenderly and nostalgically), who did not live more than a few weeks. It was a terrible blow for the young couple: in the uproar of that nightmarish summer, amidst the singing of drunken negro soldiers, the black-market and inflation, the departure of that little angel to heaven had left them desperately alone. But they had to act: they were faced with poverty and hunger. Fellini was forced to make a new commercial venture, still using his talent as a caricaturist.

'When the Americans arrived,' Fellini wrote to me in 1953, 'I collaborated with my old friends of the *Marc' Aurelio* and opened a shop called "The Funny face shop". I had never earned so much in my life. We drew caricatures and portraits, we made recordings and took photographs, we did everything for the American soldiers passing through the city. It was such a success that we opened a second, a third, then a fourth shop. Envious friends leant up against the door shaking their heads scornfully and saying that we were worse than prostitutes. A ribald atmosphere prevailed in those shops and often the Military Police beat everyone up and carried away wounded and unconscious soldiers and artists.

'One day Rossellini appeared on the other side of the window. He signalled to me to come out because he wanted to talk to me. He wanted to make a documentary about Don Morosini, who had been shot by the fascists. I agreed rather doubtfully and that documentary became *Roma, città aperta*. I made a single contract in which I agreed to produce Rossellini's film and a cartoon about the adventures of a jeep, for the sum of 10,000 lire.

'Meanwhile the Americans were leaving, and in our little shops we made a sport of catching flies and staining them with aniline. I thought Rossellini was a great man and I approached him again. We became friends and the memories of *Paisà* and the tour of Italy made with Roberto—an Italy just beginning to get over the war, Naples, Florence and the Po—are unforgettable. And I think the film is one of the few great ones in the world. I saw it again recently: the copy was old and the projection continually interrupted, but the film was splendid, it gripped me from beginning to end.'

The idea of making the allies contribute to the maintenance of Italian artists, penniless but rich in talent, came to Fellini when, by chance, he came into contact with the British military authorities. He observed how easy it was to sell caricatures to officers and soldiers: they did not look for the finer points for they thought all Italians were great artists. It was a simple matter to pass from the English to the Americans who were even more welcoming. And Fellini's shops (which grew to seven in his imagination with the passing of the years from the three or four of reality) proved to be inexhaustible mines of devices for making money. The Yankees would pose beneath a large card on which was written: 'Look! The most ferocious and amusing caricaturists are eyeing you—sit down and tremble.' Or else they would flick through an album and choose one of the many grotesque poses in which they could be photographed. They were prefabricated designs in which a soldier was fighting with lions at the Colosseum or was dressed as a Roman and kissing a beautiful girl, or squandering money in the Trevi Fountain. The G.I. would put his head into the right empty space and the card was ready to be sent home.

Fellini's partner was De Seta, a caricaturist who had been a colleague in the *Marc' Aurelio*, but soon they had to take on other artists, photographers, clerks and even an administrator. The largest proceeds came from making small recordings which the soldiers sent back to America so that their families could hear the sound of their voices in Rome. 'My dear wife, the Italian girls are mad about me: I hope you are proud of your Joe,' said the texts; or else 'Dear mother, I killed three lions at the Colosseum today.' The records were made of such poor quality material that they could only be heard once, immediately after they had been cut. And the quarrels that ended with people wounded and unconscious, of which Fellini speaks, took place when some soldier decided to listen to the record before sending it off. He would go back to the shop to protest and often the cunning salesman and the rash buyers had to fall back upon the arbitration of the military police.

Fellini met Rossellini at the beginning of 1945. Rossellini, Renzi says, had 'the face of an emigrant in search of help'. He wanted Fellini to help him in persuading Aldo Fabrizi to take part in a documentary film which had been commissioned from him by a wealthy old lady. The idea was to portray the noble figure of Don Morosini who had been shot by the fascists. Together with Alberto Consiglio, Rossellini had already drawn up an outline of the production. Fellini agreed readily. But as they progressed the film had expanded. The lady who was financing them was willing to consider a second documentary about the activities of Roman youth against the Germans during the occupation; and then Fellini and Amidei, who had joined them in the meantime, proposed to Rossellini that the two films should be fused to make a larger one. One night, apparently, they hastily and furiously wrote a new plot and a new scenario and then the economic difficulties began. The old lady was not Saint Patrick's well and they had to find other financiers: but at last, after a thousand set-backs, they went to work.

Some of the minor circumstances relating to *Roma, città aperta* are controversial, but they are not without interest in the light of the film's importance in the neo-realist movement. Aldo Fabrizi, for example, claims that Rossellini came on to the scene later, since the part of Don Morosini (limited to a short film of barely 600 feet) had been offered to him—Fabrizi—who had accepted it only on condition that the episode be developed into a full-length film. So the actor suggested that two episodes which took place shortly before in Rome should be inserted. One was about the bomb that some youths had exploded in the Prenestino quarter, and the other of a working woman who had been killed by the Germans as she was trying to take some bread to her husband and son, who had been captured during a search and imprisoned. (Fabrizi said he witnessed this event himself because it took place near his house.) The enlarged plot was then given to Rossellini, whom Fabrizi introduced to Fellini.

Fellini's version, however, is supported by all the legends of the cinema and also by those who worked on the film: the director himself has recounted and defended his statements very precisely and confidently, citing facts and dates in logical order. This is one of those cases where the solution is 'open' and will probably always remain so. Perhaps it is better that a veil should be drawn over the beginnings of neo-realism, as in the great historical and literary events of the ancient world. A faint halo of mystery and romanticism does no harm to the film which now too belongs to a distant and legendary past.

At any rate, returning to the laborious making of *Roma, città aperta*, it should be remembered that Rossellini was shooting in a large room in Via degli Avignonesi, which had once been used as a betting saloon for horse races and was not far from a *maison close*. This fact made the film famous. It was as he was cautiously leaving the *maison close* that Rod Geiger, an American officer, saw something of the shooting of what was to be *Roma, città aperta*. He was immediately interested and offered to place the film in America. With nothing to lose, Rossellini accepted and when Rod Geiger came to see the film he in his turn became a fanatical supporter of it. But nobody thought any more about him, until the news came from New York that Geiger had sold the film to the independent distributor Burstyn, who had in his turn successfully distributed it. And the echo of enthusiastic criticism from America finally convinced the Italians, who had remained indifferent until then, that *Roma, città aperta* was a masterpiece.

Fellini was one of the first to sense the beauty of the film: he remembers that at the first showing he was moved to tears. But he admits honestly that he only played a secondary part in its making. 'Rossellini did everything. I limited myself to a few ideas for the theme.' He says that the electricity needed for the making of the film was stolen from a cable at a nearby printers where a PWB newspaper was printed and that some scenes were shot at the house of the same Amidei. The film itself was, for the most part, deteriorating and this created an extraordinary optical effect which the Americans took for a fantastic discovery.

Fellini only made an authentic contribution to the birth of neo-realism in the following year—with *Paisà*. The 10,000 lire he had received as payment for *Roma, città aperta* were certainly one incentive for him to continue collaborating with Rossellini, but, as has been seen, he had come to admire Rossellini greatly: he was to call him 'maestro' from then on, never deserting him even in his darkest moments. In the course of six months spent travelling together through Italy in search of a theme and of a background to *Paisà* he made a true and firm friendship with Rossellini. Of what kind? Fellini himself has confessed: 'It was a bohemian friendship, rascally, ribald, and it was also a game, a contest in "tall stories", sometimes inspired.'

Their friendship was no less deep because they were undeniably close in temperament and character.

CHAPTER 3

Fellini Discovers the Cinema (1946–50)

MAKING *PAISÀ* with Rossellini was important for Fellini because he fell in love with the cinema and realized for the first time that his only true occupation was that of a director. ('When I weighed up my laziness, my ignorance, my curiosity, my lack of discipline and my incapacity to make sacrifices, I convinced myself that the cinema was my vocation.')

In *Paisà* Fellini was assistant director together with Massimo Mida; he was also author, scenario- and script-writer. He did a little of everything. The eventful trip across the country, in an atmosphere of disorganized freedom, enabled him to discover the intricate human values of Italy, at a time when they were most sincere and troubled. They went to Sicily first, then to Naples, to Florence, to a small convent in the Tuscan-Roman Appenines, and finally to the estuary of the Po. The film grew day by day, depending upon the brilliance of Rossellini's improvisation, which had an indelible effect upon his pupil's personality. In Sicily, Fellini watched Rossellini adapt the initial episode, which he had already roughly worked out, to the two actors who had been found by chance: the Neopolitan girl, Carmela, and the American soldier, Robert. Even in the monastery the plot was adapted to fit the characteristics of the real-life monks, who were the protagonists. And the future director of *La dolce vita* learnt a valuable lesson in how to gain help from the actors, even when they are not professional.

Fellini shot some of the scenes himself: in the Florence episode, for example, he filmed the Germans near the Baptistry, and the passage of the carboys of water under gun-fire. But more important than this practice—in which he was helped by the cameraman Martelli—was his continual contact with that magician of pictures, Rossellini, in the fantastic, unique climate of Italy in 1946. In *La Table Ronde*, Fellini is reported as saying, 'Rossellini taught me humility in living, he has faith in things, in men, in the strength of man, in reality. By looking at things with the love and communion that are established from one moment to another between a person and myself, between an object and myself, I understood that the cinema could fill my life, helping me to find a meaning in existence.'

When *Paisà* was presented at Venice in September, 1946 it was successful, not greatly so, but enough to reassure Fellini that he was on the right road. In the meantime he had agreed to write the scenario—with several others—for *Il delitto di Giovanni Episcopo* (*Flesh Will Surrender*), for Alberto Lattuada, from d'Annunzio's novel.

'I was on the way to becoming a true professional,' remarks Fellini. But he remembers little or nothing about his work in this film, or else he prefers not to remember. However, his relationship with Lattuada began with that film, a relationship which was to bear greater fruit.

Lattuada, by temperament and taste, is probably the antithesis of Fellini: when he directs he is like an architect, precise and orderly and sometimes even over-stylized. It is a mystery how they ever came to agree, but it often happens that opposite temperaments complement each other, at least to a certain extent. Anyway, after *Giovanni Episcopo* Fellini wrote the scenario for *Senza pietà* for Lattuada and then in 1949 he collaborated with others in the scenario of *Il mulino del Po* (*Mill on the Po*).

While he was working on *Senza pietà* in 1947, he met Tullio Pinelli and this acquaintance was to prove very useful. Pinelli's character is also apparently the opposite of Fellini's: he is a Piedmontese of the old school, from a noble family, methodical, rational, well-balanced, good-natured, but dogmatic in cultural matters, though life in Rome (he settled there in 1942) has mellowed him. Yet Fellini was to form a long-lasting partnership with this man, in complete harmony and understanding.

They came to know each other by chance. (Pinelli himself has written that they were reading the two sides of the same newspaper hanging at a kiosk.) They liked each other immediately and Pinelli asked Fellini to collaborate in the writing of a film by Coletti (*Il Passatore—The Outlaw*). Fellini retaliated by persuading him to become one of the team of scenario-writers for *Senza pietà*. At that time Pinelli was already an expert scenario-writer. Born in Turin in 1908, he graduated in law and went into the cinema after considerable experience in the theatre; he was remarkably skilled in writing dialogue. In the period between 1935 and '42 he was quite an *avant garde* playwright, and divided his time between this activity and the law. It was he who probably intensified Fellini's already innate sense of the miraculous and turned his mind to religious questions. Pirelli was—and still is—greatly absorbed by mysticism, an absorption which is coupled with a strong dramatic instinct. This sensitive man with grey hair, the father of four children, has a Jansenist concept of Christianity. His influence upon Fellini was, after Rossellini's, to be decisive upon the director's work: the difference being that this one influence was to grow steadily as the other declined and was to make itself felt not only in the technical and theoretical fields, but also in the very substance of a film.

The scenario for *Senza pietà*—for which Fellini and Pinelli made an expedition into the Tombolo forest, dressed as tramps—kept Fellini very much occupied, as his wife was to appear for the first time in this film. (She later received a 'silver ribbon' for her part as a minor character.) Meanwhile Fellini was given an even greater opportunity and this time it was with Rossellini again.

The creator of *Roma, città aperta* had worked out a one-act film, all in dialogue, for Anna Magnani—really it was a monologue by Jean Cocteau—called *La voce umana* (*The Human Voice*). The plot was very short and not sufficient for a whole film; it was later enlarged with an idea of Fellini's which formed the second part of the film. It was given the comprehensive title *L'amore* (*Love*). Fellini's episode was *Il miracolo* (*The Miracle*), a story that hovered between mysticism and hallucination. (The influence of Pinelli, who was one of the scenario-writers, can be seen even at this point.) At first Federico passed it off as the adaptation of a non-existent Russian short story. In fact it was a story he had heard told in the country at Gambettola, when he was a child. A wandering gelder of pigs had made a poor, mentally retarded girl pregnant; when she had given birth, everyone was convinced that it was the devil's child. In Fellini's version the man was a rough shepherd and the girl a half-crazy gipsy given to fits of ecstasy; in her pregnant state she maintains that she had experienced something like the Immaculate Conception. When the exultant girl proclaims this, they all make fun of her and even strike her. So she climbs to the top of a mountain and rings the bell of a little church to announce the event. These ignorant men understand and fall on their knees crying that it is a miracle.

In the film Fellini was co-director as well as script and scenario-writer. At Rossellini's request he also acted for the first time. He played the hero, the shepherd whom Anna Magnani in her madness mistakes for St. Joseph. In this guise he had to dye his hair platinum blonde 'partly as a joke, partly out of vanity', Fellini says. Rossellini tells how he failed to return from the ladies hairdresser to which he had gone, so he himself went to find him. He discovered that Fellini did not dare to come out because a small crowd had gathered in front of the window and were making sarcastic remarks, calling him 'Rita Hayworth'. But Fellini soon overcame his embarrassment and people remember him at Amalfi—where *Il miracolo* was being filmed—stretched out on the rocks in a rough sack-cloth tunic, with an untrimmed beard and his hair falling on his shoulders. As an actor Fellini did not do too badly, even though he never wished to repeat such a demanding experience.

After *Il miracolo*, Fellini spent the rest of 1948 working on *In nome della legge* (*In the Name of the Law*) from the novel by Giuseppe Guido Lo Schiavo: the director was Pietro Germi for whom Fellini still has a great liking, perhaps due to a certain affinity of temperament. This collaboration with Germi was fruitful: besides *In nome della legge* ('I did very little,' Fellini admits, for he had only been concerned with the revision of the scenario, together with Pinelli), there followed *Il cammino della speranza* (*Road to Hope*) in 1950, which Fellini also staged. ('It was again a question of another journey through Italy, which was more to my liking.') Later in '51 and '52 there was *La città si difende* (*Passport to Hell*) and *Il Brigante di Tacca del Lupo* (*The Brigand of Tacca del Lupo*), from a story by Bacchelli set in the southern provinces after their annexation.

In the meantime Fellini had not left the 'maestro'; in 1950 he was his scenario-writer and assistant director in *Francesco giullare di Dio* (*Flowers of St. Francis*), planned at the time of *Paisà*, made with the aid of the monks at the monastery in the Romagna mountains. Fellini affirms that he personally suggested the scene with the tyrant Nicolaio, played by Fabrizi. In any case the film was enveloped in a mysticism which the average audience thought precious, being completely unprepared for the sublime heights of St. Francis' *Fioretti*; financially the film was a resounding failure.

Fellini last worked with Rossellini in *Europa '51*, when he collaborated in the treatment: it was rather a hasty collaboration because Fellini had his own interests by now. From the beginning of the preceding year, in fact, he had begun his activities as a director with *Luci del varietà*. Now a new and marvellous world opened up before him: the Italian cinema was ready for the 'Fellini' era.

The 'Fellini' era began unspectacularly in a partnership with Lattuada; this partnership became a foursome, however, as their wives Giulietta Masina and Carla del Poggio joined them.

With *Luci del varietà*, Enrico Flajano came on to the scene for the first time. He was to join Pinelli as script writer and scenario-writer in nearly all Fellini's films. Flajano, born in Abbruzzo, highly cultured and a talented writer, is Pinelli's opposite in character and his interests too are orientated in a different direction. Just as Pinelli is serious, dramatic and full of enthusiasm, so Flajano is casual and sceptical, hating vagueness and over-emphasis, in fact, he is anti-poetic. It is he who has always played the part of the devil's advocate between Fellini and Pinelli, by avoiding excessive lyricism and anchoring himself to reality. He suggests theories for social satire to Fellini. With these balancing influences at his side, the director has been able to find a perfect team, which is rare for a cinema director.

Flajano, Pinelli, Lattuada and Fellini set to work on the script of *Luci del varietà* at the beginning of 1950. It had been Fellini's idea entirely, on the basis of his experience with Fabrizi's company. We have seen how hazy the picture is of this company and its tour, and it is not necessary to return to it: it is more a question of clarifying how much of Fabrizi's stories and memories, related to Fellini during their nocturnal wanderings, have combined with Fellini's own memories in the film. But it is difficult to solve this problem. Besides, the theme of *Luci del varietà* was a compromise between Fellini's more or less autobiographical standpoint and an idea of Lattuada who wanted to portray the events relating to the Miss Italy competition, then very much in the public eye. (This film about Miss Italy was eventually made indifferently, by another director, Duilio Coletti.)

That form of co-operative enterprise was considered, at that time, as a kind of panacea for the ills that afflicted the cinema, mainly the fault of the producers, or so it was averred. Lizzani also used this method in *Achtung, banditi!* (*Look out, bandits!*). The system was so much favoured by left-wing critics that of all Fellini's films *Luci del varietà* was the only one (except for *La dolce vita*) which the left defended to the last. But the co-operative idea had a weak point because artists cannot be expected to become industrialists and business men. Fellini especially is the negation of figures, estimates, and all the operations of accountancy. It is not surprising that such a rash undertaking should have ended badly.

A company called 'Capitolum' was formed and 50 per cent of the capital was contributed by private financiers, whilst the remaining 50 per cent was contributed in equal parts, interest free, by Fellini and his wife Giulietta on the one hand and Lattuada and his wife Carla del Poggio on the other. There were others who had small shares in the co-operative; actors in the film (John Kitzmiller, Folco Lulli), two assistant directors, the editing secretary, and the *maestro* Felice Lattuada, Alberto's father. It was a grave mistake not to have approached a bank for financial aid in the intial stages. Finally the private contributors who had good-will, but no money, put themselves in the hands of an efficient distributing company, which later failed. Then there was a whirlwind of bills, which Fellini still has not paid off, of legal injunctions, and subsequently various lawsuits. Even ten years later, Fellini and Lattuada are paying bills of two or three hundred thousand lire, which are outstanding from that sea of debts.

How did the collaboration between Fellini and Lattuada work out in practice? The plot and the scenario were kept too firmly for the first 'work-out' of the film; the next time they were entirely non-existent and the shooting of various scenes on the set proceeded from time to time. Fellini was mainly concerned with the acting and Lattuada was in charge of the technical side. *Luci del varietà* was made in summer 1950, mostly in a playhouse in Rome. The night outdoor scenes were shot at Capranica. The film cost approximately seventy million lire.

Amongst the best memories of that bygone film, Fellini counts his meeting with Peppino De Filippo, the hero, whom he had in mind whilst he was writing the plot. His work with Peppino De Filippo was interrupted for ten years, but was to be taken up again later in *Le tentazioni del dottor Antonio*. The director also recalls that in working with Giulietta, *La strada* began to take shape, with its atmosphere of a vagabond, unstable, gypsy life, the strangeness and loneliness of the people, the unknown half-mysterious countryside and certain melancholy observations made about the characters, typical of *Luci del varietà*.

The film revolves around three people: Checco Dalmonte (Peppino De Filippo) the 'wizard of fun' and the 'international magician', as the advertisements call him, but in reality an unsuccessful actor, the leader of a troupe of comedians; the sweet, gentle Melina (Giulietta Masina) who loves him and is the daughter of Achille, the director of the wandering players; and Liliana (Carla del Poggio) a pretty, scatterbrained country girl who dreams of becoming a great actress. Checco and Melina's small variety company lives from hand to mouth with a few curtain-raiser acts; one day they are about to leave a small provincial town. Melina, an expert mimic (the 'rival of Fregoli') is running through her modest repertory, while Checco is trying to amuse the lookers-on. Liliana joins the comedians on the train as they are on the point of departure. She has run away from home, with her head full of absurd magazine stories. Liliana, who has been 'Miss Spiaggia' and has won a few dancing competitions, anticipates the heroine of *Lo Sceicco bianco*, but she is more selfish and socially ambitious. Checco Dalmonte decides to take her under his wing, despite the cool reception his friends give her. But when they arrive at their destination it is Liliana who sees to hiring a cart with her last lire to take them all to the town. That same evening the girl, all dressed up, manages to get on to the stage, and after a noisy incident (when her brief skirt slips off), it is she who receives most applause.

A few days later, after she has finished her number, Liliana finds Signor Enzo (Folco Lulli) waiting in her room. He is rich and boastful, prepared to feed the whole company provided he can have the girl in his house. The entertainers accept, but during the meal the elderly Don Giovanni begins to court the girl, arousing the anger of Checco, who is in love with her by now. Later that night Enzo tries to enter her room. After a lengthy argument with Checco the puffed-up Enzo throws them all out and the players, cold and sleepy, make their way towards the town. Checco leads the group with Liliana on his arm: behind comes Melina's old father who suddenly slips and falls down in the middle of the road. His daughter seeks Checco's aid in vain and she realizes that she has lost her old suitor.

Shortly afterwards, Dalmonte leaves the company; he goes to the city with Liliana and begins to look for a 'contact' for her, in the hope of launching the girl and binding her to him through gratitude if nothing else. Liliana dreams of quite different things from early risings, depressing dawns, uncertain meals, chilly provincial theatres, and the feeble applause of a boorish audience.

No one takes any notice of Checco; he only lands himself in trouble and is forced to undergo bitter humiliations. One evening, in a dubious night-club, Liliana meets the well-known impresario Palmisano. He is struck by her legs and is prepared to give her a contract and help realize her dreams: but Checco's jealousy ruins everything. Yet it is a purely platonic jealousy because Liliana has never granted her uncouth, shabby admirer any favours.

Finally the 'wizard of fun' decides to form his own company and turns to Melina for financial help: she is still in love with him. Moved by Checco's hypocritical tears Melina gives him her savings book and Dalmonte makes a desperate attempt to stage a show. He engages an excitable negro trumpeter (John Kitzmiller), and a sharp-shooter, 'Buffalo Bill's grandson', whom he found in a public doss-house. During rehearsals everything goes badly, and the marksman all but kills the theatre manager. Checco's efforts are doomed to failure but he still hopes for a miracle that will enable him to transform Liliana into a famous star.

Just as the calamitous revue is about to go on stage, Liliana receives a telephone call from Palmisano who says that he is ready to sign a contract with her. The girl deserts the show and the luckless actor in favour of her powerful suitor. Checco leaves at dawn, believing he hears a burst of applause in the square; it is only the sound of a train passing through.

While Liliana, who is now a starlet, descends an elaborate flight of stairs like those in Wanda Osiris revues and is ogled at by lascivious men, Checco returns penniless to his old friends and to Melina who forgives him and trustingly goes to sleep on his shoulder. In the third-class compartment of the train that is taking him back to his old life, Dalmonte sees a beautiful girl arrive. As she sits down in front of him he adjusts his tie and is ready to begin all over again.

And what becomes of Liliana? Will she become the famous star of her dreams? *Luci del varietà* does not give the answer and this is one of the film's 'Fellinian' touches, the first hint of those left-open endings in the director's later films.

Undoubtedly the producers intended to portray, rather ambitiously, the much maligned world of music-hall without melancholy and decadence. They wanted to avoid facile affectation. But they did not always succeed in fulfilling their aims. There was an obvious difference in style between the first and second parts. When Fellini shot the first part of the film he kept to the scenario, but in the second half he improvised a great deal as he went along and this difficult method (which he had not yet perfected by later experience) led him to commit some errors in balance and narrative continuity. *Luci del varietà* runs smoothly in the first half, where the humorous element dominates. Indeed, it is precisely the recurrence of comical elements which are not fully exploited that finally gives the impression that the film is intended to be a series of sketches. In the second half on the other hand the tone changes abruptly and *Luci del varietà* makes heavy going and falls into a kind of nineteenth-century realism, of the 'Laugh, Pagliacci!' kind.

The nocturnal walk with the negro trumpeter, one of the first of many in Fellini, seems a pointless piece of writing; an inserted fragment which is unrelated to the rest of the work. The close attention paid to detail and the success of a few sequences were the good qualities of *Luci del varietà*, especially the sad march of the players along the road after the humiliation suffered at the hands of the rich landowner, with the sorrowful, but profoundly human, figure of Melina's father aided only by his daughter. A note of sincerity was struck and many critics noticed how Lattuada had for the first time thrown a bridge between himself and his characters, who are full of human warmth, in an interpretation which reminds one of the '*commedia dell' arte*'. Peppino De Filippo gave an excellent performance which was sensitive and effective. Nearly all the critics praised the part played by Giulietta Masina. On the other hand Carla del Poggio, who had to portray an unsympathetic character, was less convincing, despite her indisputable acting talents.

To sum up, Fellini is largely responsible for the plot, and a certain way of looking at things as if through a distorting mirror; but the structural and perspective precision seen in the individual close-ups and the many foreground shots, and the smooth movement of the cameras are unmistakably part of Lattuada's technique.

CHAPTER 4

The Misunderstood Lo Sceicco *(1951–52)*

After the dubious artistic results and the financial burden of *Luci del varietà*, Fellini had a moment's respite and returned to writing scenarios for other people. (We have seen him at work on *Europa '51*, in *La città si difende* and in *Il Brigante di Tacca del Lupo*.) Towards the end of 1950 he gathered his energies together for a subject that attracted him and in which he saw great possibilities. The beginning was somewhat banal: Michelangelo Antonioni who was then just a director of documentary films had, in the summer of 1949, written a script about the world of strip cartoons and had asked Fellini and Pinelli to write a scenario for it. Antonioni had already made *L'amorosa menzogna* (*The Loving Lie*), which had the same theme, one he wanted to repeat. He had thought up a story ironic in flavour, although basically dramatic. During these years the success of strip cartoons was phenomenal. Some publications like *Grand' Hôtel* had reached a circulation of millions of copies, appealing to a simple, unthinking public of seamstresses, shop-girls, small employers and servants who found in those books a romantic escape for desires which could never be realized.

Fellini already knew this world, in the first place from Nerbini, then from reading the 'Little Post' in *Cinemagazzino* and *Cine-illustrato*, which was printed next door to the *Marc' Aurelio*. Influenced by these memories Fellini, together with Pinelli and Antonioni, rewrote nearly the whole plot, stressing the satirical and humorous aspects. Here is how Pinelli remembers the affair: 'We vainly looked for a subject on strip-cartoons for a couple of weeks. One morning we were sitting silently at the Casina delle Rose, looking at nothing in particular and feeling discouraged. Suddenly I had an idea. "A little strip cartoon wife", I said, "runs away to see the star of her dreams." And Fellini joined in; "They are a young honeymoon couple and everything happens in twenty-four hours." '

So the first draft of *Lo Sceicco bianco* was prepared: but the producer Ponti, who was to make the film with Antonioni, was doubtful and undecided. Antonioni meanwhile had got married at Bomarzo near Viterbo where he was to film *La villa dei mostri* (*Bomarzo, Villa of the Monsters*) and had fallen ill. While he was in bed Ponti's partner persuaded him to hand over the direction to Lattuada. Even when this solution failed, Fellini, who had already been paid for the plot, began to trail it round various producers in the hope that they would give it up in turn and he would then direct it. For more than a year the rough draft of *Lo Sceicco bianco* travelled from one table to another; it was bought and then sold again until the last producer bought it for more than ten times its original price. This was Luigi Rovere. Fellini had previously persuaded Cines to buy the idea but the directors wanted Pascal to play the lead and were absolutely against engaging Sordi, whom Fellini had wanted from the beginning.

It may seem incredible today, but Alberto Sordi was disliked by producers and distributors at that time. They claimed that he was unpopular with the public because they accused him of cruelty. A radio and revue comedian, he had had little success in the cinema in *Mamma mia, che impressione*. Fellini had known him for years from the time they ate together in a snack bar and he had been very impressed by the mimic expressiveness of the actor's face. 'Fellini and I were friends,' Sordi told me. 'We knew each other throughout the war years, from '40 onwards; we were in the same class at school and were soldiers in Rome or on leave together. I was then appearing in the Za-Burn shows at the Quirino Theatre and later I worked on the radio. I had worked in films four or five times as a "lover": *Cuori nella tormenta*, *La notte delle beffe*, *La signorina*, *I tre aquilotti*, *Chi l'ha visto?*, *Tre ragazze cercano marito* (*Hearts in Torment*, *Night of Tricks*, *Signorina*, *Three Young Eagles*, *Who has seen Him?*, *Three Girls in Search of a Husband*). But I was completely different from what the producers and directors imagined.' Sordi had already built up his character of a swindling, lying, immature Italian, an out-and-out racketeer of a cruel and ruthless kind. Fellini who first led him to the brink of stardom in *Lo Sceicco bianco* employed him in his next film, and still retains a very high opinion of him. 'He could be a real clown if he were well directed,' he maintains. 'He is a first-class actor because he is sincere and vital; because he identifies himself completely with the character he plays.' Why did he not use him later in *I vitelloni*? 'I never had the chance. I would have liked him as a grotesque, histrionic "Nero", but this idea, like many others, never came to fruition.'

However, unlike the others, the producer Rovere accepted Sordi, but absolutely rejected Peppino De Filippo, whom the director proposed as the husband. They had to look for a new actor and Fellini found him by chance one day when he went into a projection room in Cinecittà, where a pseudo-Mexican film was being shown: *Sulla via di Guadalupe* (*On the Road to Guadaloupe*). As he stopped to look at the setting, Fellini saw a strange figure coming very slowly out of the distance into the foreground with what seemed an endless movement of the camera. It was a serious film (the hero was a saintly priest), but due to the actor it was irresistibly comic in parts. Fellini immediately asked who he was and learnt that the man was not a professional actor, but a well-known man of letters and a comedy writer, Leopoldo Trieste, the author of several dramas, such as *Cronaca*, *NN*, *Trontiera*. He engaged him immediately and the cast of *Lo Sceicco bianco* was completed with Brunella Bova as the wife (she had already distinguished herself in de Sica's *Miracolo a Milano* (*Miracle in Milan*), and Giulietta Masina who was destined to play the small part of a 'naïve prostitute' by the prophetic name of Cabiria.

Lo Sceicco bianco opens with a honeymoon: during the Holy Year a simple, provincial couple arrive in Rome, the inevitable destination of all honeymooners. He, answering to the very unromantic name of Ivan Cavalli, is constantly worried lest he should fall short of his own code of manners and behaves in a most dignified and authoritarian way towards his wife. He seeks the aid of an influential employee at the Vatican, who will arrive with a large tribe of relations and take it upon himself to present the couple to the Pope and act as guide to the most famous monuments in Rome, following a rigid, correct and bureaucratic programme. She, on the other hand, is cherishing a secret hope; that of being able to meet, just for a moment, one of her idols, the hero of a strip cartoon 'Lo Sceicco bianco' (The White Sheik), who way back in her secluded provincial life has given her moments of wonderful happiness. Profiting from her husband's routine nap (9 o'clock a short rest, 10–11 family council, 11 o'clock appointment with the uncles) his wife hastens to Via XXIV Maggio, to the editorial office of a cartoon magazine, but does not find Fernando Rivoli, alias the 'White Sheik', there. He has already left to 'shoot' on the beach at Fregene. Instead she finds Marilena Vilardi, editor of the paper, who is another idol of hers, and the author of *L'abisso stellatto* (*Star-studded Abyss*) and *Cuori nella bufera* (*Hearts in the Storm*). 'Reality only exists in dreams', Marilena says sweetly when she realizes what sort of a person she is dealing with. 'One must withdraw into oneself . . . like Countess Lucilla in *Love and Fatality* (*Amore and Fatalità*).' Almost insensibly the woman's words transport Wanda into the fantastic world of her dreams and shortly afterwards she finds herself being lifted on to a lorry, where the rest of the troupe (from the Fierce Bedouin, to 'Fatma, the faithful slave', from 'Ali the noble servant' to 'Egizia the deceitful maid'), is collected and they go off to their place of work.

From this moment two adventures alternate and are woven together. On the one hand there is the husband searching for his young wife, though he is more anxious to keep the scandal from his uncle and to prevent a shadow falling 'over the name of the Cavalli'. On the other hand, his wife Wanda has now found 'The White Sheik', the man to whom she had so often written and signed herself 'Your passionate little doll'. She avidly laps up his mendacious talk—the prelude to an easy conquest. So, back in Rome, poor Ivan Cavalli is obliged to follow the prescribed itinerary without his wife, in the company of his uncle and cousins. (He takes advantage of a moment's liberty to phone the hotel secretly and subsequently informs the police of her disappearance.) Meanwhile at Fregene the 'passionate doll' has now become one of the cartoon characters and has the honour of acting a scene with 'The Sheik'.

Then things take an ugly turn: 'The Sheik' invites his admirer for a trip out to sea on the 'corsair ship' which is more prosaically an old boat, used for shooting the 'picture romance'. While he is making passes at Wanda, the spar holding up the sail hits 'The Sheik', who is laid out, semi-conscious. The boat drifts for a time, finally reaching shore. Here the romantic atmosphere of the adventure is definitely broken. The troupe, furious at the delay, greets 'The Sheik' with a stream of insults. The voice of his wife is louder than the rest; she is a strong quarrelsome woman who grabs the 'passionate doll' by the hair. As for 'The Sheik', his behaviour is anything but gallant: his words, no longer full of enchantment, have become a foolish and embarrassed muttering in Roman dialect. As soon as he can, he makes off on his scooter.

Now evening has fallen on the pine wood at Fregene: the troupe goes home too, after calling 'passionate doll' in vain. She has hidden herself amongst the trees. The weeping Wanda gets back to town by a stroke of luck: her illusions about 'The White Sheik' are shattered, but those she has built up in her dreams back in the provinces are not. Convinced that she has irremediably stained the 'honour of the Cavalli' she wants to make the dignified end of all strip cartoon heroines. After a desperate telephone call to her husband, which is received by a sleepy, puzzled hotel porter, she tries to throw herself in the Tiber. The attempt is futile because at that point the water is only a few inches deep: but the nocturnal bather is observed, promptly saved and taken forcibly to the hospital. Her husband finds her here, having wandered about for half the night, eventually ending up in the room of an 'understanding lady'. But Ivan Cavalli has only one worry: he must arrive punctually with his wife on his arm in St. Peter's Square, where he has arranged to meet his uncle the next day and carry out the programme of the visit to the Pope which he has so far been able to fulfil. All explanations must be left till later: desperate and panicky the two arrive at eleven o'clock to face their relatives and walk towards the 'Great Dome' with dutiful smiles.

Lo Sceicco bianco is a reinvention of reality, evoking *Sogni Proibiti* (*Forbidden Dreams*), (another film about strip cartoons), and here and there Clair's *Un chapeau de paille d'Italie* (*Italian Straw Hat*). But a closer look will immediately reveal that Fellini's humour is different from Clair's; it is more incisive, more 'wicked', less eager to provoke smiles. The young director's greatest merit has been to maintain a constantly balanced production, skilfully giving each element its right place, without ever slipping into crude farce. If there is a farcical tone, it is, as Castello has seen, one of social farce, of pitiless lucidity, where emotion is always controlled by a virile intelligence. It is centred in the character of the husband with his 'pathetic dismay à la Ridolini and his face with its crazed, rolling eyes'. Some of the scenes have an outstanding, satirical value, the conversation between 'passionate doll' and 'The White Sheik' in the boat, the tragi-comic farewell message to the husband which his wife dictates to the hotel porter, who interprets it back to front, Cavalli's report to the police commissioner and its almost Kafkian atmosphere. Other scenes are meditative and poetic, the forerunners of many similar Fellinian ones to follow, such as the husband's frantic night in deserted Rome, and his meeting with the little prostitute who tries to comfort him. It is a film in which nearly all the director's motifs are present, but they are not well orchestrated and polished. This does not mean that *Lo Sceicco bianco* is one of Fellini's minor works; on the contrary, as time passes the film's impact grows and one becomes aware of the richness of tones, the subtle magic which reveals the melancholy vein beneath the comedy.

Lo Sceicco has been defined, because of its social satire and farce, as an 'extraordinary parade of mediocre characters', observed closely and with irony. Everyone is mean-spirited, from the three principal characters to the hotel porters, Cavalli's relatives, the periodical's 'letter post' editor, the fanciful cartoon film director (Ernesto Almirante), the star and even an odd street dandy who takes the wife home and on the refusal of his advances, utters a vulgar Milanese phrase. The Cavalli are particularly striking in this crowd of actors. It is as if they had been drawn by Daumier or by Novello: their tribe is headed by an authoritarian uncle, played by that experienced cinema figure, Ettore M. Margadonna.

The background too is original, small hotels and inns, streets in which *bersaglieri* parade to give a sense of contrast and to underline the commonplace attraction of patriotic rhetoric, indicative of the hero's mentality. (Fellini has a real passion for this type of colouring. In *Lo Sceicco bianco*, a fanfare by the *bersaglieri* in the first run-through ironically followed Ivan Cavalli's whole odyssey. Plumed *bersaglieri* also figure in the recent *Tentazioni del dottor Antonio*.) Lastly, the setting is completed by the beach at Fregene with the absurd sham world of the strip-cartoons, in an 'oriental' story which might have been thought up by Clair for the end of *Le silence est d'or* (*Man about Town*).

The heroine in *Lo Sceicco* is reminiscent of the one of *La dolce vita*, because of her disarming childish mentality, but unlike the other, she is subjected to a certain crisis. But it is a completely exterior crisis, the result of a delusion provoked by her heroes. We can well imagine that once she has returned to her provincial town she will begin all over again and build up other fictitious ideals. Ivan Cavalli also has a crisis, but this is shaped more by the shattering of his Southern prejudices, and the inevitably bad impression he makes on his relatives, than by serious, reflective thinking about his wife. His grotesque naïveté is patent above all when, approached by the prostitute, he begins to tell her his troubles and proudly shows her his wife's photograph. (By mistake he brings out a picture of her at her first communion.) The only one who has no crisis is the Sheik, Sordi, who remains all of a piece in his cowardliness, his selfishness and his thoughtless living from day to day. He anticipates other similar creations of Fellini. His magical appearance to 'passionate doll' on a flying swing in the middle of the pine trees is a brilliant impression of him: rarely has a cinema presentation been able to express so forcibly and so clearly a state of mind and a moral portrait.

The film was shot entirely in Rome and the outside shots were filmed at Fregene, between October, November and December, 1951; the cost was modest, some sixty million lire. At the beginning of March, 1952 *Lo Sceicco bianco* was ready. As it was his first real film Fellini did not fail to show it to Rossellini, while it was being edited. Rossellini has written this about it: 'During the projection I was in the grip of a thousand feelings, because I saw on the screen Fellini as I had intimately known him for many years. I felt old and disturbed because he seemed so young.'

Following Rossellini's 'thousand feelings' for *Lo Sceicco* came Fellini's own, but they were of a very different nature. The battle with the critics and with those external enemies, the distributors and contractors, had to be won. And here things took an unfortunate turn. At the end of March the director, understandably excited, presented his film to the Italian Selection Board for the Cannes Festival. It was then that I met Fellini for the first time and spoke to him. He was leaning against a radiator in a corner, half hidden, with his great head of ruffled black hair. As they took their places none of the members of the team (they were nearly all leading Italian critics, presided over nominally by the Deputy Andreotti, and, in practice, by the lawyer De Pirro) guessed that this young man was destined to revolutionize the Italian cinema. Nothing particularly recommended Fellini to us. *Lo Sceicco bianco* was one of the many films to be 'viewed' out of a sense of duty. Well-known films such as Castellani's *Due soldi di speranza* (*Two Pennyworth of Hope*), and Lattuana's *Il Cappotto* (*The Overcoat*) were destined for Cannes, whilst a third (De Sica's *Umberto D*) was outstanding for its formal grandeur.

As the film went on, we realized that we were seeing something new. This was confirmed at the commission's first deliberation, when there was a great argument because not all the members were convinced of the originality of the approach or of Fellini's powers. The proposal to enter *Lo Sceicco bianco* at Cannes was firmly opposed by some and the battle for and against Fellini was opened. Whilst the decision was *sub judice*, a few days later I broke the explicit prohibition that no member of the team was allowed to give premature judgments on the film. I published in *Oggi* (No. 15, 10 April, 1952) an article in which I analysed the film, stressing its importance and concluding, 'the Italian cinema can now rely on another source of talent'.

Many years later I do not regret that venal sin. I hoped to be of use to the director and the film, for I foresaw that the immediate future would not be easy. And I was not a bad prophet. Already discussion had become very acrimonious, within the Commission: at last the supporters of *Lo Sceicco* and of Fellini—backed also by De Pirro—won by a narrow margin. *Lo Sceicco bianco* was chosen as the fourth film for Cannes; the director and the press were told.

But when the festival began I received a depressing telegram from Fellini: the film was not to be shown, he said, but was replaced by another (*Guardie e Ladri—Cops and Robbers*) at the last minute just as the director was packing his bags to go to Cannes. Why? Unfortunately I could not tell him then, all I could do was to send him a consoling letter in which I reaffirmed my faith in *Lo Sceicco bianco* and in him personally. But I hoped that the film would recover from this set-back. Had it been excluded from Cannes by an underhand trick? Well, it would go to Venice. The 'fellinians' —a small group at that time—closed their ranks and after overcoming further opposition, *Lo Sceicco bianco* embarked for the Lido Show.

Unfortunately, the film really did seem to be dogged by misfortune. At an afternoon showing in Venice, which the director also attended, there was applause and laughter so that Fellini thought that the showing had been successful. But the next morning when he read the papers he was dismayed;

there was a flood of absurd, harsh, cutting criticism, as though each critic had passed the word to the next. Some, like so many Don Ferrante's of Manzonian memories, went so far as to predict that the author would never be heard of again because 'he had not the slightest aptitude for cinema direction'. Naturally, the jury's opinion was the same as the majority of the critics and they were careful not to mention *Lo Sceicco bianco* in the distribution of prizes.

Fellini's humiliation and discomforture were aggravated by the financial disasters suffered by the film. *Lo Sceicco bianco* was produced on a small budget and the Venice judgment, after months of hold-ups, was the final blow. The film was badly distributed by a small company and was consistently refused in many places mainly because of Alberto Sordi's presence. When shown at one of Milan's leading cinemas, it was screened for exactly three days. The public's reaction was negative, indeed there was no reaction: they simply refused to pay to go in. Things went a little better in Rome, but the film was soon withdrawn. The distributing company collapsed, and *Lo Sceicco bianco* was pursued by bankruptcy officials. It was nearly scrapped when, after a few years in store waiting for the creditors to come to an agreement, Cineriz bought the copy in 1960, after the enormous success of *La dolce vita*. The film was put back into circulation at the end of summer 1961. Fellini was famous by now, and Sordi even more so. But unbelievable as it is, this attempt failed too. The public appeared to like it and the newspapers printed long, favourable reviews, but the financial rewards were awaited in vain. *Lo Sceicco* did not even manage to cover the cost of editing and contracting. Fellini has reason then, superstitious as he is, for saying that the film was made under an unlucky star.

CHAPTER 5

Retaliation with I vitelloni *(1952–53)*

DESPITE THE practically total collapse of the hopes and dreams for *Lo Sceicco bianco*, there were still some critics and producers who had liked the film, in that melancholy autumn of 1952. Amongst the perceptive critics were Vittorio Bonicelli and Pietro Bianchi (at that time the editor of the Cinema column for *Il Tempo* in Milan) and amongst the producers the Venetian Pegoraro. So Fellini did not allow himself to be beaten by that set-back, but approached Pegoraro, who said that he was quite prepared to give him a contract for his films and a sum in advance.

Fellini easily freed himself from Rovere: the previous year (as we shall see later in a more detailed account), he had written the plot for *La strada* together with Pinelli, and confidently taken it to be read by the people who had believed in him through *Lo Sceicco*. 'You know, I wept?' Rovere said to him after he had looked at the manuscript. Just as Fellini was thanking him profusely, the other interrupted sharply: 'Yes, but it drives me mad. Whatever got into you? And what's more you want your wife to play the heroine? Come off it. . . !' Fellini abandoned Rovere and turned to others, but with no success, until he found Pegoraro. But even he, after some hesitation, gave up *La strada*, mainly because he had not enough confidence in Giulietta Masina as the heroine.

Fellini would have liked to retain liberty of action, but he was in debt to Pegoraro for the advance sums of money he had received and so he resigned himself to directing a different type of film for him.

Just at this time, during his chats with Flajano and Pinelli, he had worked out the idea of *I vitelloni* (*The Spivs*). Naturally it sprang from his personal memories of Rimini, but Fellini found them strengthened by Flajano's own memories of his youth in Abbruzzo. There was a striking resemblance between the student life of Pescara and that of Rimini; they shared the same jests, escapades, and ideas. So it was not difficult to agree about the plot which Pegoraro liked when he heard it.

Who are the 'spivs'? Fellini himself has given a brilliant description of them. 'They are the out-of-work middle-class mother's boys. Why don't they do anything all day long? They don't even know themselves. Perhaps because they all have to a greater or lesser degree, someone who supports them: a father, a mother, a sister, an aunt. A family in short. You can eat,

vitelloni—from left to right, below: 'ranco Fabrizi, Leopoldo Trieste, lberto Sordi; above: Franco Interenghi and Riccardo Fellini.

Sceicco bianco—Brunella Bovo and lberto Sordi.

Sceicco bianco—Alberto Sordi and oup of Bedouin on the beach at egene.

Le notti di Cabiria—Giulietta Masina an
Silvani.

Le notti di Cabiria—Masina and Fran
Marzi.

Le notti di Cabiria—The first scene.

strada—Giulietta Masina and
ony Quinn.

La strada—Masina and Richard Basehart.

rada—Masina and
ony Quinn.

Il bidone—Opening scene.

Il bidone—from left to right: Ric
Basehart, Franco Fabrizi and Brod
Crawford.

Il bidone—finale.

sleep and be clothed in a family; and you can even manage to wheedle some cash for cigarettes and for the cinema. Perhaps because none of them really knows what he wants to do. They scorn the dead-end jobs which the provinces offer as suitable for their limited education. They have begun their studies but have never completed them. They have no particular skill; they are always awaiting a letter or an offer, or a stroke of luck that will take them to Rome or to Milan, for some vague, honorary, and lucrative post. While they wait they reach their thirtieth birthday, passing their days in talking and playing schoolboy jokes. They shine in the three-month summer season, which they anticipate and talk about for the rest of the year. These are the "spivs".'

The script was quickly drafted because as Fellini delineated the characters, he already had in mind Alberto Sordi and Leopoldo Trieste, whom he had directed in *Lo sceicco bianco* and also Riccardo, his brother who, better than anyone, could enter into the 'spiv' mentality since he had been one himself. In fact the producers would have liked a better cast. They thought the one chosen was bad and they were especially difficult about Sordi because of the general dislike of him in cinema circles at that time. At last, however, they came to an agreement about everything.

The three 'spivs' were joined by two others; Franco Interlenghi, who with his fresh, serious, boyish face was to play Moraldo, and Franco Fabrizi. At that time the latter was practically unknown. Fellini remembers having seen him some time before when he was just one of Wanda Osiris's 'boys' in a successful revue. The director had been to a performance and had been struck by the appearance of the young man, who had been unlucky enough to slip down a flight of steps on stage. When he went back stage to speak to Wanda Osiris, Fellini had discovered the boy, very angry indeed, arguing about the incident. He had been unable to forget the face and its expression of comical disappointment and childish temper.

When the scenario was finished (the film is remarkably faithful to it, the director having improvised very little during the making of it), shooting began and went on from December, 1952 until early the following spring. The going was somewhat stormy because it was twice interrupted; from Christmas until the middle of January and again later. This was because they had to chase after Sordi who was working in Wanda Osiris's revue company just at that time. (He was in *Gran baraonda* with the famous sketches of the 'pedestrian skier' and 'Why do you insist, Wanda Osirri?'). Consequently *I vitelloni* had three different cameramen, Martelli, Trasatti and Carlini, for each one of them, corresponding to the breaks in the film, found that he was no longer free, due to previous commitments.

The interior scenes were nearly all shot in Florence. Pegoraro's associates were Tuscan cloth industrialists and they liked to be able to look in on the shooting from time to time, for they wanted to keep the film within controlling distance, although Florence was not particularly suited to winter filming. A disused theatre (the 'Goldoni') was hired where two very important sequences were filmed—the 'spivs'' carnival and Commendator Natali's performance. The outside scenes were shot between Ostia (the beach and Kursaal) and Viterbo (the streets, squares and stations). Using the two places, Viterbo and Ostia, Fellini tried to reconstruct Rimini from memory. He did not even consider making the film at Rimini (he rarely visited his home town), out of a kind of modesty. He did not wish to appear, famous as he was, a patronizing figure in the eyes of his former 'partners in crime', who had for the most part become mediocre, professional men in their provincial town. For Fellini, going back involves uneasiness and embarrassment and the acknowledged impossibility of being able to stroll about the town like any private individual without having to contend with the worry and annoyance fame brings.

I vitelloni was hardly finished when the Venice selection committee chose it for the International Film Show, this time in a less discordant atmosphere than that of the previous year. However, there was no lack of difficulties. In the meantime Pegoraro and his associates had found it hard to get hold of a distributing company for Italy. (The film was also a Franco-Italian production in conjunction with Ciné films of Paris.) Then there was the problem of the title, which made many people purse their lips. Whatever was that strange name, which could not be traced in Italian dictionaries? Fellini explained that brazen good-for-nothings are commonly called by that name in Romagna. He had heard it as a child from the peasants in Verucchio and the same picturesque word had been shouted after him by an old woman whom he and a group of friends had pestered at the time of the Rimini escapades. Flajano too affirmed that a similar word was used in the Abruzzi. So the word used in common speech, had full right to be accepted. It was a long fight but Fellini dug his heels in and the title remained unchanged.

The film had a huge success at Venice: it received genuine ovations and the 'Silver Lion' together with five other films in a year in which no 'Gold Lion' had been awarded. The reason for the award was 'a felicitous portrayal of society in the Italian provinces' and many went as far as to reverse their judgments about Fellini. Finally a distributor was found for *I vitelloni*. ENIC bought it for a few million lire—the film had cost eighty million lira—but had no faith in it, despite its success in Venice. ENIC too wanted to change the title, but there was nothing to be done about this. They wanted to rub out Sordi's name even from the credit titles, because the hirers thought he was 'poison'. In fact the name was omitted at first and only reappeared later. Then ENIC made Fellini a staggering proposal: to make another ending. The one which had been awarded the prize at the Festival was thought to be too depressing, and the film should have finished as follows; an oil well is discovered in the town, everybody gets rich and the ex-'spivs' all go to work singing. Of course Fellini laughed (he has never remade a sequence that has already been filmed, on principle; also, he says, out of laziness). Now he was in a position to refuse and the matter was not discussed any further. It was Fellini's first film to go abroad, even if the French did not accord it the welcome they later gave *La strada*.

Those who consider that the true Fellini is seen in deliberate satire, judge *I vitelloni* to be his masterpiece, because it is the film in which the director has emphasized satire and social observation most strongly and has known how to fuse the dramatic aspects with the humorous, giving the film great richness and complexity of motives. It is certainly a work of great humanity and depth—bitter, sorrowful and thoughtful beneath an agreeably, careless surface. If *I vitelloni* gives us a very accurate picture of a certain provincial society, it is not a picture confined to Rimini, but of universal significance. This is another quality of the film together with the masterly way in which the characteristics of the five 'heroes' have been combined (although they are widely different), to live on in the memory as one group. The director has handled his characters without confusion or overlapping or undue stressing of their mentality (though outside the pale of the community), so that the audience can follow the events effortlessly, as in *La dolce vita*. What Fellini failed to do later in *Il bidone* (the case is different in his other films that have a simpler and more compact narrative plan), he succeeded in doing marvellously in a film made with far less technical skill. In any event, compared to *Lo Sceicco bianco*, the style of *I vitelloni* is fully mature. As a forerunner of Fellini's most promising work, it closes one cycle and introduces another of completely different tone.

I vitelloni opens with the last festivities of the season in a bathing resort, with the election of 'Miss Siren 1953'. Sandra Rubini (Leonora Ruffo) is elected. She is the sister of Moraldo, one of the five 'spivs' who are naturally present: Fausto, the group leader and a fatuous Don Giovanni; Leopoldo, a man of letters, writer of comedies with no future; Riccardo, a singer and a good actor; Alberto, a childish type and 'a mother's darling', who lives off his sister's earnings. Halfway through the entertainment which is broken up by the first gusts of autumnal rain, Sandra faints and it becomes evident that she is pregnant. Fausto, responsible for her condition, sneaks off home to pack his bags and go away. But his father, a humble artisan who lives with his younger daughter, stops him. So Fausto is forced to marry Sandra who is a good and beautiful girl at heart, and is socially superior to him, so much so that Sandra's parents despise Fausto's father and sister.

The group is temporarily split up. After they have seen Fausto off on his honeymoon, the remaining spivs feel somewhat envious and meet in a café where they play billiards and talk of leaving. Then they go out into the streets, which are deserted because the holidaymakers have all left. To alleviate their boredom they plague the passers-by, or they break the great silence by running their fingers over the lowered shop blinds. In the end they go off singing a vulgar song. But boredom awaits them as soon as they get home. Leopoldo reacts by writing hopeless dramas in his room, or by trying to establish an idyllic relationship with the little servant girl who lives opposite.

At last Fausto returns from his honeymoon, and life resumes as usual. Fausto has brought back the latest novelty from Rome, the 'mambo', which he dances in the middle of the street and is immediately imitated by Albert. Then Fausto's father-in-law (Enrico Viarisio) makes him take a job and persuades a friend (Carlo Romano) to employ him in his shop, where he sells sacred objects. Fausto looks like a drowned rat in his working smock and his friends come and make fun of him outside the windows. On Sunday the spivs meet on the deserted beach, they go to the pier in front of the Kursaal to look at the wintry sea and dream of impossible departures. Alberto chases an Alsatian and ends up behind the bathing huts, between the beached boats, where he finds his sister with a married man. But the drama that follows is only superficial; above all Alberto is ashamed of his friends and fears that his sister will go her own way and bring suffering to their mother and consequently to himself.

Meanwhile Fausto attempts to lead a normal life and to play the part of an affectionate husband; but when he goes to the cinema with Sandra he sees a beautiful woman in the next seat and, leaving his wife with an excuse, he follows the unknown woman home. He extorts a kiss and a promise from her. When he goes back to Sandra the film has finished by now and the poor girl weeps as she confesses, 'I'm afraid'.

The great season of the spivs, the carnival, arrives. Everyone is at the masked ball in the local theatre. Alberto is dressed as a woman, Riccardo as a musketeer, Leopoldo as a Chinaman. Fausto discovers that his employer's wife (Lyda Baarova), whom he has always seen as a submissive spouse in the shop, is still attractive, and he tries to court her. Gradually the theatre empties and only they, the spivs, are left to make merry to the end. Alberto, dumb and grotesque in his woman's disguise and trailing a great papier-mâché mask behind him is dragged home by Moraldo at dawn. He meets his sister in the doorway as she is departing with her lover. At first Alberto fails to understand, then he indulges in a ridiculous scene of despair with his mother. ('And that we should have believed that she . . . for the few pence she gave us . . . I'll find a job.')

In the morning Fausto, still excited by what he has seen the previous night, importunes the proprietress in the shop, who boxes his ears and tells her husband. He calls the young man into his house. 'We are peaceful people,' he says, 'and we love each other, because that is what matters. But you can't understand that . . . .' Then he sacks him and Fausto has to make up some feeble excuse to the family. Moraldo, his brother-in-law, believes him and because Fausto has not been given any compensation he persuades Moraldo to help him get his revenge by stealing a golden angel from the shop. With the help of a half-witted peasant they load the angel on to a barrow and in vain try to sell it to a nunnery and a monastery. They leave the angel with their companion, who stands it up and falls down in front of it on his knees, in speechless adoration. But the theft is soon discovered. Signor Rubini would like to throw out Fausto and Moraldo, but Fausto tells some more lies and is forgiven once more. When the child is born they pay less attention to Fausto. Sandra becomes friendly with Fausto's father again and in one of the most beautiful and moving sequences in the film, she takes the child to her father-in-law and gives him to her little sister-in-law to hold and amuse.

A company of wandering players led by a ham actor, Commander Natali, who once enjoyed a modest measure of fame, arrive in the little town. The spivs go to see the show at once: it is a very feeble revue, with a crazy military patriotic finale acted and danced by very bad dancers. (It is another echo, genuine or fictitious, of 'Sparks of Love'.) One of the spivs, Leopoldo, wants to approach Natali and persuade him to put on one of his plays. He finds him in his dressing-room and reads him a long script, while the actor is eating and pretending to be very interested in it. His other friends meanwhile are flirting with the company's dancers and Fausto succeeds in making love to one of them. It is the first serious break he has with Moraldo, who is sickened and remonstrates with him.

Meanwhile Natali has persuaded Leopoldo to finish reading to him outside, in the street, where the wind is howling. They arrive at the dark pier, where Natali, in honeyed tones, invites the young man to go with him. Leopoldo suddenly understands, takes fright and flees.

Fausto returns home and finds his wife awake and in tears. She too has understood and leaves home with the child. A frantic search begins, because they fear that the poor girl may have killed herself. Faced with a possible tragedy Fausto sees his error and is tormented with remorse. The other spivs begin to look for Sandra too in Riccardo's father's old car but in a very different spirit. Alberto, still boyish and unfeeling, stands on the car at one point, and makes an insulting gesture to a group of men working on the road; it is meant to be an act of bravado, but he comes off badly because the car breaks down and stops shortly afterwards. The workmen give chase and throw stones at the spivs, who run away as fast as their legs will carry them. Only Leopoldo, the least guilty, is left to be a scapegoat.

Sandra is finally found in her father-in-law's home and he takes advantage of the occasion to give Fausto a good lesson based on a sound beating. Husband and wife are reconciled and the narrator tells us: 'This is the end of the story of Fausto and Sandra.' Will he reform? Will he be a man? It is Moraldo who has decided to break with that life. One morning, unknown to anyone, he leaves at dawn without knowing where he is going. At the station, as the train is about to draw out, he meets Guido, a boy who works on the railways. Although he is old beyond his years through necessity, Guido (who gets up at five o'clock every morning to go to work) is the symbol of a normal world, in which daily hard work is the rule. He is the only one to wave goodbye to Moraldo as the train slowly disappears into the mist.

I vitelloni is the first film made by Fellini that does not come to a definite conclusion; it is an unfinished tale both for Moraldo and the others. So much so, that the director, as we shall see, thought he would give it a sequel, *Moraldo in Città* (*Moraldo in Town*). He wrote the scenario for it, but never made it. Moraldo is clearly Fellini himself, but the others too are part of Fellini, and a certain understanding on the part of the creator towards his characters is only logical, even when he discovers their faults and condemns them. This understanding, which has been exaggerated and called dangerous condonement and even complicity, does not exclude the protagonists from a severe moral condemnation which is evident in the finale.

Besides, the five protagonists are more insensitive than guilty and without hope of redemption: they are not 'dead souls' but merely torpid ones who can be awoken when they come into contact with the harsh reality of life. This is what happens to Moraldo; he too is weak, he plays an active part in stealing the angel, he always 'covers up' for Fausto, but something begins to stir within him when he comes into contact with the little railway worker, the boy who earns his bread by getting up at dawn. Each one of the five has had, like Moraldo, a favourable chance which he has not taken: Fausto when he comes into contact with a worthy couple, his employer and his wife; Alberto when his sister leaves, Leopoldo's disillusionment with Natali. This last sequence—whose premises and conclusions are echoed in *Le notti di Cabiria* where Natali is replaced by D'Onofrio—is artistically one of the best in the film. Leopoldo's face which expresses amazement, confusion and embarrassment and in the end real terror, contrasts with the repulsive and viscous sweetness of the leading comedian, which is accentuated by his position in the scene; Natali is lower down on the dark pier with his devilish leer lit up only in flashes and Leopoldo is above him on the landing stage barely illumined against the light.

French critics have rightly stressed that one of the greatest qualities in the film is the exact fusion between reality and poetry, which Fellini has brought out in a kind of Proustian search after time lost. The spivs, men who have never emerged from childhood, wander about the streets at night, in a melancholy way, and have an intuitive sense of their condition, but they also feel prisoners of themselves; later, on the beach they have the same feeling of anguish and isolation. Mlle. Agel has observed that it reminds one of the world of Tati—in *Les vacances de Monsieur Hulot* (*Mr. Hulot's Holiday*), but the resemblance is questionable. It is not the same beach nor the same problems.

Instead the main episode in *I vitelloni*, the key to the film, lies in the tumultuous gaiety of the carnival, where the five mistakenly believe that they are expending their fruitless, dynamic energy to some purpose and they stifle their loneliness in an atmosphere of frenzied gaiety. The change from the frenzy of the ball to the bitter awakening of the morning as the pitiless light of day reveals the shape of Alberto's grotesque mask leads to the spiritual climax of the film. The influence of Dali and Bosch have been detected in these scenes but perhaps no artist would be able to portray that precise state of mind as Fellini has done with the camera.

I vitelloni has been described as 'a despairing world, a world of dust and ashes'. In fact this is a tragic film with a tragic rhythm, a subtle cadence of anguish. Although tragedy is ever threatening, it never breaks out because there is no thunder with the storm. For this very reason the atmosphere in *I vitelloni* is all the more heavy, tense, unnerving and dramatic. Fellini has shown amazing mastery in the gradual development of this atmosphere.

Naturally there are faults in this dense, compact atmosphere. Fausto's amorous advances may be exaggerated, Sandra may appear affected, certain 'fortuitous' coincidences are not very likely. (Someone has pointed out, amongst other errors of taste, Sandra's faint at the beginning, and Fausto's meeting with the unknown woman in the cinema, just at the critical moment of his repentance.) Moraldo may seem the odd one out amongst his friends and it is easy to foretell his revolt; the symbolism of the angel is unwarranted and uncalled for. But taken as a whole the spivs' characters are vital and sincere and are made so by everyone's perfect acting, especially Alberto Sordi, who was faced with the most difficult character.

The film is made up of minute details, of original observations, of unexpected illuminating touches, between the sleeping walls of the town: one only has to think of the mambo danced in the middle of the street, of the narrowness of Fausto's home-life, with the moving figures of the old man and the little girl who are always united and ready to help one another, contrasting with the other's selfish absenteeism. Even the famous 'workmen' sequence, whose facile and direct comedy contributed so much to the success of the film, has a moral purpose which should not be overlooked. Nor did the director want to abandon his customary themes, such as the supple precision of conventional elements, for instance, shown in the crocodile of priests walking across the beach and standing out against the background of the sea, and in Fausto's search for Sandra.

I vitelloni, as sustained as a beautiful song, with sadness, pathos and magnificent photography, closes the first cycle of Fellini's films. Now, a trilogy is to be initiated by *La strada*, followed by *Il bidone*, and culminating in *Le notti di Cabiria*. But first the director made, partly for amusement, partly for a bet, a short sketch in the film *L'amore in città* (*Love in the City*). The sketch was *Agenzia matrimoniale*, which was shown at about the same time as *I vitelloni* towards the end of 1953.

Agenzia matrimoniale was not a very compelling film, and we shall therefore deal with it rapidly before passing on further. It was initiated by Zavattini, who, since the first visual issue of his 'cinematic reviews', *Lo Spettatore* had championed a 'film-inquiry' (a film with a journalistic approach) delegated to various directors who were to develop six short 'articles' or chapters on the theme 'Love in the City'. Zavattini also had other themes in mind, but they did not materialize. The Emilian writer upheld the necessity of an 'integral, uncompromisingly realistic cinema, which would portray man in his everyday activities'. 'Even,' says Zavattini, 'the banal purchase of a pair of shoes.'

In *Amore in città* real events were to be related, with the real-life characters in those events, talking about themselves in front of the camera, without the interference of the director. It was to be, purely and simply, a documentary. To imagine that such a formula and the imposition of a theme which he could in no way exaggerate would please Fellini—and what is more at a time when Zavattini was conducting a vigorous campaign against invention, against the cinema of fantasy, just as Fellini was thinking about making *La strada*—seems really bizarre to those who know the director. What is more surprising is that Fellini should have adhered to this programme.

But Fellini—despite the fact that at the beginning of the film he goes to great lengths to explain that the adventure really did happen to him—had originally agreed to make a film with an imaginary story, contrary to the plan, therefore his episode is out of tune with the rest. The other directors had obeyed, to a greater or lesser extent, the dictates of the formula: Lizzani had directed *L'amore che si paga* (*Love at a Price*), (the titles are revealing and indicative of the subject matter); Antonioni *Suicidio tentato* (*Attempted Suicide*); Lattuada *Gli italiani si voltano* (*Italians Turn Round*); Maselli and Zavattini *Storia di Caterina Rigoglioso* (The Story of Caterina Rigoglioso); Dino Risi *Paradiso per quattro ore* (Four Hours of Paradise) (against a background of 'Sunday dance halls'). They are not surpassingly good episodes, destined to live on; in fact, they are almost forgotten now, including Fellini's own 'rebel' episode, proving that the formula, although it testifies to the good faith of the promoter, was neither effective nor vital.

In his non-conformity over *L'amore in città*, Fellini conducted himself in much the same way as he was to do eight years later when he directed *Le tentazioni del dottor Antonio* within the framework of *Boccaccio '70*. He did not concern himself greatly with the formula of this film, and he was personally disinterested in the work of his fellow directors.

In *Agenzia matrimoniale* a somewhat cynical journalist—a shadowy predecessor of Marcello in *La dolce vita*—investigates for his paper the small bureaux where marriages could be arranged, for cash. He comes across an unfortunate girl who is ready to marry a man suffering from lycanthropy for the sake of regulating her future with a piece of paper. The journalist takes pity on her, but goes away without interesting himself further in the sad affair, leaving the solution to the protagonists' conscience.

'The plight of the woman,' says Renzi, 'was portrayed with an exceptional modesty which triumphed over the ludicrousness of her awkward manner, her speech defect, and the very nature of her calculated intentions.'

Yet the film is cold and soulless without the impact and sincerity that

Fellini imprints on all his work. Although the director remembers the film affectionately he did not keep the scenario. (On the other hand, Fellini generally prefers to forget his scenarios, hiding them or giving them to his collaborators, 'through a kind of rogue's complex', he says.) The music, written to emphasize the exceptional nature of this experiment, was by Nascimbene and the photography by Di Venanzo. The actors were none of them professional, but students from the Experimental Centre.

CHAPTER 6

The Lonely Heroes of La strada *(1954)*

After the enormous success of *I vitelloni*, it should have been easy for Fellini to launch his old project, *La strada*. But it was not so. Pegoraro who had made a handsome profit from the success of *I vitelloni*, was very willing to produce a new film with the director, but he adamantly refused to allow Giulietta Masina to appear as the heroine. Rather than make concessions on this important point, Fellini deserted Pegoraro and for some months he vainly knocked at the doors of various producers, who generally wanted sequels to *I vitelloni* (even with the title *Le vitelline*), or else kindly advised him to make *La strada* into a book rather than a film. But at last he found someone—Carlo Ponti—who was willing to partner the enterprise with Dino de Laurentiis.

Ponti was enthusiastic when Fellini told him about the plot: but his enthusiasm suddenly faded when he learnt that the director wanted Masina and Anthony Quinn to act in it. Why not have Silvano Mangano and Burt Lancaster instead, since they were so much more 'commercial'? Fellini said he was ready to tear up the contract which had already been signed; then a compromise was put forward. Masina yes, Quinn no. 'He is little more than an all-round actor,' the producers maintained, when they talked about the American. Fellini, who had at first thought of an actor taken from the street, perhaps a real 'strong-man' to play Zampanò, was adamant this time too and at last he triumphed. The American Richard Basehart, Valentina Cortese's husband, was brought in to play the 'Madman'. He was accepted without difficulty because he had had a great success in Hathaway's *Fourteen Hours*.

However, the film was begun in an atmosphere of suspicion ('They treated me like the last of the orphans,' comments Fellini), and amidst a thousand troubles. Nearly all the film had to be made outdoors and the season was already drawing to an end with winter on the doorstep. Then there was an accident which aggravated the situation: in December, 1953 when shooting had just started, Giulietta fell and dislocated her ankle bone while she was acting a scene with Quinn. Everything had to be stopped, until February of the following year, 1954. In the meantime the cameraman Carlini left and was replaced by Martelli.

For the second attempt (the successful one) the company installed itself in Viterbo, where a Convent of the Clare sisters, centuries old and partly in ruins, had been found. The scene of the nuns giving Gelsomina and Zampanò shelter was set there. Afterwards shooting took place at Ovindoli, ten miles off the Aquila road, where the death of the 'Madman' was filmed. But at that time—the end of March—there was no snow on the roads, as the script demanded and artificial snow had to be made with thirty sacks of chalk. As these were not sufficient two entire villages were ransacked to find a hundred clean white sheets to use as a basis for the chalk. A strong wind began to blow and the fake snow began to whirl about in the air.

At Bagnoregio and Viterbo, in April, the procession and the 'Madman's' display on the rope were shot. A professional acrobat was naturally chosen for the latter, dangerous performance. They had to prevent him knowing that his wife had her first labour pains that night, for fear that he would be worried or even leave the troupe in the lurch halfway through.

Filming stopped again for some time because Quinn went out of circulation, and it was at that moment that the film backers acted in a way which Fellini always remembers with emotion. Knowing the setbacks with which the director was struggling and convinced that an unusual film was being made, they approached Fellini and said: 'Don't worry about your debts to us. Let's pretend they were a joke, buy us a coffee and we'll forget them.'

Anthony Quinn's frequent absences, the main cause of the delay, were due to his making another film, *Attila*. Despite all this, after three months, about May, the first phase of *La strada*—completed by other outside shots in small towns in Southern and Central Italy—had ended. The two immortal characters, Gelsomina and Zampanò were born.

How did the idea for the film come about? Today it is not easy to follow its tortuous evolution. At any rate, whilst the hypothesis that it had been harboured in Federico's mind since his far-off 'flight' with 'Pierino's' circus, is not really tenable, we can say that its shapeless form had existed since Fellini had known Aldo Fabrizi and had heard his tales. These memories subsequently underwent a strange transformation: after meeting Pinelli, Fellini began to cherish the idea of portraying a mediaeval knight errant who wanders all over Italy and after many adventures dies alone and forsaken in the open countryside. An imaginary character within a historical framework? It was probably the vestiges of an experiment carried out with Rossellini in the film about St. Francis. But it is still a fact that Fellini and Pinelli did some research in libraries in order to bring the character to life. When the plan was definitely abandoned, the timeless fairy-tale setting stayed in Fellini's mind and he did not forsake it in *La strada*.

Fellini places the real creation of the heroes of *La strada* some time in 1950, whilst he was filming the outside scenes for *Luci del varietà*. Already the climate was favourable to the subject that was taking shape. He relates how one evening he had gone out into the country and had seen two nomads camping in the open. While the woman was stirring soup in a pot over the fire the man waited, apart from her. They never exchanged a word all the time Fellini watched them. For the first time the director understood directly the inability to communicate between two people destined to live together. He had noticed this in many peasant couples, especially in Southern Italy. Some time afterwards he and Giulietta were staying in the Alps and they happened to come across another gipsy couple. The man was driving a heavily laden cart along the snow-covered road, whilst the woman was patiently pushing behind.

While Fellini was reflecting on all these ideas in the autumn of 1951, Pinelli returned from Piedmont and told him that on market days he had wandered on foot around the towns near Turin. He had collected many observations on wandering gipsies who gave displays in small village fairs. By combining their observations the two friends immediately began to write a preliminary plot and then a detailed version. It was a compromise between the carefree tone Fellini had in mind and Pinelli's more dramatic one. However, although this first version of *La strada* (which we still have) contains nearly all the themes of the definitive scenario, the treatment is more sombre and legendary than that of the actual film. Zampanò was a real wolf, not the cur he became in the later version. Gelsomina was more innocent and immersed in a kind of somnambulism which verged on madness. Zampanò owned a cart, not a motor-bike and the magical elements were accentuated. In fact one reads sentences like: 'Suddenly the storm dies away as if by magic' or 'Gelsomina takes the flute, brings it to her lips and makes strange, mysterious music on it. Where and when did Gelsomina learn to play the flute? She does not know herself.'

In November, 1953, when it had been decided to produce the film, Ennio Flajano was asked to collaborate on the scenario. His job, in his own words, was to 'say derogatory things about *La strada* for three months'. 'I condemned a vagueness of atmosphere, certain affectations in the characters and I insisted that the story, though very beautiful, should come down to earth and that the symbolism should be integrated with the narrative.' This contribution is far from negative and produced the final scenario for the film. It still differs from the film in some respects, but it does reflect generally what Fellini, Pinelli and Flajano wanted. Flajano is the first to recognize the greater contribution of the other two. 'The praise,' he explains, 'goes to Fellini and Pinelli and especially to Fellini, who later found himself alone, after the battle with the production, having to master the elements, characters and purpose of the story to make it into a film. He had to find a balance between the true world of the road, and the poetic world of his imagination.'

Brunello Rondi also gives evidence of the director's work before and during the making of the film. 'From the beginning Fellini fought against the literary temptations of the theme and against the obstacle created by picturesque elements inherent in the atmosphere. He changed the sea-side village at the beginning of the film several times, because he found it was too picturesque.' Before he filmed the ending Fellini wandered about Rome all night with Rondi, talking over possible solutions.

The selling of Gelsomina to Zampanò for 10,000 lire is the prelude to *La strada*; the background is a heath bordering on a deserted beach. Gelsomina's mother, who had already given another daughter, Rosa, to Zampanò, learns of Rosa's death and feels momentarily guilty, but this soon recedes at the sight of money. And so Gelsomina, who is a little simple ('It's not your fault, you're not like other girls') gets on to Zampanò's motor-bike and finds herself in another town at dawn. Gelsomina makes her first timid attempts to free herself from her 'master'. 'I'll go back,' she says humbly, 'don't worry . . . I'll walk back.' 'Come on, move!' is the only reply. Then Zampanò begins his display, which is always the same and consists of winding an iron chain around his naked chest and breaking it with a jerk by inflating the muscles of his thorax. 'The dilation of the lungs, blowing them up like a tyre,' he proclaims in his incoherent Italian, 'could make a little internal artery burst and then I'll spit blood. In Milan Ettore Montagna, an athlete weighing 118 kilos, lost his sight through this trick, because there is a great strain on the optic nerve. . . .' Gelsomina is very impressed and full of admiration for this feat, but her good will is immediately dampened. Zampanò begins teaching her by ramming a worn-out hat on to her head and thrusting a tambourine into her hands, which she must beat, as she cries 'Zampanò is here!' Because Gelsomina is slow in learning he beats her. At night he forces her to sleep with him inside the 'wagon' despite her shy reluctance.

Now one display follows another, with comic interludes. 'Good day, Miss Gelsomina, do you like my trifle?' 'Not trifle, stupid, rifle!' And Gelsomina with the hat on her head and a military overcoat and a tambourine round her neck, pretends to be a quail and falls to the ground with her legs in the air, when the gun-shot is heard. But Zampanò can also be generous and takes her to eat in a real restaurant. Gelsomina is enchanted and does not notice that her man has made a date with a casually encountered woman. 'Wait here, you,' he says to Gelsomina, making the woman get on his bike. 'Where are you going?' asks Gelsomina, who has not understood. 'Wait here.' The next morning, the poor girl 'as scruffy as a stray cat', is still there waiting in the middle of the street and she replies to the kindly questions of the passers-by with a rough impatience which hides her despair. ('Auffa! Auffa!') At last she finds Zampanò drunk and while she waits for him to wake up, she digs up some earth and plants tomato seeds, believing in her simplicity that they will grow.

The two wanderers are then taken in at a prosperous farm, where a wedding is being celebrated. While Zampanò is getting ready to make love to the old farmer's wife in order to earn himself an old hat (and he even goes so far as to wink at Gelsomina, in amused complicity, while she returns the wink in good faith), a little girl leads Gelsomina to the bedside of a poor paralytic, Oswald, 'of no definite age, but pale as a white mushroom'. Gelsomina's guide wants her to make the little sick boy laugh with her comical gestures and Gelsomina, although she is upset, tries to please him. Then she goes to sleep in the barn where she takes the fate of a strange horse, who trembles all night, very much to heart. Lying beside Zampanò she desperately tries to converse with him. 'Do you believe in spirits?' 'Go on with you, go on!' her companion grunts. 'Spirits! A lot of rubbish! When you die, you're dead.' Gelsomina does not give up. 'Why don't you teach me to play the trumpet, Zampanò?' The man pays no attention to her and Gelsomina drowns her solitude in weeping. 'What's the matter with you?' Zampanò asks her, exasperated. Gelsomina thinks about rebelling, in her own way of course. 'Auffa!' she replies, and huddles up. The next day she goes off alone. Zampanò's only farewell is 'Well, go away then . . . go to hell!'

Gelsomina makes for the town and meets three musicians on the causeway. They are going to play in a religious festival, as it is Christmas Eve. In the town the girl sees the 'Madman' for the first time, as he gives a tightrope display, while the statue of the Virgin is carried along the road. Meanwhile Zampanò has taken Gelsomina back and has joined Colombaioni's small circus, which is working in the town. There the two meet the 'Madman' again, who bears an old grudge against Zampanò and does not lose the chance of goading him spitefully. ('You did well to take him on, we needed animals in this circus.') The 'Madman' cannot help interrupting Zampanò's act with jibes and jokes, but Gelsomina is enchanted by the way the acrobat plays the violin and despite Zampanò's threats, she persuades him to teach her to play the trumpet, which Zampanò has never allowed her to do. A violent quarrel breaks out between the two men, and perhaps there is a spark of jealousy in Zampanò's violence and a little love or pity for Gelsomina in the 'Madman's' provocation. The 'Madman' throws a bucket of water in Zampanò's face and Zampanò attacks him with a knife. Both of them end up in prison, but the acrobat comes out first and goes to find Gelsomina.

At this point comes one of the most poetic scenes in *La strada*, although the film is certainly not devoid of poetry elsewhere. Gelsomina does not know whether to follow the circus which is striking camp or to stay with Zampanò. She laments in her childish voice: 'If I go with them it's the same, if I go back to Zampanò it's the same. . . . I'm no use to anyone.' Then bitterly 'Auffa! I'm sick of living!' But the 'Madman' comforts her and even makes her laugh, alternating gentleness with sudden changes of tone. ('And you're plain ugly,' he tells her.) Then he asks her, 'Would you come with me?' Gelsomina is hopeful for a moment, but the other replies immediately, 'But no, I won't take you.' Then he says, 'Zampanò is an animal, he doesn't think. He's like a dog, even if they want to talk, they bark.' Gelsomina tries a last defence. 'He's made like that, it isn't his fault.' Then the 'Madman' expounds his personal philosophy for the girl's edification. 'There's nothing useless in the world. You see this pebble? Everything has a use, even this pebble.' 'What use?' asks Gelsomina. 'How should I know? If I knew, d'you know who I'd be? I don't know what this stone does, but it's useful. If it isn't useful then even the stars aren't useful. That's what I think.' Gelsomina bursts out, 'One day when he's driving I'll set light to everything inside and burn it all up. That'll teach him. . . . He gave 10,000 lire for me, then put me to work. And he beats me, is that right?' The 'Madman', half serious, half joking, renews his proposal that she should go with him, then as Gelsomina is about to accept he hurts her again. 'But I don't want to lumber myself with a girl, I don't need one.' Then he hands Gelsomina a little medallion, 'Have this! It's a souvenir. Cheerio!' So ends the only idyll in Gelsomina's grey life.

Later when she has gone back to Zampanò, Gelsomina tries to make some affectionate advances to him, in her own way. 'Now my home seems to be with you.' But Zampanò does not take it up. 'That's a good discovery, considering the thrashing you got at home.' Gelsomina makes a last effort the night when Zampanò, having asked for shelter at a convent en route, lies down beside her. The girl, struck by the serenity of the nuns and the calm of their refuge, keeps Zampanò awake with provocative questions. 'If I died, Zampanò, would you be sorry?' 'Why don't you ever think, Zampanò?' But Zampanò is annoyed and only replies 'For all you understand . . .' 'Blockhead . . .' 'Go on with you, you mad woman.' At Gelsomina's last, low-voiced question, 'Do you love me, Zampanò?' he does not even reply, probably he did not hear. He is thinking about stealing a silver votive offering, but he asks for Gelsomina's help in vain.

Now the gulf between Zampanò and the girl grows ever wider and becomes unbridgeable when, the next day, they meet the 'Madman' on the road. He is changing a tyre on his broken-down car when Zampanò attacks him wildly and, perhaps without meaning to, kills him, whilst Gelsomina looks on helplessly. He hurls the body and the car down a railway embankment and takes off with the girl at a frantic speed on his motor-bike.

From now on Gelsomina is no longer herself. During their act she murmurs as if hallucinated, 'The "Madman" is ill.' She doesn't want to eat and one day she throws herself to the ground trembling. She is feverish and moans feebly. Zampanò, torn between fear that the wretched girl will divulge the crime and a kind of rough pity, finally leaves her in a little chapel, covered with an old blanket. Beside her is the trumpet on which she has learnt to play a single, melancholy tune. . . .

Some years later Zampanò, aging and tired, with none of his old arrogance, comes to a little sea-side town. Suddenly he thinks he can hear the tune Gelsomina used to play on the trumpet. A woman is singing it and she tells Zampanò she learnt it from a wandering girl. 'A little thing, only so high. . . . She was always crying, she never ate. . . . When she was a little better she would sit in the sun over there and play on the trumpet and thank us. Then one morning she didn't wake up. . . .' Zampanò, filled with remorse, tries to obliterate Gelsomina's ghost with wine. Kicked out of the inn, with an expression of bestial fury on his face he pummels his fists against a tree and then gives a great howl into the night and makes for the beach. An unknown terror has seized hold of him; he rolls on the ground in despair and the scenario ends like that. 'A sob fills his chest and shakes him all over. Zampanò is weeping.'

The true meaning of *La strada* is to be seen in the ending. Zampanò—who does not think and who lives only through his senses—becomes a human being again through anguish and suffering in recollection of Gelsomina: he feels for the first time, not the love vainly dreamt by his companion, but at least an intuition of loneliness and an attempt, through weeping, to give vent to the tangle of confused feelings within him. Basically his is a self-confession, he is aware of his own sad plight and understands that it is the cause of his unhappiness. Zampanò's repentance also justifies the Catholic interpretation which was immediately put on the film. The ending was therefore necessary to clarify the complex problems interwoven in the plot, but from a stylistic point of view *La strada* should have ended with the desertion of Gelsomina, which is one of the most successful scenes, while the last scene for several reasons (narrative slowness and over-emphasized symbolism for instance) is not convincing.

In *La strada*, Fellini attempted to make a film along Chaplin lines, with all the bitter desolation of *The Little Man*, *The Circus* and *City Lights*. And his success is all the more astonishing in that Chaplin's sentimental warmth is missing. However, the two chief characters have a human sympathy which goes far beyond the poetic ideas in their conception. For, without betraying the original theme, and still remaining a film which refuses to compromise with the demands of entertainment, *La strada* is not a dull formal exercise, but a work of poetry, anchored in reality. When one speaks of the lyricism of *La strada*, one must not forget that the film is strongly realistic, despite its framework of fantasy. Gelsomina, Zampanò and the 'Madman' are symbols, but first and foremost they are living characters who move and disturb, but always arouse feeling within the spectator. The atmosphere, deeds and events come to life and develop in a very concrete way. So the accusation brought forward by some critics that Gelsomina and Zampanò merely typify a state of mind, and are fated to be destroyed by the very nature of their symbolism, is not justifiable. The public did not accept this criticism, for the whole world gave its support not to the success of those symbolic ideas, but to a story which had struck deep, precisely because of its artistic truth.

Of the three characters of the triangle, Gelsomina is definitely the most successful. She is an absolutely new figure in the history of the cinema and Italian culture. She had not even been attempted by Fellini himself, previously, because the peasant girl of *Il miracolo* was only a crude, remote image of her. Gelsomina, even in the earliest stages of the film, is a character who gradually becomes aware of herself in the most beautiful scenes in the film: the procession, the meeting with the sick child, the idyll with the 'Madman' (in which she glimpses spiritual love), her advances towards Zampanò in the convent (in which she cautiously reveals her womanly feelings), in the killing of the 'Madman', when she is faced with the horror of death. Through a multitude of unfulfilled desires, Gelsomina is a martyr to loneliness and to lack of love and charity. She is the complete expression of Fellinian ethics at their highest point. Giulietta Masina's interpretation was outstanding, above all in being able to convey, from within, the destruction of the character's reason. She started from nothing and expressed the ecstatic madness of the ending with an irresistible force. And at the same time she has remained natural, with all the shyness, the wayward gestures (the exclamation of 'Auffa!'), the diffident advances. She has avoided the danger—which Fellini feared—of portraying only a pathetic half-wit.

From certain points of view Zampanò was easier; the symbolic interpretation of his character (inability to communicate, the loneliness of a chained animal) was more natural, with less need of restraint. He is also the continuation of a certain argument begun in *Lo Sceicco bianco* and continued in *I vitelloni*, made concrete in the two unfeeling, unloving characters acted by Sordi. But here naturally, the character has greater possibilities; he breathes deeply and vigorously. Fellini can make him say all that he feels, he can express through him all his revulsion of a way of life which leads only to a dog's death, soon forgotten were it not for redemption through remorse.

Did Zampanò really love Gelsomina, even when he illtreated her? It is a reasonable doubt, but it does not basically alter the question. Certainly Fellini, by slightly changing the original idea, preferred not to stress Quinn's bestiality too crudely (perhaps he exaggerated a little in the tragic brawl with the 'Madman') and he wanted him to show some degree of understanding. This is explicable, as the director saw something of himself in Zampanò. Anthony Quinn acted the part with exceptional powers of expression. He did not succeed in being as primitive as Fellini had wished ('He was too handsome physically,' comments the director) but he has given a wonderful interpretation of that dark chaotic creature, Zampanò.

Of the three the 'Madman' is the least successful, not only because he carries a heavier burden of symbolism, which often goes beyond artistic reality, but also because Richard Basehart, a sophisticated American actor, has not been able to introduce his character in the wholly Italian style of the other two. The 'Madman' should be Tuscan and should have the lightness, the restlessness, the unprejudiced nature of Tuscany. And I do not think he acquired this despite Fellini's efforts. In the famous 'pebble dialogue' with Gelsomina he is really effective, but in comparison with Giulietta Masina one is conscious of his cultured, literary background. What does this irrational hero represent? An angelic creature, as someone has suggested? Or has he not, rather, the earthly failings of one who, although not incapable of love, cannot be steadfast in affection and ends up as selfish, in his way, as Zampanò? Essentially, the 'Madman' deceives Gelsomina. He arouses her feelings, only to repudiate her: from this point of view he is no less guilty than Zampanò and he pays for his uncertainty and instability with death.

The melancholy heroes of *La strada* are therefore angels and devils. They are courageously drawn in depth, with a firmness of which only Fellini is capable. As we have already indicated, their surroundings and background have been stripped, almost ferociously, of every picturesque element by the director, so that only the essential remains, the lonely atmosphere in which the true nature of his characters can be expressed. Here are stretches of bare sand, a desolate countryside, typical of Southern Italy, deserted roads and great empty spaces. Then there are the interior scenes (the farm, the convent): the whole film takes place on the main roads, in the open, and one feels in one's bones the morning dampness, the nightly squalor, the burnt, bitter taste of soup hastily cooked in the dark in an old rimless pan.

We leave the film with our limbs aching like Gelsomina's as she gets up from the uncomfortable shake-down in Zampanò's motor-bike. The greatness and beauty of *La strada* lies in having known how to place this story of human beings in an extraordinarily clear atmosphere, without blurring, without a psychological or stylistic fault, a climate in which the sharpness of the image brings 'things' that are already in the thoughts of the spectator into the foreground. Fellini and Martelli succeeded, also, in their undertaking because of their technical skill; the extended camera movements throughout the film show the director's passion for following the character, moving with him, assisting and guiding him directly towards the public.

La strada proceeds rhythmically and solemnly, sometimes too much so, but the rhythm is always exact and deliberately articulated. Nino Rota's music, as we have said, gives it a special force, a singularly efficacious quality. (The famous 'Gelsomina's song' was recorded and sold nearly two million copies in France.)

Fellini has rightly said: '*La strada* will remain the crucial point in my life.' And immediately the film had been edited he declared: 'I do not want to make statements, I think I have already said all that I can weep for, laugh, suffer or hope for in the film. I have exhausted myself.'

On the evening of 11 September, 1954, *La strada* was shown to the public for the first time at the Venice Festival and received very warm applause. Fellini, suffering from nervous exhaustion, waited for the inevitable battle between the critics. And indeed there was one which raged for many months, with bitter, ungenerous attacks.

From the beginning Catholic critics aligned themselves with Fellini and his film: the left-wing critics were against him. Each side had a theory to support. The Catholics maintained that the film was genuinely Christian, arguing (on the basis of the *finale*) that *La strada* was a parable about Christian charity, love, grace and salvation. The Marxists declared that it was a serious attack on neo-realism in the cinema. Both were basically wrong. The Catholics had exaggerated the religious significance of the film, whilst their opponents, in their destructive fury, failed to realize that they were upholding ideas which they would have to retract years later. The invective often became absurd. 'They even accused me,' Fellini remembers, 'of having justified political oppression through the character of Gelsomina. In fact Gelsomina accepts blows and suffering passively. But won't these gentlemen understand that Gelsomina is made much stronger by this acceptance than by revolt?'

In any event the real value of the film was lost in the midst of all this criticism. Venice preferred Castellani's cold, formalistic *Romeo e Giulietta* (Romeo and Juliet), and in the distribution of prizes only awarded *La strada* a silver lion. Great injustice was done to Giulietta Masina who received no official recognition, although the prize for the best actress of the year was not awarded! But time and above all the reception of the public and foreign critics avenged those rash, hasty judgments. First in France, then in England, and later in America, truly fanatical praise was showered on *La strada*. The film was shown in New York for over three years and takings were one and a half million dollars. Fellini was acclaimed the greatest figure of the post-war cinema and Giulietta was placed alongside the greatest actresses of all time. *La strada* was awarded an Oscar shortly afterwards, together with a whole shower of prizes, whilst the couple undertook a series of triumphal tours throughout the world to launch the film. Everywhere dolls, cigars, restaurants, shops, articles of every description were named after Gelsomina and *La strada*. Everywhere Giulietta and Federico were the object of boundless, emotional admiration as avalanches of letters arrived and the actress was forced to become a journalist in order to reply to everyone in the newspapers.

'With *La strada*,' says Fellini, 'I made at least thirty people in the world rich; small independent distributors who believed in the film. But I'm not envious. I gained nothing or hardly anything from a material point of view. But I was at peace with myself and my pride as an artist.'

CHAPTER 7

A Step Backwards—Il bidone *(1955)*

AFTER *LA STRADA* various roads lay open to Fellini: to continue the thematic development of the world of Gelsomina and Zampanò, to make a sequel of the adventures of the Moraldo of *I vitelloni* or to try to enlarge his own horizon with new perspectives. The first two were real steps backwards and Fellini vaguely felt this, so that after long deliberation about *Moraldo in città* he finally abandoned the project. But instead of choosing the third scheme, he preferred to go back to the first and was influenced by the 'contacts' he had made during the making of *La strada* and the success of the film.

Moraldo in città was born in the wake of *I vitelloni* and related the adventures of the young man after his departure from his native town, during his stay in Rome. Moraldo lived by expedients: he joined up with Lange, a penniless artist, and with 'Gattone', an unsuccessful writer. He knew the wretched life of little boarding houses, of snack bars, of makeshifts of every description. At one time in the hope of making his way into journalism he was kept by Signora Contini, a writer of romantic short stories and the editor of a periodical. In the end he became engaged to Andreina, a lower middle-class girl, for love of whom he was persuaded to take a job, which he promptly abandoned. Hating to be tied, he deserted Andreina too and after a visit from his father (which is a distant forerunner of the scene later made in *La dolce vita*) and a party which filled him with disgust, he contemplated suicide. 'What am I looking for? What am I? I've some vices, but not too many, a little of the middle-class mentality, but not too much. . . . What am I waiting for, what do I want?' But having wandered towards the outskirts with these confused thoughts he returned renewed, after an enlightening colloquy, back to the city and to the life which no longer appeared hostile, 'With its unexpected riches of encounters, affairs, people and adventures.'

The outline of *Moraldo in città* was published at the end of 1954 in the magazine *Cinema* and lively discussion about it ensued. But Fellini had already grown tired of it, perhaps because of the great conjecture it had aroused, while all his films had been prepared in the utmost silence and often in an atmosphere of absolute secrecy. There was, however, another reason for abandoning *Moraldo*. In this plot there was no trace of the lyrical, enchanted climate of *La strada* and the director wanted to repeat it in a new film. Besides, Fellini, while he was shooting *La strada*, had gathered together a lot of information about the life of nomads and their ways, which naturally he had not been able to use—given the structure of the film—but which he did not want to see wasted.

He remembers in particular how one evening he was having supper in a restaurant in Ovindoli and had got to know a 'wool dealer'—a traveller of second-grade materials which he passed as pure wool—who had told him the story of his life. This gave Fellini the idea for a film in which three tricksters tour the Italian provinces swindling simple folk. The term '*bidone*' had long since come into the spoken language, to mean a low trick played upon those who will not denounce it for fear of looking stupid. Fellini chose it at once as an ideal title for his film.

Pinelli relates that in the beginning the film was to be one with an all-embracing setting, adventurous, picturesque, rich in characters and situations and that, from this point of view at least, it would be like *I vitelloni*, so much so that the director had thought again of Sordi and Fabrizi, joined by Peppino De Filippo, as the actors. As usual the theme of loneliness and the inability to communicate would have been the crux of the plot, telling the story of a woman, abandoned by her husband, dragging her children from fair to fair, selling shoddy goods. At the end, the death of a *bidonista* provokes a terrible fight between her two companions, who discover all the degradation of their position in the cruel struggle.

With this plan in hand, Fellini went to see many producers and found one, Goffredo Lombardo of *Titanus*, who was ready to give him a contract for a number of years as well as finance the film. But before he began the real scenario Fellini wanted to make a careful investigation of the world of the 'swindlers'. He also wanted to avoid the danger, which someone pointed out to him, of reproducing in its entirety the atmosphere of *La strada*, complete with wandering gipsies and a swindler owning an old broken-down car in place of a 'strong man' with a motor-bike.

At this point, after investigations in which hundreds of swindlers in Rome and its surroundings were interrogated, with the help of 'Lupaccio' (the Wolf) whom Fellini had opportunely remembered, the results were unexpected. The world of the 'swindler' was much less romantic than had been foreseen. It was more sterile, full of merciless opportunists who were not content to earn enough for the day but who wanted to get rich quick and were prepared to fight to the death with each other. Instead of being happy rogues, the swindlers were sinister and pitiless; their stories were all the same and they were not in the least amusing. For the most part their pitch was not the country or the little town, but the great city which they travelled around in 'junked-up' cars, frequenting low night-clubs and places open to every vice. It was a hard blow for Fellini and Pinelli and at one point the director considered giving up the film.

Fellini took heart again and decided to centre the whole story around one swindler (supported by two minor ones) and to avoid direct description of that atmosphere which had deeply revolted him and was by now entirely alien to him. This was the first breach in the film, the first miscalculation, because the story was based on the hope that the public would be moved to pity by the long agony of an old, tired swindler who begins to feel remorse for his deeds. But because of this set-back, a much more human, pathetic figure needed to be built up than the one that had emerged from the complex labours of research, and everything had to be thrown overboard with the resultant risk of creating an indeterminate character. On the one hand was Zampanò's primitivism, for which much could be forgiven, on the other the cynical slyness of Augusto (as the hero was called) who in fact became—as has been rightly observed—another Zampanò but with only his negative qualities.

This unstable, ill-defined character, whose loneliness was irremediable and for whom the only solution was a final despairing death, had as companions two friends, who were even less clearly portrayed: Picasso and Roberto. And the description of their despicable tricks was not designed to reconcile anyone to them.

People say that while Fellini was writing the scenario he had Humphrey Bogart clearly in mind for the role of Augusto. But Bogart, already undermined by the illness that was to kill him, could not accept. The director had thought of Pierre Fresnay, but was forced to fall back on Broderick Crawford, whom he had never seen act and of whose success in Rossen's *All the King's Men* he had heard only an echo. Crawford was joined by Basehart and Franco Fabrizi, who were now approved, and Giulietta Masina in the unusual part of a 'good' wife.

Finally—and this was not the last reason for its mediocre success—*Il bidone* was hurriedly made and even more hurriedly edited, so that it would be ready at the beginning of September for the Venice Festival. Shooting started late in May 1955; first of all the night scenes were shot at Marino, then the swindlers' party in Rome, followed by other outdoor scenes in Rome (Piazzo del Popolo, Il Cinema Flaminio) and later, at the beginning of July, the hovel scene in the authentic village of broken-down huts propped up against the ruined arches of the Felice Aqueduct; and finally Augusto's last trick at Cerveteri. It was very hot: the script required a winter countryside. Carbonic acid spread with a pump had to be used for the snow. On 16 July, the last day of the filming, Augusto's agony in the deserted stone quarry was filmed in the 'studio'.

Editing and cutting were also done somewhat hastily, in August (this time the editor was Serandrei instead of Cattozzo). Over one thousand metres of film were cut and whole scenes were shortened or sacrified, like the long scene with the 'big wheel', which was not one of the less successful.

Il bidone was shown on 10 September at Venice, where expectation was great. In the preceding days Fellini was very nervous because a daily paper had suddenly published the incredible, false statement that Giulietta Masina had run away with Richard Basehart. Five hundred journalists besieged the director day and night, asking for statements or denials. Intimacies of his private life were ferreted out, lawyers came on the scene and quarrels abounded. *Il bidone* was thus presented under circumstances anything but calm, and naturally the hint of scandal did not help it. During the whole showing the public—usually very generous with its applause—maintained a deathly silence. At the end of the film a very violent storm broke outside the Palazzo del Cinema and the thunder and the sound of rain were mixed with the sound-track of the film, overpowering it and sometimes becoming part of it. A few whisperings were heard, but in truth there was not even any discussion: some feeble applause was heard at the end and then, heads down, people began to crowd out leaving Giulietta and Federico in the theatre with the bitterness of an icy reception.

Il bidone had fallen and was not to rise again, despite subsequent attempts to restore it (especially in France) and the author's strenuous defence of it. But now, with his mind at peace, Fellini admits that it was not a completely effective film, because he was paying the reckoning for its intial errors.

What is the plot of *Il bidone*? We have seen it briefly, now let us look at it in detail. The film opens with a noisy *coup* on the part of the three swindlers: Augusto, Picasso and Roberto. The first dressed as a prelate, the second also in ecclesiastical dress as his pretended secretary, and the third in chauffeur's uniform, arrive in a long black car at a country dairy farm run by two old sisters. The false prelate tells them that a dying man has informed him that a treasure is buried in their field, the loot from a murder. Once their initial diffidence has been conquered, the sisters fall into the trap and dig a great hole in the place indicated. At the bottom, under a few bones, a box really is discovered, having been buried there the previous day by an accomplice. The treasure consists of a quantity of jewels of little value which the women believe to be real. The prelate stipulates that the booty, as the dead man decreed, shall go to the owners of the field, provided they have a certain number of Masses said for the soul of the testator. The peasant women pay out nearly half a million lire and the swindle is accomplished. The three go off in a hurry to divide the spoils.

In town, after the swindlers have boasted the success of the undertaking in a night-club, where Augusto amuses himself with a little dancer, they plot a second *coup*, this time even more despicable because it is against the poor people who live in the hovels. With the prospect of being allotted a house, a sum of money is extorted from these wretched people, who ruin themselves by paying it. The swindlers arrive at the village in the usual car and neither the sight of such poverty nor the emaciated faces of children clinging to their mothers' necks holds them back. However, Picasso, who at this stage of the swindle is in charge of payments begins to feel guilty and admires Augusto's careless ease. An unsuccessful painter, Picasso always gives the earnings from the thefts to his wife Iris, who knows nothing of the activities of her husband and lives a life of drudgery with little Silvano, of whom her father is very fond. Picasso is basically the best of the three, even if he is weak. He will be the first to revolt against this life.

The opportunity immediately presents itself when, following a chance meeting with an affluent swindler, the three are invited to memorable festivities at the former's house in the evening of San Silvestro's day. Even shy Iris takes part. While on the one hand Augusto realizes how modest his frauds are in comparison with those of his host and vainly humbles himself in offering his own services, Iris begins to realize what her husband is and Roberto (the most stupid and callous of the three) can do no better than steal a gold cigarette case. He is immediately found out and is harshly compelled by the owner of the house to give it back. The party reaches a pitch of crude eroticism, and culminates in a frenzied dance where everything seems to be possible. But the ending is bitter for Iris, and her husband follows her outside weeping and begging forgiveness.

A little later the trio pull off their last swindle together with a quantity of overcoats of poor quality which tear as soon as they are put on but are sold as if they are made of pure wool. That evening at Marino, not knowing how to pass their time, the three go to a little fair to amuse themselves and they try out the thrills of the 'big wheel'. Picasso, who is drunk, feels ill and on the steps of the fountain of a deserted square he confesses to Augusto his repugnance at continuing to work for him. Augusto vainly tries to persuade him, for deep down he is not convinced of what he says and is gripped by uneasiness. After he has rebuked Picasso for having a family, he says to him: 'And how can we have families? We must live alone, each one for himself. When one is young freedom is everything. You are afraid of being alone even now when you are young. What will you do when you are old?' Bitterness chokes him, at this hint of the spectre of loneliness. So Picasso leaves Augusto and goes back to the city and to Iris, and we do not see the painter with the innocent face again.

Meanwhile Augusto, in search of new ideas, happens to meet his daughter Patrizia in the street (Lorella De Luca). He has not seen her for years because she lives with her mother apart from him. He is astonished to find her grown up and, suddenly seized with paternal tenderness, he takes her out to supper in an open-air restaurant. Patrizia who knows nothing of her father's 'profession', tells him she is looking for work and needs a certain sum of money to deposit as security for a job as a cashier.

Augusto promises to help her: father and daughter go to the cinema but here Augusto is recognized by someone whom he has defrauded and is brutally arrested before Patrizia's eyes.

When Augusto comes out of prison he is changed. Bereft of his old friends (Roberto too has settled down) he seeks out new companions and organizes the safe old trick of the prelate and the treasure, in a mountain cottage. But he carries it out ill at ease, without confidence in what he is doing. Moreover, one of the victims is a little paralytic girl, on whom the money was to be spent for an operation. The girl, believing that the man really is a bishop, wants to speak to him: she begs his blessing and kisses his ring. Augusto, perturbed and overcome, takes flight and considers returning the stolen money. Back in the car with his friends he tells them he gave back the money to the peasants (though in fact he still has it on him, for his intentions are still confused) and his accomplices suspect that he is betraying them. Furious and suspecting that he wants to keep all the loot for himself, they beat him up badly. As he is trying to escape their wrath, Augusto falls and breaks his spine. His companions leave him, he rolls to the bottom of a rocky escarpment and laboriously tries to climb up again. He calls on the name of God, is seized with panic and in moments of lucidity he recalls his wicked life. As he tries in vain to reach the road by clutching the rocks with his nails, he hears the distant sound of bells, the noise of vehicles, the voices of people who go by without noticing him and he understands that his end has come. At dawn two terrified young peasants find him and to the dying swindler they seem like a last earthly vision.

This ending, of a crude and perhaps unnecessary realism, makes the mistake of being too long drawn-out. Fellini did not want to spare us anything of Augusto's prolonged agony and has gone beyond the point of equilibrium at which he usually halts, instinctively. We have spoken of the other structural defects: the insistence on motifs previously exploited (the nocturnal scene in the square at Marino); the weakness of Picasso's character—Richard Basehart—which relies too much upon the trite expedient of family affection to form an unconvincing contrast with the rascally world of the swindlers; the very nature of the frauds which are actually only two or three in number, cruelly ingenuous but lacking in subtlety; and above all the fundamental deficiency in moral content which makes the whole film questionable.

In some parts *Il bidone*, with its heritage from *La strada*, is lightened by happy recollections (the opening with that airy sense of the wild, re-echoed in more sombre tones in the conclusion; Augusto's meeting with his daughter and the little paralytic). In other parts, especially in the middle, it is *I vitelloni* which has the upper hand and we watch the hellish 'mambo' at the party in the house of the parvenu, and the development of an atmosphere which recalls that in which Alberto's grotesque revelries come to a climax. But it is just this fusion of contrasting themes which damages *Il bidone* and deprives it of its originality. Besides, the great quality of *I vitelloni* was the perfect harmony between the five protagonists and here this harmony is missing. The film is centred first upon Roberto, then Picasso and finally upon Augusto alone, while the others are lost on the way. So the apparent richness of motifs gradually fades away, without the film ever acquiring the moving, poetic tone of *La strada*.

The hovel sequence reminds one, in its general appearance, of De Sica's *Miracolo a Milano*, but has a less ambitious development because, in conformity with Fellini's character, there is no social interest whatever. One of the best and most original scenes was that with the 'big wheel' in which, with Augusto as a spectator, Roberto and Picasso were spun giddily by the diabolical machine of a 'Luna Park'. Here Franco Fabrizi could effectively display his mimicry of a 'brazen-faced child'. For Augusto it was the final confirmation of the squalor of his life, seen in the contorted faces of his two friends tossed about on the 'big wheel'. But for various reasons the scene was almost entirely cut in the editing process and in the copies that circulated in France it did not even appear.

Having emphasized the defects, the many good and valuable qualities of the maltreated *Il bidone* must also be stressed. First, the film is in no way unworthy of the great 'trilogy of loneliness' begun with *La strada* and ending with *Le notti di Cabiria*: it is a point of less resistance, a defective link in the chain, but it is still a link of iron, difficult to break despite the most violent attacks. In *Il bidone* the image adheres firmly to the substance;

there is a strong thematic quality which re-advocates courageously and lucidly the motif of the isolated man and of salvation. The parable of Augusto who comes near to renouncing his wickedness is developed gradually and convincingly; Augusto himself, and the others have, Pietro Bianchi observes, a full-blooded power and live with vital intensity. The orgy at the swindler's house is an extract from an anthology, a hell without hope and the atmosphere in the hovel sequence, of a miracle that never comes, is, according to a French critic, a long outcry of grief in destitution. Even if they are not well co-ordinated, all Fellini's qualities can be detected in *Il bidone*: extravagant, baroque, lyrical—they are all there, so that just this one film would give a complete idea of his style. The photography, with surprising chiaroscuro effects, the scenery, the music, all come across effectively in an unappealing and uncompromising film, but one worthy of respect. A final revision, which was Fellini's intention but which he never in fact accomplished, would have had a beneficial effect.

CHAPTER 8

The Message of Hope in Cabiria *(1956–57)*

FELLINI WAS beset with new problems at the sour reception of *Il bidone* by the public and critics, and it seemed advisable to pause and review the plans he had already sketched out rather confusedly. He abandoned two ideas which were still in embryonic form, the first about the life of a man who has several families and cavorts from one to the other; the second (in an atmosphere of miracles) about a 'little nun' who is snow-bound with three other sisters on a mountain convent, without food, yet who amazingly manages to survive.

Instead Fellini concentrated for some time on the idea of adapting for the screen a novel by Mario Tobino, *Le libere donne di Magliano*. The book was about the life of a psychiatrist in a mental hospital. The American actor Montgomery Clift was to play the hero and negotiations with him were begun. But Lombardo, the producer of *Il bidone*, was not very well-disposed towards Fellini and gave the director to understand in no uncertain terms that he did not like the subject or the actor he had chosen.

So Fellini thought of developing another idea, which had been growing little by little over the years. The dropping of *Le libere donne di Magliano*, however, does show that the theme did not appeal to him. This is not surprising considering that it was a question of using someone else's book as a basis, which is entirely out of keeping with the director's character and a thing which has never happened in his directing career. It was not the producer's objections which made him change his mind; when he is quite convinced about a subject the director will move heaven and earth to film it. And he succeeds. But in this case the uncertainty about Tobino's text was coupled with the certainty of having found the right path in another direction: the one that led to *Le notti di Cabiria*.

There were at least four stages in the creation of Cabiria as a character. The first is far back in 1947, when in place of *Il miracolo* Fellini suggested to Rossellini for the second part of *La voce umana* the pathetic story of a prostitute from the city's outskirts who, despised by her high-ranking colleagues, has a magical adventure with the actor Amedeo Nazzari. It is easy to see that the best part of *Le notti di Cabiria* was already contained in this idea. The character was determined a few years later, as we saw in *Lo Sceicco bianco*, where her identity-card already had the name filled in.

Flajano states that in the autumn of 1951, while the film was being made, Fellini had decided then to base another film entirely on Cabiria. The director and scenarist went to the Villa Borghese to interview 'one of those girls' who told them about her miserable existence.

But it was while he was directing *Il bidone* that Fellini had a decisive meeting with Cabiria (the third stage in the development of the character) in the sequence of the shanty village which huddled against the old Roman aqueduct. The woman whom Federico immediately identified with his ideal picture of Cabiria was called Wanda. The director recalls that she was a pathetic little prostitute who lived in a water-tank with two holes for windows. At first she was very hostile towards the company. She shouted at Fellini in highly coloured language and she even tried to dislodge the camera track. Fellini ordered everyone to treat her kindly and he sent her a little basket with lunch in it. Wanda softened and condescended to talk about herself. 'Her wild, violent behaviour hid an enormous need of affection,' says the director.

A few months later, on completion of *Il bidone* (autumn 1955), the fourth and final act of the search for Cabiria began. As for *Il bidone* an inquiry was conducted, this time on prostitution. The disappointing results of the first investigation did not deter Fellini; this time not only numerous but positive results were obtained. Hundreds of street walkers and their protectors were questioned; an old prostitute, the 'Atom Bomb' who had once been extremely beautiful and who died during the making of the film, was approached. Every corner of that squalid world was investigated. For many nights, together with the architect Gherardi, who had been engaged as the scenarist, Fellini walked the streets of Rome, especially in the Passegiata Archeologica quarter. The director was even present at a dinner in Bologna organized by one of the best-known brothel-keepers. He wanted to meet the 'man with the sack', the mysterious benefactor of whom the papers were talking and he followed him on his nocturnal travels amongst the needy in society: to the Pantheon, the Palatine, the Colosseum, wherever there was poverty and suffering to alleviate.

Meanwhile the treatment for *Le notti di Cabiria* was taking shape during the daily sessions with Flajano and Pinelli. Lino del Fra says that at first Fellini no longer wanted to use the Nazzari sequence and it was Flajano who fought to reinstate it in the plot. Then while Federico was beginning to think of the 'Divine Love' scene, Flajano remembered the terrible crime which had been committed the previous summer at Castelgandolfo when the headless body of a woman, who was later identified as a servant, had been found in the lake. Immediately Pinelli suggested ending the film at Castelgandolfo, with the death of Cabiria. But Fellini and Flajano, having accepted the ending in principle, wanted Cabiria to be saved. However, when the ending had been thought out, the whole film was constructed round this; it was only the opening of the film which provoked doubts and lively discussion. (In the early stages ideas for the beginning included Cabiria setting fire to the house of her enemy Matilda, or appearing in *Aida* at the Caracalla.)

Meanwhile Fellini concentrated on designing and then buying the entire wardrobe for Cabiria and the other characters at the Porta Portese street market: the striped costume, the jacket with the feathers, the gaudy kimono which Giulietta Masina later wore. The architect Piero Gherardi was of invaluable assistance at this stage; later he was also to play a great part in the making of *La dolce vita*. Gherardi—an adventurous Tuscan who adores the East and goes there each autumn—began to work with Fellini, interpreting the quick notes the director handed him: Cabiria's hovel=cube, Cabiria's jacket=hen, Cabiria's dress=beetle.

But while it could be said that the film was well under way the question of the producer was not only still at sea, but in very stormy waters. For many months from the end of '55 well into the spring of '56 Fellini battled with his usual tenacity against a wall of refusals and half-offers which were immediately retracted. The story of the producers of *Cabiria* is a chapter in itself in the history of the film, and Narciso Vicario, Fellini's 'aide' has told it with great vivacity.

When Goffredo Lombardo of *Titanus* had read the outline of the plot he called for Federico and their conversation is reported as being something like this: 'It is a dangerous film. . . . Let's be quite frank. . . . You have made films about "queers" (he was alluding to *I vitelloni*, thinking of Natali perhaps), then one on rascally gipsies, another on swindlers. You wanted to make one about madmen. Now you present me with one about prostitutes. I'm wondering what your next film will be about!' 'About producers!' Fellini replied irritably. Lombardo objected that the censors would never have let *Cabiria* pass and gave the name of De Pirro, a general director in the cinema. Fellini hastened to De Pirro, his admirer of long-standing, who assured him that as far as he was concerned he would not have raised any difficulties.

Fellini decided to forget Lombardo and then there began an extraordinary roundabout of at least ten different producers. The first was some outcast on the verge of prison, the second was prepared to set to work, but he had not a penny. Another two were afraid of the censors, a fifth, a big stable owner, was for ever waiting for one of his horses to win before

Le tentazioni del dottor Antonio (Boccaccio '70)—Peppino De Filippo about to charge Anita Ekberg.

Le tentazioni del dottor Antonio—Fellini explains the plan of execution to a small film critic.

Fellini at the Cannes film festival, 1960.

'ellini blowing
ıis own trumpet.

The making of *La dolce vita*—Marcello Mastroianni, Anouk Aimée, Luise Rainer, Federico Fellini, Anita Ekberg, Yvonne Fourneaux.

La dolce vita—Fellini with Polidor the Clown—the Balloon scene.

La dolce vita—Anita Ekberg.

La dolce vita—Fellini instructs a waiter, dressed for the part.

he decided but unfortunately it never did. Another producer (the sixth) in a moment of enthusiasm gave the forty millions necessary to cover the expenses which had been incurred meanwhile, but then he wanted Fellini to undertake not to exceed 180 million for the whole production which the director could not do. It was now a question of taking back the script and in addition, to repaying the 40 millions debt. The fifth producer appeared on the scene again, the horse owner, but after his assurance, 'I am going to Turin to get the money, and I'll be back immediately', he was not seen again. At one point the Americans came into the picture: a big combine promised a minimum guarantee of at least 100 million, which was immediately cut to 45 million after a telephone call to the central office in Paris. Instead Richard Basehart arranged a meeting with a diminutive American producer dressed in black, who took notes on everything. 'It's a deal,' he said, 'all we need is the release of Swiss francs.' But the francs stayed where they were.

Finally, someone suggested that Fellini should approach a Swiss financier who was reputed to control the whole of the Italian cinema through exchange deals. The financier was an old man, but still vigorous; his great passion was golf. He received Federico one evening and, opening a safe, he showed Fellini many envelopes on each of which the name of a well-known producer appeared, all his debtors. 'This one owes me 30 million,' 'This one 50 million,' and so on. The next day at dawn he telephoned the director after he had read the treatment. 'Wonderful, marvellous, I've still three pages to read, but let's make the film.' At ten o'clock in the evening another telephone call: 'Bring me the estimate. Tomorrow I'll put 100 million in the bank.' Fellini and his collaborators stayed up all night to draw up the estimate when the phone rang a third time. 'I can't make the film anymore, I've just read the last three pages and I've discovered that Cabiria doesn't get married. I'm sorry, but it's impossible.'

Some time later a humiliated Fellini was at home one rainy evening, when, in the road below, he espied Dino de Laurentiis' car in front of his door. The famous producer, who knew all about the vicissitudes of *Cabiria* had come to visit him. During the visit Fellini showed him the script. De Laurentiis looked at it quickly, then he said, 'What a man . . . you go to everyone else and you forget me. . . .'

Later Fellini also showed him the favourable judgments on the rough script of *Le notti di Cabiria* made during its whirlwind tour of the producers, some of whom had shown it to cinema critics whose opinion they trusted. One of the judgments—perhaps the most favourable—I had given in

March, 1956, and I remember that De Laurentiis himself confessed to me that his final decision to make the film rested partly on the impression made on him by that enthusiastic review.

From that moment, the camera went into action rapidly on *Le notti di Cabiria.* Fellini had never doubted the name of the heroine. Cabiria had been Giulietta Masina in *Lo Sceicco bianco* and her husband had always had her in his mind as he worked out the character. François Périer who had already played in René Clair's *Le silence est d'or* was engaged to play the leading male role. Fellini had been puzzling a long time over this character and had held many tests to find the right actor. Here is how he himself describes the choice of Périer: 'I had stuck François' picture up on the wall of my office, I would look at it now and then without being able to make up my mind. Then, one day, I painted a moustache under his nose and a Robespierre shirt round his neck, and I thought the flabby character of the accountant was just right for him.'

Flajano worked out in detail the Passeggiata Archeologica scenes and the incident with the film star. Pinelli looked after the more dramatic scenes, those of the 'Divine Love' and the ending. The writer Pier Paolo Pasolini was also engaged and he wrote the dialogue for the 'Divine Love' (which was destined to undergo certain changes in the shooting) and he gave a romantic note to the 'walkers' dialogue. Pasolini had also suggested a new sequence, that of a nocturnal ride in a car with Cabiria and certain robbers, which after various considerations was not used because, for one thing, De Laurentiis was against it.

The shooting, interior and exterior, lasted four and a half months, all summer '56 and part of the autumn. 56,000 metres of film were used, leaving various solutions open until the decision was made in the editing. This last stage and the cutting were carried out amidst greater calm than in *Il bidone*, to the benefit of the whole film. Despite inevitable hold-ups (Giulietta Masina fractured her knee during shooting and the film was held up for fifty days; the cameraman Tonti had to be replaced by Martelli for the last three weeks) *Le notti di Cabiria* was ready at the beginning of March, 1957. It enjoyed great success when it was selected for showing at the Cannes Festival and Giulietta Masina was awarded the prize for the best actress. But then the film was 'stopped' for a few months, with the object of planning its 'launching' in the autumn undisturbed. In October, 1957, *Le notti di Cabiria* appeared on the Italian screen, repeating the triumphant success of Cannes.

In substance the film, stripped of inessentials, is built up around six principal episodes: the first attempt to kill Cabiria, the quarrel in the

Passeggiata Archeologica, the adventure with the actor, the pilgrimage to the Madonna of Divine Love, the sequence with the illusionist, the meeting with the accountant d'Onofrio and the final scene at Castelgandolfo which results from it. In between are a few linking scenes, so that one can say that *Le notti di Cabiria* is one of Fellini's most unified films, perhaps only to be compared with *La strada* in this respect.

The film opens against the background of a large, uncultivated field on a creek of the Tiber between St. Paul's and the Magliana quarter. The young man who has brought Cabiria to the river bank relieves her of her handbag with some excuse, gives her a push into the water and then runs off. Cabiria falls into the mud, but she still has not understood as she cries out trustingly, 'George! I'm here! I haven't hurt myself.' Then the supports on the bank give way and she is carried out into the middle of the river. Fortunately some young lads save her and revive her; Cabiria is more angry than scared and is careful to tell everyone that she fell into the river by herself. Some children recognize her, 'It's Cabiria . . . she lives past the filling station. . . . She's a . . .'

Her aggressive attitude, strengthened by her wounded pride, is not modified at home, where her friend Wanda tries to console her. 'I was on the river you see . . .? And I fell. . . . And he was very frightened . . . and ran off.' Her pathetic attempt at dignity finally makes her quarrel with Wanda, but in the end the poor girl can bear no more and bursts out, 'But why on earth? . . . Why should someone push me into the river for 40,000 lire.' 'But why? Why did he need to? . . . I gave him everything. . . .' Then suddenly she is frightened, she takes one of her chickens on to her lap, strikes it, and holds it close against her in a craving for affection, murmuring 'And if I were to die. . . ?'

The following evening, on the Passeggiata Archeologica, Cabiria takes up her old life with her friends; there is Wanda, fat, lazy and warm hearted, Marisa who has 'acquired' a new 600 which everyone wants to try, and Matilda, Cabiria's professional enemy. The girls' 'protectors' laugh and make a great deal of noise, one of them dances the 'mambo' with Cabiria, just as in *I vitelloni*. Then there is a terrific tussle between Matilda and Cabiria and they fight each other fiercely. Marisa's 'protector' drives the battered Cabiria off in Marisa's car, and dumps her in the Via Veneto. Here the girl meets with disdain from the elegant prostitutes in the vicinity, but she assumes an attitude of offended dignity which is her source of strength. She stops in a night-club doorway (the 'Kit-Kat') where a uniformed commissionaire tries to shoo her away. . . .

At that point a famous film-star (Amedeo Nazzari) and his blonde friend (Dorian Gray) come out of the night-club; they are quarrelling, and Cabiria watches the scene with great interest. Jessy slaps the star and as he gets angrily into his car, he catches sight of Cabiria and invites her to get in. They make for another luxurious night-club where Cabiria has a great deal of trouble and embarrassment, leaving her umbrella in the cloakroom. The actor, who only now appears to be aware of Cabiria, dances with her almost defiantly amidst the ironical comments of the others present. Then he takes the girl back to his house: but first of all Cabiria wants to get her revenge on the elegant prostitutes who snubbed her before, and leaning out of the windows of the powerful car she shouts at them.

The film-star's house, a villa on the Appian Way, is sumptuous in a rather vulgar way; with majordomos, white telephones, mirrors, statues, swimming baths, and electrically controlled cupboards. Cabiria is overwhelmed. To impress her, the star puts on a Beethoven symphony on the record player ('I'm fanatical about him'), then he orders a trolley loaded with every delicacy to be brought in. ('Help yourself, caviar, lobster . . .') Meanwhile he questions Cabiria who, always very much on her dignity, having admitted that she frequents the Passeggiata Archeologica, explains, 'It's more convenient. . . .' she adds proudly. 'But I have made myself a home, I've got light, gas. . . . Of course it's not like this. . . .' She begins to eat, tormented by the thought that her friends will not believe her when she tells them of her adventures. Suddenly the internal telephone rings; the film-star's girl friend wants to come up at all costs to make up the quarrel and the actor can find no better way out than to hide Cabiria in the bathroom. Then Cabiria listens to the ensuing quarrel and sides with the man, and yet she cannot help feeling ecstatic and moved when she realizes they are reconciled. At dawn she is still sitting in her prison, and the embarrassed star lets her out furtively while his girl friend is sleeping. Cabiria tries to get out of the house on all fours, succeeds in finding her inseparable umbrella, crashes into a big window and at last goes out into the road in a daze and walks to the bus stop.

Some time later at the Passeggiata Archeologica the girls and their protectors decide to go for an outing to the sanctuary of the Madonna of Divine Love, on her feast day. The reason is that one of the boys, a cripple, wants to beg a favour from the Virgin. Cabiria joins the party, which proceeds amidst a swarm of cars, buses and motor-bikes. The crowd of pilgrims at the Sanctuary is overwhelming: people are shouting, the women are half-suffocated in the crush, the stretchers with the sick can hardly break through the throng. There is an atmosphere of hysteria at the expectation of a miracle. Wanda tells Cabiria to ask for a favour, but her friend replies, 'I don't need anything. I've got everything. . . . Oh yes, I'll ask that the planning control will withdraw the order to pull the house down.' And then she adds quietly, 'And I'll ask for something else too'. After a visit to the church, the group goes to a field nearby to eat their lunch on the grass. Cabiria is exuberant, she has been drinking, she dances, jokes and kicks the football belonging to some young lads who have started a game.

Later Cabiria goes to a cinema in the suburbs where an old magician (Aldo Silvani) is performing in frock coat and top hat before the film begins. When the man comes to some experiments in magnetism ('I'm taking no risk, these are experiments recognized officially by science') he asks Cabiria to come up on to the stage too. The girl watches fascinated as five young men are hypnotized. They sit on a bench and the magician makes them believe they are in a boat, going through a storm, and all suffering from sea-sickness. Then the conjuror turns to Cabiria: 'Miss or Mrs?' Cabiria becomes aggressive again and tries to defend herself, but finally, amidst the laughter of the audience she is forced to admit that she lives in the village of St. Francis. Insinuatingly the charlatan goads her on: 'You are not married, but would you like to be married? I know a fine young man . . . a lively boy, who is looking for a wife, and would be very happy to marry you.' And he calls out, 'Oscar!' while the notes of a waltz strike up. By now Cabiria is completely under the conjuror's hypnotic influence and thinks that she really can see Oscar who is gallantly introduced to her. Whilst the audience is sniggering, poor Cabiria is indued to dance with the elusive Oscar and pirouettes about the stage in ecstasy. The 'magician' continues speaking for Oscar in oily tones. 'I am rich, but lonely and unhappy. . . . My intentions are honourable; I want a home and children. . . .' 'So it is true,' babbles Cabiria, 'you're not deceiving me. . . . Do you truly love me?' Amidst renewed applause from the audience the illusionist senses that the act is getting out of control and awakes Cabiria. She finds herself in the street, furiously angry, and suspects that she has been made a laughing-stock.

At that moment an unknown man approaches her. 'Excuse me, signorina. My name is D'Onofrio, I am an accountant.' He is very polite and mellifluous. . . . 'Excuse my boldness . . . you have all my sympathy. . . . I was in the theatre and I felt I wanted to talk to you. . . . I was very moved.' And he insists on taking her to a bar, continuing to intoxicate her with words. 'I was passing through this quarter on business . . . the hand of fate in everything is so clear that I am troubled.' Cabiria is still suspicious. 'What do you want of me?' 'Perhaps you will understand better if I tell you my name. . . . Oscar! . . . of all names, that imposter had to choose Oscar. I don't mind telling you that I was very struck by that.' In short, he manages to persuade Cabiria—who has not told him her true profession—to meet him the following evening. Cabiria is reassured when, as she is about to get on to the bus, the accountant bends to kiss her hand.

Further meetings follow in which D'Onofrio continues his diabolical plan of seduction. ('I am a state employee. I was born in the provinces. Now I am alone . . . loneliness weighs heavily. . . .') Cabiria is puzzled and confides in Wanda. 'He tells me everything . . . he says that I understand. . . . He is educated . . . a handsome man. . . . He pays for everything, ice-cream, cakes, cinema, flowers.' Finally in the decisive meeting the accountant unexpectedly asks her to marry him. 'But is it the done thing . . . you don't even know me . . .' Cabiria replies, becoming diffident again. But D'Onofrio soothes her, lulls her with his kindness and generosity. 'I haven't asked you for anything, I don't want to know anything. I don't care about prejudice. . . . I understand you, I have studied you.'

Cabiria agrees, sells the house, takes her hoarded savings out of the bank, and after a moving farewell to her friend Wanda, she runs to join the accountant who takes her to an inn in the Alban Hills, overlooking the lake. When they have eaten—it is dark by now—Cabiria takes the roll of notes ('My dowry') and wants to give them to d'Onofrio. 'Anyway, what's mine is yours—it's all the same.'

Then she goes off with him, through the woods, down to the lake, and now, at the height of her happiness, she tries to tell him about her life in broken sentences. 'The rough treatment I've had! The types that come after girls to rob them of their money. . .! But you, you wouldn't know what they do.' During the walk, the two sing together, but suddenly the accountant breaks off. They have come to the lake shore and as Cabiria exclaims, 'But yes, there is justice even in this world! One suffers, goes through all kinds of things, but then the moment of happiness comes,' she notices that the man is trembling slightly. D'Onofrio asks her if she can swim and suddenly Cabiria, who remembers how she was thrown into the Tiber, begins to understand. She moves away from the shore, shrieking in terror, 'You want to kill me! . . .' Terror immediately becomes desperation. 'Kill me! Throw me in! I don't want to go on living!' The shattering of her illusions is greater than her will to live. But the man shakes off Cabiria, throws her to the ground, grabs the bundle of notes and runs.

For a long time Cabiria remains motionless on the ground. Then she slowly gets up, and like an automaton goes back through the wood and comes out on to the road, wandering at random in the moonlight. Soon some girls and boys join her as they come out of an alley, playing harmonicas and guitars; they dance and sing round about her. At first Cabiria does not appear to hear them, but when one of the boys smiles at her, she smiles in return and her step becomes more resolute. Then she too begins to sing.

As we have said, *Le notti di Cabiria* was developed in greater detail at one time: the film is one in which the actual screen version has deviated most from the script, or, rather, one in which Fellini has improvised to a great degree. The progressive alterations which were made to the film did not even cease during the shooting. Amongst the episodes which were cut—or not even staged—were Cabiria's meeting with a group of pilgrims who are visiting sacred places; the adventure of Cabiria and Matilde who are taken home by two farmers while their wives are away and are then abandoned in the country; Cabiria's and Matilde's last adventure with two thieves, who also finally leave them in the middle of the road; Cabiria's discovery of charity and human fellowship as she follows the man with the sack, on his nightly tour (in which the old 'Atom Bomb' is also helped); a trip to Viterbo with two lorry drivers. None of these episodes would have added anything to the film and Fellini wisely resisted the temptation of including them, thus achieving that perfect balance which is one of the film's qualities. Above all in one of these scenes (that with the thieves) Cabiria almost becomes an accomplice in a theft; in the episode of the 'Atom Bomb' she reveals the malevolence beneath the surface and the episode of the 'man with the sack' resulted in the opposite effect of sugary sentimentality.

In fact the film is extraordinarily well balanced. The author has been able to restrict a difficult and knotty subject within a strictly moral framework, showing a singular respect towards the people concerned. Cabiria is a little prostitute, neither good nor bad, with the obvious defects of a woman of her background and education and with the virtues of a generous heart which, in spite of everything, has remained as pure as that of a child. Cabiria is in fact a human being in the widest sense of the word. If, in Fellinian reasoning, Gelsomina and Zampanò separated after *La strada* and gave life the one to Augusto of *Il bidone* and the other to Cabiria, it is not to say that this process of identification continues *ad infinitum*. It is true that Cabiria and Gelsomina have in common their desire for love and their loneliness (besides certain 'magic' sequences like that of the illusionist) but they differ profoundly on one point; Gelsomina was more of a symbol and less of a person, living in the shadow of Zampanò's overbearing nature, while Cabiria follows in her own footsteps; in spite of her simplicity, she is very much a creature of flesh and blood.

Even in *Le notti di Cabiria*, Fellini did not intend to depict a social phenomenon—prostitution—because it was the human case, Cabiria's own, that interested him. Cabiria, to a far greater extent than Gelsomina, unconsciously mirrors the sad state of thousands and thousands of beings who, in every corner of the world, lead the same unhappy life. From this point of view, *Cabiria* is of greater value than *La strada* and represents a reconciliation between the director's world and the old tendencies of neo-realism. A reconciliation or a conclusive ascendancy? This dilemma has been expressed by many critics: those of the left have understood it in the first sense, finally deciding to forget their reservations and praise Fellini as a director for the first time. Others have seen *Le notti di Cabiria* as the neo-realist swan-song, others again have given the film a Christian interpretation because of the motifs of salvation and hope in the ending, which were already evident throughout in Cabiria herself.

But it would be unfair to maintain that the poetry in Cabiria is less effective than that in *La strada* because it takes its themes from the solid reality of everyday life, instead of from the emotional lyricism of Gelsomina. The ending, for example, of *Le notti di Cabiria* is more artistic although here, by a touch of hopefulness in Cabiria's smile as she prepares to face the struggle for existence again, Fellini has avoided the danger of over-dramatizing, as all great creators are able to do. The delicacy, almost humility of this finale is comparable to the films of Chaplin, who certainly cannot be accused of rhetoric.

Where the director has above all displayed his skill is in the treatment of a subject which could have been conventional and banal, of mediocre literary worth, such as would not have tempted the imagination of the average artist. The sentimentality of the theme could have been a trap; but Fellini has been able to work out each character, each situation with a simplicity and originality which are astounding. It is not so much the acute observations, aimed at highlighting characters and facts, which is astonishing, nor the sense of narrative and rhythm, because these gifts had been apparent for some time in his films. But to have fused characters and background so perfectly, isolating Cabiria in an atmosphere from which she cannot escape because it is created from within the spectator himself, is amazing, and it is this which gives the film its impact of truth and emotion.

Cabiria is a great character, hovering between vulgarity and charm. She is disarming, yet at the same time victorious over the strongest who surround her. She has her own nobility in a pride and dignity which remain intact even in her most painful moments. Thus, proud and indomitable, she reacts against the humiliating position in which society has placed her. Far above its documentary aspect, her character has an indisputable poetic reality.

Yet *Le notti di Cabiria* lives through other characters, also, who are all unforgettable; from the famous star to Wanda, from the cripple to the suburban conjuror, and the accountant D'Onofrio, who is one of the most sinister and tragic figures the director has created. He, the last person to shatter Cabiria's illusions—magnificently portrayed by François Périer—is without doubt deprived of independent action except within the heroine's sphere, and yet Fellini has made him into one of those characters whose power enables them to transcend the limitations of the screen.

In places the background of the film has the magic of *La strada*, especially in the second part which is mysterious and a little strange. But elsewhere it is extraordinarily concrete, in the darkness of the Passeggiata Archeologica, or amidst the blinding dust of that sad, anonymous quarter where Cabiria lives. And the staging has also depicted the ridiculous ostentation of actors' villas on the Appian Way, with biting satire. The direction has its share of technical skill in the famous sequence of the 'Maddona of Divine Love'. Here there is on the one hand, a hint of Fellini at his less convincing, more attached to the 'poeticizing' lumber of the past, but the narrative power is also exceptional, an exasperated outburst in a mixture of the holy and the profane, of emotional pity and irreverent malice, a chiaroscuro in harsh relief.

What of Giulietta Masina the actress? In *Le notti di Cabiria* her acting is more conscious and mature than in *La strada* and she is to be praised for having diversified, by tone, gesture and mimicry, a character out of 'the people'. All the other actors live up to Fellini's masterpiece, from Franca Marzi who plays Wanda, Cabiria's gentle, bovine friend, to Aldo Silvani and Amedeo Nazzari who, with great courage and skill, has caricatured himself or at least the 'type' identified with him from a series of films.

Le notti di Cabiria enjoyed an enormous success, not only in Italy, but in all Europe (particularly France) and in the U.S.A. Together with the Oscar for *La strada*, Fellini received another Oscar from America and then, also in 1957, he was awarded the Hollywood Director's prize. It was John Ford, the doyen of his colleagues across the ocean, who presented it to him personally. In a speech he explained why Fellini was the only director in the world who deserved this mark of recognition. Then at the end of a solemn dinner, a colossal marzipan cake was brought on to the table.

('Tremendous', Fellini calls it.) It had a life-size model of Zampanò's motor-bike on top, together with the statues of Cabiria and Gelsomina. In this ingenuous fashion the cinema world of Hollywood intended to honour the man whom they now recognized as the greatest of the new artists of the screen.

CHAPTER 9

The Universal Vision of La dolce vita *(1958–60)*

AFTER *CABIRIA* Fellini's plans were again rather confused. When the 'trilogy of loneliness' was completed, a change of direction was necessary in order to avoid repetition. So, towards the end of 1957 and at the beginning of '58, many ideas were studied, some of them completely new to Federico.

First of all he thought of making a film of the biblical *Barabbas* by Pär Lagerkvist, conceived by Fellini as a kind of historical Zampanò, to the extent that even the actor had to be the same (Fleischer later made this version of *Barabbas* with Anthony Quinn, but in a different style). Then a modern version of Casanova was considered, with episodes taken from his 'Memoires', and possibly Orson Welles as the hero. The 'Decameron' was contemplated, or Don Quixote in the person of Tati, and even a small piece by Flajano which was later put on the stage with mediocre success: *Un marziano a Roma*. But Fellini did not spend long considering these ideas. He was more tempted by plans for a script for Sophia Loren, provisionally called *Viaggio con Anita* (*Journey with Anita*) or even *Viaggio d'amore* (*Journey of Love*). Gregory Peck would have played opposite Loren: but the plans fell through because of Sophia's tempestuous marriage in Mexico to Carlo Ponti and the troubles which ensued.

Then Fellini began to examine the old plan for *Moraldo in città*. But he found that it had deteriorated and become lifeless: the problems of the former spiv were no longer of interest because times had changed so much. It all had to be thrown to the winds, and a *Moraldo '58* had to come into being which would reflect contemporary disquiet. During spring and summer 1958 Fellini—who rarely takes a holiday—turned the question over in his mind and contrary to his usual habits frequented the cafés of Via Veneto. And it was there, seated at those little tables, that he saw a great panorama passing before him which he had never closely observed before, the clamorous panorama of wealthy society.

The beginning of summer 1958 was characterized by feverish society happenings, scandals big and small, attacks on photographers, and sensational 'reports' which flooded the glossy weeklies. The 'Society Café' in Via Veneto was enjoying an ephemeral popularity and was admired by some, condemned by many, but continually watched with great interest not only in Italy but throughout the world. Rome had become (in contrast to her traditional character as the Catholic capital) a cosmopolitan, worldly city. Fellini observed all that and he watched the parade of beautiful women and elegant idlers. That year the outrageous 'sack' had become fashionable for women, and was becoming an apotheosis of bad taste and exhibitionism. Fellini said later: 'I realized that women dressed like that were becoming desperate elements of that nightmarish aspect of humanity which I was considering. Unreal, false apparitions; stylized butterflies, icy, mysterious, geometrical figures.'

So gradually the idea of *La dolce vita* was born as an atmosphere which was to surround the new Moraldo, who kept his old name—Rubini—but acquired another: Marcello. Under the influence of the boom in journalism and with the photographic-reporters of Rome in his mind, Fellini gave Marcello a real-life profession as a journalist, or better still, a society reporter, with more serious but as yet unfulfilled hopes of becoming a writer.

The development of the idea and of the film—for which various testimonies exist, especially Tullio Kezich's valuable book—took a decisive step forward when Fellini confided in Pinelli and Flajano. At first Pinelli was uncertain and today he still admits that he raised many objections. He was finally convinced, and with the help of Brunello Rondi, a treatment was written. At the beginning of September, 1958 the narrative outline of *La dolce vita* was nearly complete: there were only two episodes in addition to those which were later filmed (the episode of the writer Dolores who protects Marcello and the tragic one of the sea-picnic where a girl is burnt to death) and there were two missing: the miracle faked by the lying children and the aristocrats' party, which Fellini devised later.

The nucleus was made up of a few episodes of *Moraldo in città* but they had been much altered. The scene of the father's visit, the character of Steiner, evolved from the writer Gattone; the same figure Dolores, who in *Moraldo* was called Contini; and finally the orgy at the end which was only hinted at in the film that was never made. All these were taken from *Moraldo in città*. The Steiner tragedy was suggested to the director by a similar happening in France, of which he had read in the newspapers.

From the beginning Fellini had decided on Marcello Mastroianni to act Marcello; it was Mastroianni who had automatically suggested the name of the hero of *La dolce vita*. Fellini had great plans for the other actors who were to conform to the international character of the society depicted in the film. One part was to be assigned to Anita Ekberg who was known to the London cinema ('She is a little girl, no more than twelve years old, but in her way she is a powerful personality'). The part of the father was reserved for Maurice Chevalier and Henry Fonda was to play Steiner. The authoress was to be either Edwige Feuillère or Greer Garson or even Luise Rainer, the famous actress of *The Good Earth*. Other actors he had in mind were Silvana Magnano or Madeleine Fischer for Maddalena, Peter Ustinov and perhaps Barbara Stanwyck.

But matters still had to be settled with the producers. Dino de Laurentiis did not appear to be enthusiastic about the film and he had made available the seventy million lire for the first payment against his will. He thought the scenario was chaotic, the story too gloomy and long drawn out. His major objection was that Mastroianni was not suitable for this most demanding part. He suggested Paul Newman instead as he was well-liked in America. But Fellini had no intention whatever of giving way over Mastroianni. He wanted the hero to be Italian, otherwise he did not feel that he would be able to consolidate all the fragmentary and scattered arguments that the film presented at first. There were violent differences of opinion with De Laurentiis and in the end the producer asked for the arbitration of three experts about the rough script: Ivo Perilli, Gino Visentini and Luigi Chiarini. Fellini knew that a film, still less a work of art, cannot be made on the strength of arbitration, but, curious to see the result, he agreed. The result was unanimous; a negative judgment on *La dolce vita*. The three critics thought the material was too untidy, that it had no 'balancing elements' and so on.

Fellini had to look for a new producer. Fortunately there was no lack of willing support because word had spread that the film was entirely about the Via Veneto and would contain spicy and even downright scandalous scenes. In vain did the producer attempt to bring things back to reality. Meanwhile the rounding-up of producers continued. There had been eleven for *Le notti di Cabiria*, in this case there were seven, but the ones who really counted were the last three. Between September and October, 1957, Goffredo Lombardo, Fellini's old producer, Arturo Tofanelli, the director of *Tempo* representing a Milan group, and Peppino Amato representing Angelo Rizzoli, came forward. At one point the director became so muddled in his negotiations that he realized with horror that he had become involved with all three and had some difficulty in freeing himself. Goffredo Lombardo promised him four hundred million lire, Amato–Rizzoli six hundred million, and Tofanelli the same. Fellini went to Lombardo first, with the news (which was true), that both Chevalier and Fonda were unable to act in *La dolce vita* because of other engagements and he persuaded him to annul the contract, explaining that otherwise he would have made a bad deal. It was easy to say 'no' to Tofanelli, who had announced his arrival by plane, because he had not the seventy million which were immediately necessary with him. Amato was left; after he had contacted Angelo Rizzoli Fellini signed a definitive contract on 28 October, 1958, with 'Riama' (the Rizzoli–Amato Company).

The meeting with Angelo Rizzoli was very important for Fellini. At last the director had found a refuge from the 'brainstorms', expedients and uncertainty which had characterized his films till then. He found a broad-minded man who really respected and had faith in him. Fellini declared several times, during the shooting of the film and again later, 'Rizzoli is an ideal producer, without him I could never have made *La dolce vita*'.

Disagreement came instead from Rizzoli's associate Peppino Amato. Quite a legend has been built up around these arguments because Amato is a fiery, picturesque Neopolitan and Fellini, for his part, is a man with a lively imagination. Thus the rumour ran that Amato had threatened to tear up the contract one day and had in fact begun to do so. Another time, it is said, Amato, having protested that they wanted to strip him naked, actually began to take his clothes off. Another time he is supposed to have drunk the ink which was to be used to sign a certain clause he considered ruinous for himself.

La dolce vita was making progress despite these diverting complications. Between November, 1958, and March, 1959, the scenery and costumes were prepared under the direction of the architect Gherardi, who gave the film an Eastern touch in certain parts, in accordance with his personal tastes. The script was perfected and the cast was chosen. Here there were many difficulties as most of the actors Fellini had considered at the beginning of September were no longer available and others had to be found. Annibale Ninchi was chosen to play the father; he had already played the hero of *Scipione l'Africano* (*Scipio of Africa*) and had then left the cinema because he had become disillusioned in that far-off epic with its fascist, imperialistic touches. Ninchi who comes from Pesaro, and has very much the same mentality as the director, proved to be an excellent choice. Fellini approached Elio Vittorini for Steiner, but he refused and only when the film was in its last stages did he discover Alain Cuny, 'as imposing as a gothic cathedral', who had already acted in Melle's *Les Amants* (*The Lovers*). He had thought of Enrico Maria Salerno before that and the choice had to be made rapidly. For Maddalena his first choice after Magnano, was Madeleine Fischer and then the slight and timid Anouk Aimée whose real name is Françoise Sorya. For Emma, Marcello's jealous girl friend, Yvonne

Fourneaux's name was put forward; she had acted for Antonioni in *Le amiche* (*The Girl Friends*).

Many other parts remained in suspense; indeed when the first camera began to turn on 16 March, 1959, at 11.35 in Theatre 14 of Cinecittá the film was being made with only Marcello Mastroianni and Anita Ekberg. In that first take was filmed Sylvia's (Anita's) hasty climb up the stairs inside St. Peter's dome. This had naturally been reconstructed as had most of the 'genuine' background of the film. A young man, destined to become very important not only in the film, but in Italian life, was working with the actors: Walter Santesso. He played Marcello's regular photographer under the name of Paparazzo, and followed him in all his adventures. Paparazzo—who was soon to baptize the whole category of photographers with this stupid name—is a mixture of Roman and Venetian. Walter Santesso is in fact a Paduan. At the time of *La dolce vita* he had been working at the University theatre and directing a few documentaries. He was to prove one of the most intelligent actors in the film, synthesizing the frenzied hunt for a picture, for a story, which was typical of Italian journalism at the time.

Another example of modern 'public relations'—the film-star's press conference—was the subject of the next scene, which was filmed immediately afterwards, again with Anita Ekberg. Here too the photographers played a considerable part. All the scenes in which Anita Ekberg appeared were shot first (during March) as the Swedish-American actress could not stay in Rome any longer. So work was begun on *Caracalla's*, a fictitious night-club set in the famous baths, and Sylvia's husband, played by Lex Barker, appeared on the scene: he had played Tarzan till then but was a success in *La dolce vita*. Indeed Fellini confirms that he was one of the most sensitive actors: amongst other things he had to slap Ekberg, an incident which was later repeated in real life between Ekberg and her husband Anthony Steel.

This group of spring scenes ended with Ekberg's and Mastroianni's bathe in the Trevi Fountain. It was a very trying performance for the actors, because it had to be shot at night (as had nearly all *La dolce vita*) and mostly in very cold weather, which was exceptional for the time of year. Naturally the scene required several retakes.

In April, the night-club episode with the father and the dancer (Magali Noël), which had been roughly sketched in the script, was considerably enlarged, together with the sketch featuring the old clown, played by Polidor. Then the outside shots of the house of the prostitute who gives Maddalena and Marcello hospitality were made at the Tor di Schiavi in the

Tuscolano Quarter. (The inside shots, in which a flood effect had to be achieved, were taken much later and, after some hesitation, made in Cinecittá's bathing pool.)

In May Fellini worked on the episode featuring the aristocrats, in Don Livio Odescalchi's sixteenth-century palace, at Bassano di Sutri on the Cassian Road, twenty-five miles from Rome. The palace only needed minor alteration (the number of ancestral busts was increased), while real aristocrats took part in the sequence, such as Prince Vadim Wolkonsky—whom the director called an instinctive actor—Doris Pignatelli, Eugenio Ruspoli and various others.

Halfway through the month *La dolce vita* ran the risk of coming to a full stop because of the 'Rainer affair', which was now coming to a head. This was the situation: Fellini had chosen Luise Rainer (whom he had met in Rome, and immediately declaring himself her fanatical admirer), to play the writer Dolores, an old and lonely nymphomaniac who becomes infatuated with Marcello, and shuts herself away with him in an isolated refuge by the sea, persuading him to write a book. But when Rainer returned to America and read the part at leisure she found the character 'sordid' and 'hateful' and in February, 1959, she wrote to the director from New York, explaining her misgivings and suggesting modifications. Fellini replied with a telegram in which, amongst other things he said: 'I vouch, on my honour, for the integrity of the character.' Later the heroine of *The Good Earth* came back to Rome and insisted that the part should be radically altered. She herself tried to rewrite the part that concerned her. Fellini—who is very unwilling to accept alterations from actors, still less if he is not convinced about them—was very kind about it this time, but Rainer proved ever more difficult to please. At the end of May the situation was like this: on the one hand the actress was still unconvinced and, moreover, in disagreement with the production over some financial questions, and on the other the director had become very doubtful about the character, because he said she had lost every trace of humanity as a result of excessive alterations. By now the scenes had to be shot, but Fellini put them off 'to think about them'. Time went by and he was beginning to feel that above all, Dolores would duplicate Steiner, and at the beginning of July he considered loosening the Gordian knot by cutting the whole episode from the film, to the great annoyance of Luise Rainer.

In June meanwhile the Via Veneto scenes (the most expensive) had been reconstructed in Cinecittá and were being filmed. Then the false miracle was made in the Tivoli Gardens. This had been suggested to Fellini through a photographic feature by Tazio Secchiaroli published in a weekly magazine. The report depicted two little peasants from Maratta Alta, near Turin, who claimed they had seen the Madonna.

The Steiner drawing-room scenes—in which the writer Leonida Repaci had been introduced at the last moment, after plans for filming the Strega prize award had been abandoned—were shot at the beginning of July as soon as the actor Alain Cuny had been 'found'. Then the difficult scene of the 'exhausted and useless orgy' as Fellini calls it was started. In the middle of August at Fregene the last sequence was made, when the fish monster was dragged up on to the beach at dawn. Fellini took a long time to decide on the final scene. He had kept an open mind about an alternative solution, in which all Marcello's friends drive away by car after the orgy, leaving him drunk and alone.

The last feet of *La dolce vita* were used up on the 27 August at Passo Corese near Rome. Now the film was finished. Work on the set had lasted almost six months and the cameraman Martelli had run through three hundred thousand feet of film. Eight hundred actors and thousands of walk-on characters had been under Fellini's orders for 150 days in scenes that had almost all been shot at night. The director himself had had almost fifty sleepless nights. The film had cost nearly seven hundred million lire.

Clemente Fracassi had given an immense amount of help as 'factotum' and had been a source of invaluable encouragement. Fracassi who had left direction after one or two small successes (*Romanticismo*, *Sensualità*), is a tireless worker, despite very bad health, and in *La dolce vita* he cleared the way for the director, smoothing out unavoidable obstacles and helping him to solve innumerable problems. Fellini gives him credit by saying that *La dolce vita* is also his triumph. When the film was finished the editing and cutting began and Fellini was aided by Cattozzo and Rota for the music.

In November the film was ready and the only doubts that remained concerned the inclusion of some particularly alarming scenes, such as the murder of Steiner's children. *La dolce vita* was eighteen thousand feet long and lasted over three and a half hours. Some cutting was therefore necessary, despite the director's reluctance. The film was at last cut to seventeen thousand feet, then again reduced by several hundred feet to its final length. At this time there was serious disagreement with Amato, who wanted to force certain of his ideas on to Fellini, and Fellini had to defend his work tooth and nail. But thanks to Angelo Rizzoli's forceful intervention, all the difficulties were solved and in the middle of November *La dolce vita* was given a private showing in Rome to a group of cinema critics and intellectuals at the time of a literary congress.

The film made a deep and immediate impression on that distinguished audience. Two Nobel Prize winners and the flower of European culture were present. It was described immediately as a 'new language' and I myself was one of the first to write an article (which appeared in *Oggi*, 25 November, 1959) in which I stressed the great ethical value of the film and acclaimed *La dolce vita* as a 'masterpiece'.

The final touches occupied Fellini during December and January, and at last, in February, 1960, *La dolce vita* was presented to the public. From the beginning it had an enormous success but at the same time, as always happens with all genuine works of art, there was a battle between the critics and moralists, a controversy which lasted the whole year. Generally, independent criticism was favourable and the public understood the true moral significance of the harsh condemnation of a society that has lost faith; yet in some cases there was isolated, noisy and violent criticism. At the première in Milan for instance *La dolce vita* was hissed and protests drowned the applause of one part of the audience. At the exit, Fellini, who had been in the auditorium, was insulted and spat upon by a small group of hotheads. This vulgar and unfair gesture depressed him, but he recovered and immediately began to argue calmly with his adversaries.

This time his opponents did not come from the left, which had joined to support *La dolce vita* for various reasons, but from the most conservative Catholic circles; yet there was a clear division amongst the Catholics. A critic such as Gian Luigi Rondi fully approved the film both morally and aesthetically. At one showing, which was followed by a debate organized by the Jesuits of the Centro San Fedele in Milan (who openly supported Fellini), there was audible agreement and praise on the part of priests who were certainly not prepared to compromise on moral questions. The Genoese *Colombianium*, headed by Padre Arpa, fought to make the spirit of the film understood; if it was not in line with Catholic dogma, at least it was not against it. But many of the clergy conducted a campaign against Fellini and *La dolce vita*, even from the pulpit. In most cases, they had not seen the film and based themselves on the negative judgments given by the Centro Cattolico Cinematografico, which had classified the film as 'unsuitable for all'. There were also noisy protests from the diocesan board of the Azione Cattolica in Rome, from the Collegio dei parocci dell'Urbe, and harsh criticism from the *Osservatore Romano*.

I had occasion to be near the director at the height of the storm. He had come to Milan to explain his position to the Archbishop. (For various reasons, the matter had no outcome.) One morning in February, I walked with Fellini through the old streets in the centre of Milan, from his hotel to San Fedele where those priests who had compromised themselves by generously defending the film in all good faith, awaited him somewhat nervously. Fellini confessed, as we went along, that he felt ill at ease, because it seemed that everyone was looking at him and pointing to him. Then he regained his old confidence and he made evident once again, very lucidly, that his aim in making *La dolce vita*, had been the complete opposite of the one attributed to him.

In the meantime a similar battle had blown up in Parliament where certain deputies and senators had submitted that the film be withdrawn or at least that it should be drastically cut in parts. The Under-secretary for Entertainment, however, replied with great good sense and refused to take any action against *La dolce vita.*

For months half Italy discussed Fellini's work, with the result, certainly unforeseen by the director and deprecated by him, that the flavour of scandal aided the film's success with the public. People queued up to see it and the Milanese, finding it impossible to get into their local cinemas, drove into nearby towns to see the film. In all this hubbub the film's true value was often lost sight of, as always happens when a work of art becomes a battle sign. Then little by little the fury died down and the film could be evaluated more calmly. It had meanwhile been awarded the Cannes Festival Prize.

La dolce vita is created around a dozen episodes and principal characters: some are compact and highly-developed (Sylvia, Steiner, the father); others are more fragmentary and less complete. Marcello and his photographer Paparazzo link the various sequences. Fellini himself says that many more stories could have been told in *La dolce vita* ('It is a film that could last all of ten hours') and people suspected that while the film was being made he never wanted to finish it, but aimed at a continuous story as the ideal though unattainable goal of his 'journey into disgust'.

La dolce vita begins with the shot from a helicopter carrying a great statue of Christ the Worker over Rome. Marcello and Paparazzo are in the helicopter. As they fly over, groups of girls in bathing costumes wave from a terrace and both their exclamations and Marcello's are drowned in the throbbing of the motor. The beginning, as will be seen, deliberately balances the ending of the film; here too there is a sharp contrast between two worlds.

Here, immediately afterwards, is the world of 'dolce vita': a fashionable night spot, where half-naked dancers perform an oriental dance against an indeterminate and unnerving background. Marcello is there looking for society gossip for his paper and he meets Maddalena, the daughter of a rich industrialist. She is a wilful, restless, man-hungry girl, and he has his first squalid adventure with her.

Along the road they pick up a prostitute in Maddalena's luxurious car and they take her home to the far outskirts of the town. The house is half under water and the woman, who has not understood Maddalena's obscure intentions, offers to make some coffee. Maddalena has an irresistible impulse to give herself to Marcello in the prostitute's over-worked bed and degrade herself with an almost mercenary embrace.

When he goes back to his flat, Marcello discovers that Emma, the jealous Calabrian woman with whom he lives, has tried to commit suicide with barbiturates. He takes her to hospital, where she is soon out of danger. Then the reporter's job involves him in another sensational whirl; he has to rush to the airport because Sylvia, the celebrated American film-star, is arriving. A ridiculous producer from the South, Totò Scalise, has made great plans and ordered an enormous pizza for the actress. But he arrives late, upset and perspiring, and has great difficulty in getting through the vast crowd of photographers. 'Welcome to Rome. . . . Very happy,' he stutters in broken English to the film-star, and he cries angrily to the others, 'Flowers! Pizza! Hurry up, get a move on!' At last with a silly smile of triumph he gives Sylvia his surprise: 'Neopolitan pizza!'

After the photographers have followed her in cars, there is a press conference in a large hotel. The reporters' questions are the usual idiocies, even when they try to be witty and original. The actress's replies are equally stupid: 'Is it true that you bathe nude in ice?' 'Oh yes, every day!' 'Do you sleep in pyjamas or a nightdress?' 'Only in a drop of French perfume.' (An allusion to Marilyn Monroe's famous reply at a press conference.) Meanwhile Emma has grown even more jealous and telephones Marcello, who has difficulty in keeping the woman and the producer Scalise (to whom he has promised a series of photographs) at bay. Shortly afterwards Sylvia is shown round the interior of St. Peter's where, with unsuspected energy, she leaves everyone behind on the stairway, climbing to the top with great agility. When she gets there she asks Marcello where Giotto's bell-tower is.

That evening at 'Caracalla's' night-club in the famous baths, Sylvia talks to Marcello who whispers to her in Italian not one word of which she understands, 'You are everything: you are Eve, mother, sister, lover, earth, home.' Then the actress shows off with Frankie, an American colleague, who turns up by chance and, pretending to be a fawn, drags her round the place, unnerving her fiancé Robert who is sitting at a table. Suddenly the actress takes off her shoes and a waiter dressed as an ancient Roman carries them to Robert. Hiding his rage the latter coldly says, 'I don't think this is the correct costume: it's a stupid Roman-Phoenician distortion'. When Sylvia comes dancing back with Frankie, Robert talks to her scathingly and the actress walks off offended. Marcello offers to go and get her back, but then succumbs to the temptation of taking her with him for a drive beyond Rome. While Marcello is meditating on a method of approach, a dog begins to howl in the night and the actress imitates it. Impressed, the journalist takes her back to town and the two end up at dawn near the Trevi fountain. The film-star has found a kitten, decides that it wants some milk and presses Marcello to go and get some. When he returns disconsolate, Sylvia has climbed into the fountain fully-dressed. He is puzzled, but then shaking his head and saying, 'Well, perhaps she is right and we are all wrong,' he too gets into the water. They are kissing when suddenly the fountain, as if by magic, stops playing.

Shortly afterwards Marcello takes Sylvia back to her hotel: Robert is drunk and asleep in the car and the photographers having unkindly taken pictures of him from every angle, awake him and tell him what is going on, in the hope of witnessing a quarrel. They are not disappointed: Robert slaps his fiancée and quarrels with Marcello.

One morning while the journalist is taking photographs of fashion models, he sees a friend of his, Steiner, go into a modern church in the suburbs. He joins him and finds him playing the organ, immersed in a peace which makes Marcello dream of a world quite different from that in which he lives. Steiner reminds him of his ambitions, of the book he had begun. Marcello is embarrassed and changes the subject, promising to go and visit him. To find some peace for his writing Marcello goes to a seaside inn where he meets Paola, an Umbrian girl who waits at table and who has a beautiful profile. 'You look like one of those little angels in paintings,' Marcello tells her. This meeting has awakened in him distant echoes of a peaceful life.

But soon he is caught up again in the vortex of his occupation and he leaves Rome with Emma and his usual following of photographers to trace the facts of an alleged appearance of the Madonna to two children. One realizes from the beginning that this is a trick organized by the parents to exploit their children's lies. But things have taken on huge proportions: television cameras, the press and an enormous crowd, hysterical and excited, are there ready and willing to believe anything. Only the priests remain sceptical. While the children are reciting their contemptible 'piece' in a darkness broken only by powerful arc lights, it begins to rain heavily and there is a mass exodus. In the confusion one of the sick who has been carried there on a stretcher dies, and as dawn breaks over the place of the false miracle the body is lit up, abandoned in the middle of the field with a priest reciting prayers.

Marcello has kept the promise he made to Steiner and gone to see him at his house, where his friend holds a rather snobbish and exotic literary salon frequented by odd English intellectuals and mysterious Oriental women. Steiner plays his guests records he has made of the 'noise of the wind' and other sounds of Nature. However, it is Steiner's wife and two children who make Marcello more aware that he lacks a family and many other aspects of a sane and stable life.

His next conversation with Steiner is a self-pitying confession: 'I do not like my work . . . I ought to change many things. You know, your house is a real refuge. I am wasting my days away. Will I ever manage to do anything? Once I had ambition but perhaps I am losing everything.' Steiner's reply is somewhat disconcerting. 'The most awful life is better that a sheltered one, in a world where everything is in its place. At night this darkness and peace weigh on me; it's the peace that frightens me. I fear that above all. I feel it's only superficial and that it hides some danger. They say the world is wonderful. What does it mean? Suddenly a telephone rings and everything is lost. One ought to succeed in loving outside time, beyond time. Alone. To live alone and in isolation.'

Just at the moment when Marcello is longing for a normal existence, his father arrives unexpectedly in Rome from the provinces. He is a simple, old-fashioned man, yet he does not want to make a fool of himself and he tries to act like a man of the world. He says to Paparazzo, who looks at him as though he were a Martian, 'Ah, you're a photographer? A photographer. . . . It's interesting work, artistic work in a way. . . .' And to Marcello: 'By the way, a friend of mine who came here told me there was quite a nice place, a kind of cabaret. . . . Oh you know, just to see what it's like.' In the night-club which is jaded and second-rate his father likes the dancers who file past as they put on tiger skins. When Marcello suggests calling over two of them—Lucy and Fanny—to their table, though Paparazzo mutters, 'Even an orange squash is too much for these two tarts', the father gallantly insists on buying everybody champagne. He and Fanny have a pathetic attraction to each other: 'For heaven's sake, signorina, forget about age. Don't let's revive the grief and desperation which weigh heavy on my heart. Do you know what makes us grow old? Boredom.' 'He's nicer than you are, you know.' Fanny remarks to Marcello and she dances a waltz with his father. Then she takes him home while Marcello hangs about in the street. When he eventually arrives, Fanny is frightened and tells him that his father feels ill. Ashamed in front of his son, the old man is turned towards the window and asks him to shut the door: 'Come on, come on,' he whispers. 'Where are we? Which quarter is this? There is a train at six o'clock, I could catch that one.' Despite Marcello's insistence he goes away alone shortly afterwards.

Marcello is pulled back into the orbit of the Via Veneto. One night he is bundled into a car and, together with some others, driven to a party in a castle belonging to one of the aristocracy. He knows hardly any of his companions who form a group of different nationalities (there is even a Lithuanian, or Finn). When they arrive at the villa his host's youngest son ('I'm the third child and by far the least important') introduces him to his father, Prince Marescalchi, who, in the midst of Babel, looks abstractly at him. 'Papa, this is Signor Rubini, who really does serious work.' 'Indeed? Good evening. How are you? So you see. Je vous presente. . . .' And the conversation continues like that, half in French, half in English, in meaningless phrases. Then Marcello finds Maddalena again and whispers words of love to her. 'I like you like this, when you are sincere . . . I really need you,' and he asks her to marry him, through the echoes of an empty fountain placed between two adjoining rooms. Maddalena appears to agree but just then she allows an unknown passer-by to embrace her.

The guests are invited to visit an outbuilding of the castle, which is full of mice and bats. It was built by an ancestor, a Pope, in the sixteenth century. A spiritualist séance is held in a dark room in an atmosphere of morbid hysteria. Many couples are kissing in dark corners and Marcello finds himself embracing one of the guests. At dawn, tired and disgusted they make their way back to the castle; it is a grotesque procession because some of them are wearing mediaeval costume. As they look at one another along the road they see embarrassment and nausea in each other's face. Heads down, with the Prince leading them, they arrive at the castle and hear the sound of a bell; the old Dowager is going to Mass and she does not even deign to look at them.

A few days later, after a noisy scene with Emma in EUR, the telephone awakens Marcello who hurries to Steiner's house where there has been a terrible tragedy. He has murdered his two children in their beds, and then killed himself. The investigation squad is already at work, with the confidence, efficiency and anonymous indifference of men who are doing their duty. Marcello is questioned and offers to go and meet Signora Steiner who knows nothing and has not yet come home. His agonizing task is made all the worse by the crowd of photographers who, with almost inhuman cruelty make Steiner's wife pose for their own purposes as she gets off the bus. The poor woman does not realize what has happened, she smiles and at last Marcello and the Inspector force her into a car and tell her the truth.

The death of Steiner and the end of a world he had learned to love, drives Marcello back into the depths of his degrading existence. An orgy takes place in a Villa at Fregene and he is one of the principal characters. After a 'strip-tease' and other such scenes, the grand finale is an assault on a poor drunken girl, covered with feathers. This time disgust reaches its culminating point and as Marcello goes out on to the beach he is horrified with himself. But he is weak and cannot free himself from his slavery. He listens abstractedly to a depraved wretch who is dressed and made up as a woman. He skips about behind Marcello and talking rapidly, says seriously, 'I think we shall all be like this in 1970, completely corrupted. It will be worse than the Apocalypse. Lord, what an abomination it will be. . . .' Meanwhile on the beach some fishermen have dragged up a hideous fish, a sea-monster with a great round eye, which no one can name. All the participants in the orgy gather round, and stare at the sight. At this moment Marcello catches sight of little Paola, a long way off on the other side of the beach. She is shouting and waving to him. Because of the wind and the distance Marcello does not understand; he makes signs back and in the end Paola stops her attempts and runs away laughing with her friends as Marcello starts to go towards her. Then one of the women takes Marcello's hand and leads him back towards the group.

Between the first appearance of Steiner and the miracle episode Fellini had placed two other episodes; one was with the writer Dolores who entertains Marcello in her tower by the sea and the other the nautical picnic of Marcello and Maddalena, which ends tragically because a girl (Sandra) dives into the water from a motorboat which is leaking petrol and dies in the flames carelessly caused by a cigarette stub. As we have said the two sequences were never made (one of the reasons was that Sandra's death would have anticipated Steiner's), but Fellini enlarged others instead such as that of the miracle, Steiner's salon, the aristocrats' scenes and that of the final orgy. A great deal of improvisation was thus used on the set. Some scenes were altered at the last moment. For example, Steiner's wife was told of the murder by Marcello and the headmaster of the school where she teaches.

What is the essence of *La dolce vita*? From the beginning people spoke of a 'great fresco' and 'a cosmic window on the world', of 'a baroque merry-go-round' and a 'terrifying panorama of our times'. Fellini himself confirmed that against a background of spiritual ruin, where all ideas and institutions are crumbling, where men and women move like automatons awaiting one does not know what, he wanted to present the moral condition of humanity as an epic narrator of the second millennium might have done, objectively, but without irony.

It is precisely because of this that *La dolce vita* represents primarily a stylistic change of direction in the history of the cinema, with the ambition of surveying an unusually wide sector, through many dramas which do not only involve the individuals who act in them but the whole of humanity. Fellini had to free himself from the usual plans for a film with a plot and yet he had to avoid making a documentary. While the events in a film are usually extraneous to the spectator and the world created for his illusion ceases to exist as he returns to reality, the world Fellini has created in *La dolce vita* seems to have existed already in one's imagination and will not fade away at the end of the film. It is a dark world full of unknown quantities, lit up from time to time, as it were, by the flashes of a photographer's camera. These moments of blinding light correspond to the principal episodes in *La dolce vita* and are connected by phases of subdued lighting which serve either to prepare us for the intense glare to come or to relax us and create an atmosphere for Fellini's next target. Marcello is sometimes in the foreground, sometimes partially obscured by the shadow of events, but he is always looking through the window of the 'dolce vita'. He mirrors the director's own curiosity, and is a reflection of the director himself, with his virtues and faults. In the role of implacable and exact witnesses of *La dolce vita*, are the photographers, the expression of a society which has modelled them in its own image and likeness, in order to satisfy an inexhaustible thirst for sensation. They are the violators of every secret and the absolute masters of the streets and piazzas.

The ending follows a kind of downward curve without the slightest attempt to give the narrative a more satisfying solution from the public's point of view. Fellini's own sincerity and innermost coherence have not allowed it. The moral conclusion is suggested to the spectator and is not imposed; but is the ending really without hope, as it first appears? Or is not hope implicit, not only in Paola's appearance to Marcello, but also in the creator's courageous resolve to lay bare the deepest roots of evil and expose their terrible nature? Certainly this aspect of *La dolce vita* is a warning more solemn and lasting than that of any sermon and indirectly the film is a passionate accusation against those who think they can abstract themselves from divine law and take refuge in an absurd materialistic philosophy. It is the lack of faith and love of one's neighbour which makes *La dolce vita* so squalid, and leaves not only the hero ever unsatisfied, but also all those who believe they can stifle the irrepressible needs of the human mind in the midst of pleasure. And it is precisely the terrible nihilism of the film which gives birth to the desire for redemption. In *La dolce vita* Fellini launches a desperate appeal to all those who can be saved in time. He invites all to a last examination of their conscience. When one leaves the film the feeling of discouragement does not last long. *La dolce vita* arms one for the fight, because the very presentation of evil in its most manifest and nauseating forms pushes the spectator to the edge of the abyss with its terrifying depths so that he can hear the cries of the damned.

But the authoratitive Jesuit review *La civiltà cattolica* did not agree with this interpretation of the moral significance of the film. The periodical's cinema critic, Padre Baragli, in the September and October numbers of 1960—more than six months after the release of the film—made the strongest attack against the film. With a great show of erudition Padre Baragli attempted to dissect the film to prove its immorality. After the critic had posed the problem of whether *La dolce vita* was a Christian, Catholic or at least religious film, he concludes that despite numerous religious references, the film must be classed as 'irreligious' or at least 'religiously ambiguous', although 'the few genuinely human values that are vindicated in it are not extraneous to the Christian message'. The writer discusses Moravia's comparison of the film to *Satyricon* (which was taken up by others) and observes, 'Yes, more than in *Satyricon*, *La dolce vita* is filled with weariness and disgust at vice. But on deeper reflection, never once does this disgust take on patently Christian values, that is to say it does not show evil as a sin and aspire towards Christ's grace. . . . In fact it is heaven that is missing.' Later *La civiltà cattolica* concentrates on Fellini's strictly moral purpose and maintains that too many other elements are present which obscure the director's good intentions: 'It is as if artistically there is no delineation between the poet, the disinterested spectator and the provincial who has become a city dweller and "viveur"; he despises and condemns the life and world into which he has embarked, but only on condition that he continues to live that life and enjoy that world . . .'. 'One can recall,' Baragli went on, 'the monstrous amalgamation of ostentation and wealth, of frenetic living, luxurious eccentricity, oppressive sensuality, patent corruption, unmitigated passion, blasé attitudes towards work and the meaningless trivialities which compose that world, essentially feminine, that he has chosen. He has presented his world and set it in motion with excessive emphasis, multiplying surroundings, situations, behaviour and actions which are almost always shamelessly indecent, often violent and base . . . above all one should remember the director's ambiguous if not equivocal identification with his characters. . . .'

Whilst he admits that *La dolce vita* is denunciatory, Baragli rejected it just the same because 'We mistrust condemnations which for the most part are concerned with erotic and sexual immorality and we mistrust even more the condemnations of those who, in their denouncements, do not lose money, but profit by them'. Basically *La dolce vita* is 'an effective contribution towards spreading the evil it denounces' because in it 'evil itself is too generalized'. The film carries no message of hope, except perhaps in little Paola.

Fellini was troubled by *La civiltà cattolica*'s criticism, especially at the hint of profit, a matter to which he is entirely indifferent. Besides, before it was released *La dolce vita* was considered both by the owners, distributors and producers to be a financial failure. (Its success was an enormous surprise for everyone.) But although Father Baragli's opinion reflected some of the more intransigent Catholic groups, it remained a relatively isolated voice. As we have seen, other Catholics, no less authoritative—the review *Letture* for instance—defended or continued to defend *La dolce vita.* For his part Fellini has never stated that there is a truly religious spirit in his work. Instead he is eager to point out that his condemnation (for despite Father Baragli's doubts one can certainly speak of condemnation) in fact coincides with some Christian dogmas. At any rate it has a solid moral basis. It is completely untenable that the author could condone those evils portrayed in the film.

The controversy over the question of the film's morality continued for a considerable time. In lay circles especially, Croce was much quoted. But although he stated in his *Brevario d'estetica* that art itself is neither moral nor immoral because it is above morality, he had clearly given to understand that under the rule of morality 'the artist's position as a man and his attitude towards the subject he is treating must be evident'. When *La dolce vita* reached the United States in spring 1961, the critics were generally favourable towards the film, showing an enthusiasm unknown in Europe. They faced the ethical problem, regarding it as the first yardstick in their judgment and came to those conclusions Fellini had always maintained. 'An exposure of the spiritual void of a certain wealthy class lacking ideals.' 'A warning cry against an all-devouring paganism' and so on. Bosley Crowther, the famous cinema critic of the *New York Times*, said that the 'titanic film' is 'one of the most important and serious works made for the screen', Archer Winsten of the *New York Post*, wrote: 'the whole film is centred around Steiner, the symbol of the sensitive intellectual, forced to face the challenge of the modern world. If there is a message it is this: that loss of faith in this age has led to a destruction of human will.'

On closer examination of the different parts of *La dolce vita* it is clear that apart from the disparity in ethical values, the film is an excellent example of unity, achieved through a rhythm that has not one superfluous note. The history of the cinema has few films so stylistically complete; every sequence, every setting is linked to the other like the pieces of a mosaic, thus creating a perfect harmony. This balance, produced by a fusion of language and imagery, becomes especially evident after two or three showings of the film. Then one becomes aware of so many small details which otherwise go unnoticed beneath the general impressiveness of the whole. One realizes that various elements contribute to the unity of *La dolce vita*, from the acting to the scenery, the musical commentary to the dialogue. The latter is completely alive and sincere, reflecting the director's own integrity. The dialogue is very human and devoid of all rhetoric. It is never literary, which could be dangerous for the film. In the sequence of the aristocratic festivities, the vapid, unfinished conversations are surprisingly effective in the jargon of the 'international set', where every line of dialogue reveals their mentality. So, too, in the scene with Marcello's father emotions are enhanced by the felicitous union of sound and image. And what of the intellectual salon in Steiner's house, where the impression of vapidness in the guests' conversation is no less than that of the 'Café Society' in Via Veneto? It should be remembered that Fellini condemns that section of society no less severely; in fact perhaps even more severely, for these intellectuals have abjured their duty as leaders by taking refuge in a shameful abstractness and withdrawal.

Steiner's succinct revelation of his hidden drama is indicative of this situation. The conclusion ('To live alone, in isolation . . .') illuminates the problem so often confronted by Fellini. It is a fatal malady which affects not only the wandering Zampanò's, but many contemporary intellectuals. How many of them, anxious and tormented by complexes enlarged by their imaginations, dreading the tomorrow of an over-organized world, have not experienced just Steiner's fears? The nature of the crime is clearly revealed to Marcello, who attempts to drown his meaningless existence in an erotic, loveless affair. Thus, as many people have realized, Steiner is one of the central characters of the film.

After Marcello, Steiner and the pathetically regretful father, the character most clearly delineated is the film star. She is a creature of instinct, simple, almost primitive, who without fully realizing it, provokes the least noble of human passions. Fellini has treated Sylvia sympathetically. She is a distant connection of Gelsomina and Cabiria, with an even more disturbing vitality and the sensual fascination of a mythical woman.

Even the most well-disposed critics of *La dolce vita* were least enthusiastic about the false miracle sequence. The episode is too long drawn out because while making it the director was forced to rely so much on improvisation. It recalls the similar sequence of *Le notti di Cabiria* ('The Divine Love'). But the emotion of the imagery never loses evocative power, finally reaching dramatic heights rarely achieved in films. Wilder's *Ace in the Hole* has been quoted as a similar example, because of the obsessive excitement of the crowd. In Fellini's settings, which are at first sight confused, there emerges in reality a coldly rational order, which completely fulfils Fellini's aim of condemning certain aspects of contemporary life. The corpse lying in the dawn light is an accusation and a sinister reflection of social egoism, masked by false pity.

One of Fellini's most beautiful sequences has been inserted like a jewel in the episode with Marcello's father, a chilly oasis of melancholy intimacy. This is the scene with the balloon acted by the old comedian Polidor. It is a gently lyrical extract amidst the harsh, bitter poetry of the film. Here the note of fantastic enchantment loved by the director of *La strada* has its own particular development, and Fellini appears reluctant to abandon it. But *La dolce vita* presses on; it is necessary to return to reality. There follows the episode's unexpected ending. With a sharp turn of the rudder Fellini steers the ship far away from the harbour which the spectator imagined and perhaps desired, towards a more painful yet more truthful solution. Immediately afterwards, through design and love of contrast, he placed the bitterly satirical aristocrats' party, which assumes the character of an absurd carnival revelry, vaguely alluring as long as it is enveloped in shadows and illuminated by candlelight. When daylight surprises the long line of characters as they retreat shamefacedly like a defeated army, one perceives the extent of their moral poverty.

Again the tragedy in the Steiner household is a pretext for the disturbing illustration of a scandalous news 'case'. Everything is seen there subjectively with the dead man seated in his chair, always in the foreground and to all appearances, still living. And round about him the 'analysts of the crime' are busy at work like so many insects (ballistic and medical-legal experts, inspectors): they are a chilling aspect of our bureaucratically controlled age and a symbol of what Steiner feared.

Although the acting is centred around the superb Marcello Mastroianni, others too have had the chance of demonstrating their acting ability.

The actors employed were—with a few exceptions—not well known before this film for their acting talents. Fellini has known how to encourage not only Ekberg, but actresses like Anouk Aimée, Magali Noël, Yvonne Fourneaux, Nadia Gray (as well as a host of walkers-on and people who had never seen a camera), who were considered mediocre, to give laudable performances. Martelli must be credited also because he has expressed the director's grandiose conception in images that are impressive and significant.

The music has already been discussed. It only needs to add that Rota has used other composers' themes very skilfully, in addition to the melancholy 'dolce vita' theme. In the first part after the 'little song', the 'nocturne', the 'Cadillac' theme and 'Caracalla's', we hear 'Arriverderci, Roma', 'Patricia', Donaldson's 'Lola', and 'Stormy Weather'. The scene with Polidor and the balloons is an arrangement of the slow waltz 'Parlami di me'. In the second half several previous themes recur, together with a beautiful 'morning' theme for the end of the aristocrats' episode. The Fregene orgy is accompanied by an arrangement of 'Patricia' and 'Jingle Bells' amongst other tunes.

Does *La dolce vita* depict extreme cases? In reply to this last objection which has been made by some critics, it could be said that all literature and theatre—leaving aside the cinema—is based on extreme cases, for they alone are of interest to writers and in them the only truth is the artistic one. Hamlet, Macbeth, Don Quixote, and Raskolnikov would not exist without these premises. Nor could *La dolce vita* have been created.

CHAPTER 10

From Le tentazioni del dottor Antonio *to* $8\frac{1}{2}$ *(1960-62)*

AFTER *LA DOLCE VITA* new horizons opened before Fellini. With the help of Angelo Rizzoli he was able to fulfil his old dream of setting up a production company—called *Federiz*—which was designed to produce not only the director's films but more especially those of young men who were worthy of help. Naturally Fellini did not concern himself with the finance or organization, which were put in the hands of his factotum of *La dolce vita*, Clemente Fracassi. In practice things went less smoothly than Fellini had foreseen; through an excess of scruples the company remained inactive because none of the projects submitted were considered to be safe or worth making. And yet the plots for films that have since been successful in the Italian cinema passed through the *Federiz* office, amongst them Ermanno Olmi's *Il Posto* (*The Job*) and Pier Paolo Pasolini's *Accattone* (*Beggar*). But the hesitations of the prudent (and sceptical) Fracassi and the inability to satisfy Fellini, prevented them from taking advantage of favourable chances, justifying—for a while at least—the criticism that Fellini only likes his own films.

Meanwhile, after the shattering impact of *La dolce vita*, the director decided to wait for his ideas to mature so that he could make his next film at leisure. Consequently he was won over by the team that was to make a film of short episodes entitled *Boccaccio '61* at first and later renamed *Boccaccio '70* to free it from any immediate chronological associations. The best Italian directors from Visconti to De Sica and Monicelli had agreed about the form of the film. It is quite probable that the film would have become a contest of skill, in which Fellini would have been victorious. But Fellini did not accept the proposition in this spirit. He had already had experience of episode films, when he worked on *Amore in città* and normally he would have had no desire to repeat it. But Fellini was in a rather unusual frame of mind when the proposal for *Boccaccio '70* reached him. He had not forgotten the harsh attack of *La civiltà cattolica* and he had had a long battle with the censors in order that *La dolce vita* should not be cut. Besides, right at the end of 1960, violent criticism about the liberty of expression in the cinema had broken out in newspapers and in parliament. Even if it did not directly concern Fellini—Visconti was involved for *Rocco ei suoi fratelli* (*Rocco and his Brothers*) and Antonioni for *L'avventura* (*The Affair*)—he was nevertheless alarmed.

Under these circumstances the chance to make a film which was not very demanding, but which was centred around the problem which most interested him at that time, encouraged Fellini to begin work again. The scenario having been written at speed in winter and spring 1961, the director completed his episode in the summer of that year. He himself had called it *Le tentazioni del dottor Antonio*, a clearly symbolic title. The principal parts were played by Anita Ekberg, who was indispensable for the kind of woman she had represented in *La dolce vita*, and Peppino De Filippo, who resumed his successful collaboration which had been interrupted after *Luci del varietà* for reasons beyond Fellini's control.

The film was ready by the autumn despite subsequent expansion during shooting, when it had assumed proportions greater than those of the simple 'sketch' intended to form part of the larger canvas of *Boccaccio '70*. *Le tentazioni del dottor Antonio* lasts almost seventy minutes (nearly 5,000 feet of film)—nearly as long as a normal feature film.

As the other episodes were generally the same length, the elimination of one of them (Monicelli's) had been considered at one point. Later, however, the producer Carlo Ponti and the distributing company *Cineriz* decided to maintain the film's original structure and Monicelli's contribution took first place in the film—or rather it became the first act—whilst *Le tentazioni del dottor Antonio* became the second act.

Boccaccio '70 was presented to the public (on the evening of 22 February, 1962, in Milan at a gala performance) as a 'scherzo' in four acts from an idea by Cesare Zavattini. It lasted over three and a half hours. Apart from a vague, thematic connection—love—the film is somewhat heterogeneous and obviously varies enormously in style. Once again the weakness of Zavattini's formula for a 'film-review', or 'programme' was evident. None of the episodes, except de Sica's, was really like Boccaccio. The others were: a slight, trifling comedy by Monicelli called *Renzo e Luciana* which portrayed the typical life in a modern factory (the girls were forbidden to marry, under penalty of dismissal); Fellini's social satire, dramatically depicted; an elegant, theatrical film by Visconti called *Il lavoro* (*Work*), acted by Romy Sneider and Tomas Milan. De Sica's episode, *La riffa* (*The Raffle*), with Sophia Loren as the heroine, came closest to the original idea, perhaps because Zavattini himself had collaborated in it.

Monicelli's episode was immediately judged the weakest; Fellini was said to have paid most care and given greater perspective depth to the narrative; Visconti had handled his actors most successfully, and de Sica

—Back to school.

$8\frac{1}{2}$—The Hot Baths.

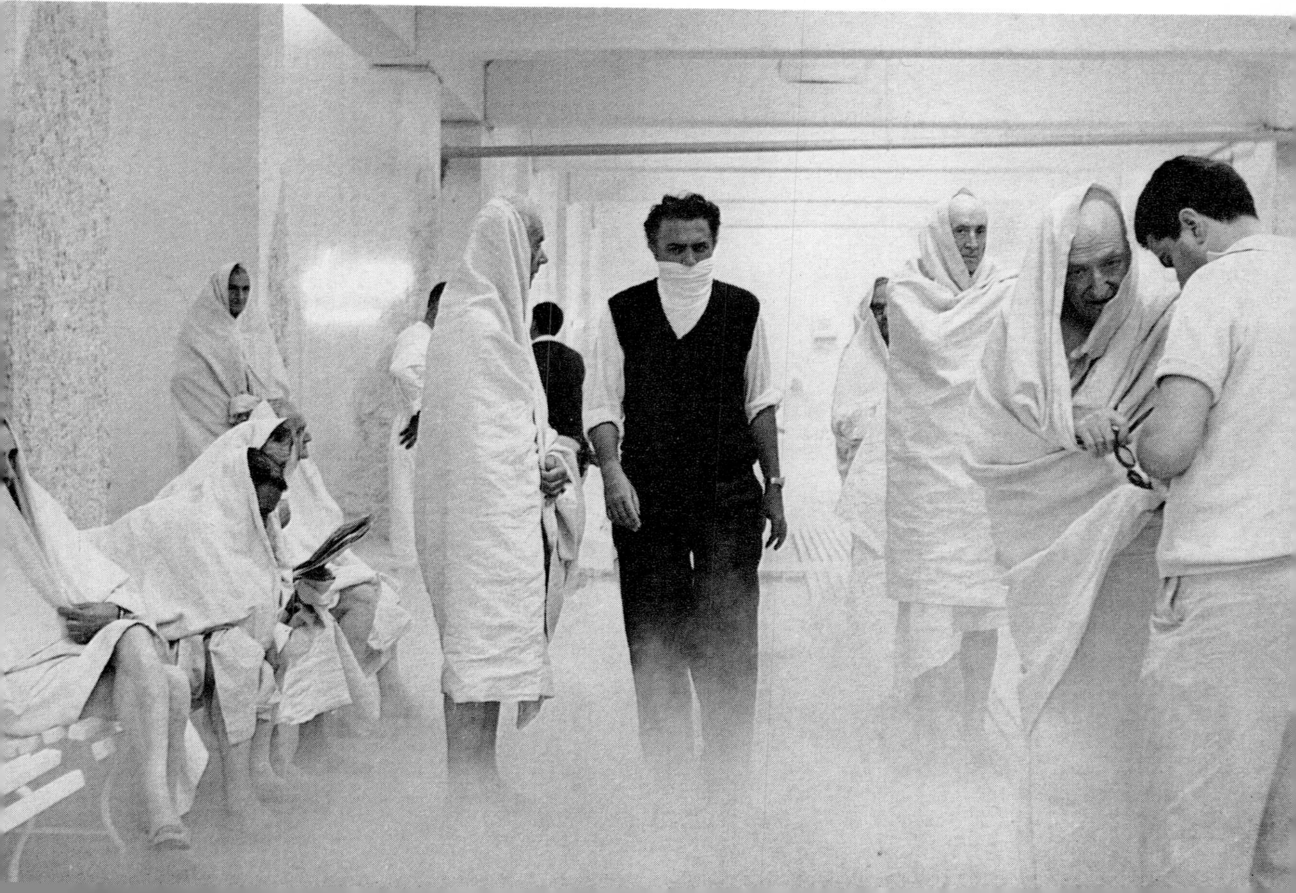

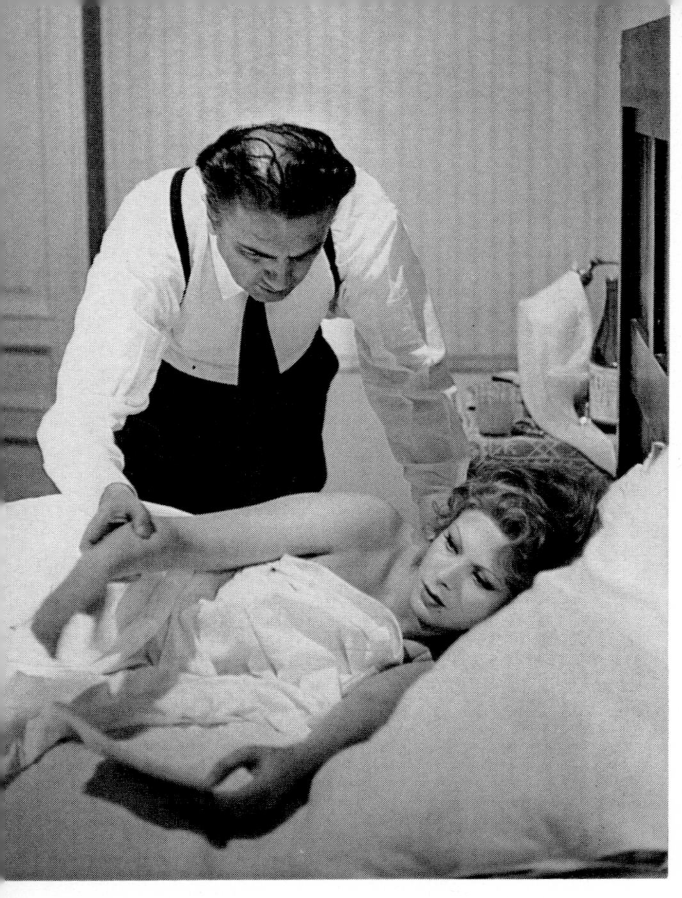

$8\frac{1}{2}$—Fellini with Sandra Milo.

$8\frac{1}{2}$—The spaceship.

had recounted a very spirited and flowing story, with perhaps the most gratifying result from the public's point of view.

Fellini engaged nearly all his old collaborators for the film, except Gherardi, who was replaced by Piero Zuffi. Besides the usual scenario-writers Pinelli and Flajano, Brunello Rondi and the writer Parise also joined the team; Rota contributed the music, which was similar to that in *La dolce vita.* (In fact here and there the central motif of that film was used.)

Le tentazioni del dottor Antonio is openly satirical in the capricious vein so dear to the director. In certain respects Fellini goes back to *Lo Sceicco bianco* and *I vitelloni*, although he profits also from his recent artistic experiences. It is a light-hearted, paradoxical film on the surface but deep down it is bitter and dramatic. In it a particular mentality and a certain way of behaving are condemned more thoroughly than in the director's previous work. Fellini is aiming at hypocritical moralists and especially those who, in good or bad faith, consider that sex is the basis of all human ethical problems, and dream of crusading against a low cut dress or a pair of legs. Even if this idea was conceived in a moment of resentment, the director's attack is an answer to the opinion of a certain section of society today. But society has changed so much in the last ten years that whoever battles against social trends, becomes isolated by continuing to reason in the light of an outdated code. In this way Doctor Antonio, the hero of the film, joins the gallery of Fellini's characters who are isolated and incapable not only of true charity towards their neighbour, but of genuinely communicating with the outside world. Unlike all his other films, Fellini allows this hero no hope, and he finally becomes the victim of his own madness.

In the opening scenes of *Le tentazioni del dottor Antonio*, the protagonist is presented. He is an old clerk, embittered by his fight against vice, which he mistakenly sees in advertisements centred around the feminine image, in magazine covers and short skirts. Dr. Antonio Mazzuolo lives alone with his spinster sister, who is continually suffering from attacks of hysterics. He spends the day destroying licentious periodicals from newspaper stands, or arguing with over-made up or eccentrically dressed women. He would have been a harmless creature, pitied for his phobias even by those who tell him he is right to his face and go so far as to encourage him (while continuing to do as they like in private) if one day Dr. Antonio, in the middle of delivering a moralizing sermon to some boy scouts, had not become aware of something which made him turn pale. Right in front of his house, in a large, uncultivated field which is to be built upon, a group of workmen are putting up an enormous hoarding, one hundred and twenty feet wide and twenty-five feet high. It is the portrait of a very glossy film-star, stretched out in a provocative manner, with a glass of milk in her hand, the advertisement hoarding for a milk producers co-operative completed by the caption 'Drink more milk'. Perhaps no one else would have thought of it but Dr. Antonio immediately and maliciously links the slogan with the actress's somewhat pronounced bosom and begins to inveigh against the colossal advertisement.

His first efforts are fruitless because even the 'high-ups' cannot find the means to act and an important ecclesiastic whose help is invoked confines himself to sending his secretary. Meanwhile, however, poor Dr. Antonio rants and raves, watching the advertisement from behind his windows. It is even illuminated at night by powerful arc-lights. During the day a provokingly gay tune springs out of it and is relayed by speaker. Finally, he decides to arouse a public scandal in the name of morality and he rushes out to shoot ink pellets at that great painted phantom. The flying squad arrives and this time the authorities order the advertisement to be provisionally covered with strips of white paper.

While Dr. Antonio is celebrating the victory with a little party in his flat that evening a fierce storm breaks and soon the water washes away and dissolves the perishable covering so that the star reappears in all her glory, with a provocative smile. Dr. Antonio is greatly disturbed: he spies on his enemy from his window and thinks she is making mocking gestures at him and assuming different poses. That night, his resistance breaks down, and he goes out into the field below and begins to abuse the star. At last the woman replies, or at least appears to do so to Dr. Antonio's excited imagination. Anita (the actress) tells her enemy to leave her in peace; then she comes to life, leaves the advertisement and begins to walk about the empty ground and through the streets.

Now Dr. Antonio is horrified, all the more so when Anita threatens to undress before him. He is caught up in her gigantic shoe and he sees her first layer of clothing fall down on him. At the same time he is irresistibly attracted by her charms, and he goes through all the diabolical temptations of a desert hermit. At one point Anita grabs hold of him and sits him on her breast. The doctor loses his umbrella which ends up in her low-cut dress and he begins a farcical struggle to free himself. After he has been placed on a second floor window-ledge he manages to climb to the ground in a pitiful state. Then he puts St. George's armour over his long pants, he lowers his lance, and charges Anita, piercing her chest. The star vanishes immediately and in her place Antonio sees an enormous bier arrive, surrounded by all the people he has known in life. Anita is dead and in his nightmare he is officiating at the funeral. Then, in a burst of sincerity, unable to withhold himself any longer, he shouts 'My love!' But now we are at the end: amidst the blare of ambulance sirens, we see Dr. Antonio, half naked, gesticulating and yelling unintelligibly, as he sits astride the poster, while a small crowd has gathered below. It is morning and we are back to reality. The firemen and ambulance men have reached the poor man and when they have put him in a strait-jacket, they load him into the ambulance, which drives swiftly towards the madhouse. A cupid, with bow and arrow, is perched on the ambulance, laughing maliciously.

Fellini has shown his skill in this work by a perfectly natural fusion of the fantastic, magical element with reality: the development of the situation is such that we feel no gap between these two opposite worlds. And the series of surrealistic, almost impressionistic episodes, is directed with great technical mastery, through a well-devised set of tricks. So besides the thirty-foot high statue of Ekberg, the scenery maker Zuffi minutely reconstructed, in an open space in the Old Appian Way, the EUR quarter where the action takes place, on a reduced scale of one in six. While Peppino De Filippo moves about the real EUR, Anita acts inside the minute plastic reconstruction, which thus creates the impression of a giantess. The work of building EUR in new dimensions cost over sixty million lire, while nearly thirty million were spent on the great advertisement placards.

Yet I do not feel that the second part of *Dr. Antonio* quite comes off; here and there it becomes a little slow, because of the stress Fellini has laid on the grotesque elements of Anita's fantastic walk through the streets of EUR. It is almost as if the director, enchanted with his own discovery, did not want to detach himself from it and blew it up beyond the proportions he had foreseen. The beginning of the film is more balanced and so are the central sequence with the hoarding—varied, colourful, and full of movement—and Mazzuolo's visit to an employee who explains the different gradations of licentious advertising. ('This is American', 'that's French', 'that's Turkish'.)

The film not only contains the director's observations on behaviour and atmosphere, but also the study of a contradictory psychological case, like that of the hero, who at one point falls in love with his enemy and although he sees her in a diabolical form, is so influenced by her erotic personality that he falls headlong into the abyss of madness. In this sequence of contrasts, always sustained by a touch of caricature which does not slow up the development of an insistent pathological drama, Fellini has been able to maintain the rhythm without a break, directing it to the purpose of the film. He has achieved this because the figure of Dr. Antonio, a misguided moralist and censor, is aligned with those impenetrable symbols of humanity who remain obstinately in the spectator's memory.

Boccacio '70, however, was just a holiday for Fellini, a break in which he could relax, a heaven-sent alibi that enabled him to bide his time: in fact few people knew that since autumn 1960 the director had been thinking about the outline of an ambitious new film. He began to toy with the idea after a visit to Ischia, where he had contemplated human beings half-buried in the radioactive mud of the Lacco Ameno baths belonging to Angelo Rizzoli, his producer. He wanted to portray different aspects of a man whose life was meaningless and who was attempting to come to grips with his problems at a fashionable bathing station. He would have liked Sir Laurence Olivier or Charlie Chaplin to play the leading man. The story would necessarily have a vein of bitterness, but would be fundamentally comic; indeed when he talked to his friends about it, Federico laid great stress on this comic note which he did not elaborate further, as he shrouded his new film in the greatest mystery.

Then, partly for treatment of his liver, partly to collect some facts, the director went to Chianciano, where deputies and solid late nineteenth-century Roman society patronized the baths. Chianciano is the opposite of Ischia in many respects, but the place appealed to him since Ischia and Chianciano, the mud baths and floral surroundings together inspired the setting of the future *8½*, a setting which Fellini did not change. It was at this time that he wrote a long letter to Brunello Rondi, which already contains the complete skeleton of the film: the hero is a writer or professional man, or perhaps a theatrical impresario. The letter has enabled Fellini to refute the accusation levelled at him that he was influenced in the choice of setting (a large dilapidated hotel) and of the theme (a kind of anti-novel in two or three dimensions), by Alain Renais' *L'an dernier à Marienbad* (*Last Year in Marienbad*). 'Marienbad' in fact, was only shown at the Venice Film Festival in the September of the following year (1961), when Fellini was engaged on *Boccacio '70*, and he swears that he has never even read Robbe-Grillet's book, nor seen the film in question.

Is he to be believed? Certainly there are some surprising resemblances to Renais' film, but to mention one amongst others, constructing the *anti-novel* around the journey of memory into the past, alternating with the present, was not entirely new to Fellini's work. Indeed one can say that in certain aspects, it first came to light in *La dolce vita*. Be that as it may, in autumn 1960 Fellini concluded the letter to Rondi (reproduced by Camilla Caderna in her book on *8½*) with the following words: 'What is all the fuss about? Really! Flajano suggests the title should be 'La bella confusione'

('*A Fine Muddle*'), but I don't care for that much. It has to be a fantastic, enchanted ballet, a magical kaleidoscope. . . .'

Meanwhile, throughout the spring and summer of 1961 he gave it no more thought, occupied as he was in directing *Le tentazioni del dottor Antonio*. However, he began to work on the idea again in October, 1961. He had added other motifs to the original nucleus of the plot: two episodes in particular, the first a moment of crisis in the life of the hero, who tries in vain to resolve it by seeking the aid of a cardinal (also a guest at the baths) and the second an extraordinary airship, the symbol of our fearful modern technology and of man's arrogant defiance of the skies; Breughel's painting *The Tower of Babel* had suggested the latter interpretation to the director.

When in November, Fellini visited London to meet Olivier he already knew in his heart of hearts that Marcello Mastroianni would play the lead again. Why did he go then? To mark time, to put his conscience at rest with the thought that he had 'done something' towards replacing the actor. The whole of Federico Fellini can be seen in such actions as this, for he even contradicts and deceives himself. In fact he did not even see Olivier and to console himself he declared afterwards, 'At heart I was afraid of Olivier and of that cruel mouth of his. And, what is more, how would I have induced him to change over to a 'country-harem'? I should have felt that Hamlet, King Lear or Richard III was walking into the midst of my odalisques.'

In the same way, at the beginning of 1962, he began to look for the leading lady (Carla) and pushed the joke as far as putting advertisements in the newspapers and giving a physical and moral description of her. 'Somewhat old-fashioned, one of the old almanac type, with a pink and white complexion and a small pea-hen's head on a Rubens' body, very soft, flowery, maternal and opulent.'

All the women of Italy became excited and thousands of photographs of fat women poured in; an interminable procession of massive ladies who had deserted their worried husbands and children came forward. 'Enormous women,' Camilla Caderna says in her book 'they were like gigantic wardrobes, like elephants on two feet, or half-reclining whales boasting that they weighed more than sixteen stone'. I saw Federico between one or other of the bombardments by these battleships while he was on a journey that took him to Northern Italy, to Turin, Milan, Venice and Trieste in search of extraordinary women whom he had no intention of engaging. He told me that the new film was a mystery to him also, but he promised that I should be the first to know its title and theme.

In fact I, like everyone else, had to wait nearly a year to know its content in detail. The title was soon made clear when the newspapers announced that the film would 'provisionally' be given a trade name, *8½*. Knowing Fellini one could be certain that it would never be changed, despite rumours circulating to the effect that the final title would be *Il labirinto* (The Labyrinth); this was the opinion I expressed publicly shortly afterwards in a review when some criticism was voiced as to the advisability of retaining what then appeared to be the strangest and most irritating of titles, indeed an outright 'anti-title'.

In order to justify himself Fellini maintained that since he had made eight films so far, and only counted the short film *Boccacio '70* as half, *8½* was merely the next number given to the new film during production. ('An unpretentious title that is almost an archive reference.') The truth is, however, that Fellini's films as we have seen are nine in number, if one includes *Luci della ribalta* made together with Lattuada and the short film *L'amore in città*. So to be precise, 9½ should be written instead of 8½. To solve this difficulty and satisfy logic and mathematics a compromise is the only solution. *Luci della ribalta* and *Agenzia matrimoniale* also count as a half so that with the addition of another half supplied by *Le tentazioni del dottor Antonio* a total of one and a half may be added to the seven films which Fellini considers to be entirely his own (*Lo Sceicco bianco*, *I vitelloni*, *La strada*, *Il bidone*, *Cabiria*, *La dolce vita*, *Otto e mezzo*) and so the title of his latest film is, generally speaking justifiable.

I must apologize to the reader for this strange digression, which may appear pedantic, but sometimes Fellini presents such unexpected problems that one must attempt to solve them in the light of common sense. To return to our story of the birth of *8½*, it goes without saying that the producer had decided to construct everything in the studio, as he had done in his previous films, because the work had to be completely faithful to the visions of the imagination alone. In this respect he had spoken to someone of 'ordered chaos', saying: 'This film will be the ultimate in autobiography: it will be a kind of purifying flame.'

In April, 1962, he rejected the eager aspirants weighing over sixteen stone and decided upon Sandra Milo, whom he had in mind from the beginning. Milo, who had only just made a 'come-back' in the clamorous failure at Venice of Rossellini's *Vanina Vanini*, had almost decided to leave the screen in disappointment. She responded immediately to Fellini's call and declared that she was willing to put on as much as twenty pounds by eating six specially prepared meals a day, enough to give her gout or kill her. Otherwise the cast was not particularly original; it included some of the old actors with whom Fellini liked to surround himself—Anouk Aimée in particular, who took the important part of the hero's wife. Annibale Ninchi appeared again (he was indispensable for the part of the father, which he had already played in *La dolce vita*) and the pathetic Polidor, for whom a small part had been reserved. The newcomers were Claudia Cardinale, Rossella Falk, a gifted stage actress, Barbara Steele and Pisu, Caterina Boratto, an ageing actress of the Italian cinema of the 'white telephones' era, and Guido Alberti. This last, who was to play a famous cinema producer—in some ways very like Angelo Rizzoli—was himself a well-known industrialist, the producer of the famous liqueur 'La Strega' and the founder of the Strega Prize, the goal of Italian writers. After *8½* Alberti seems to have found his true calling in the cinema and has made his mark in important films like Ros's *Le mani sulla città*.

At this time another character was born, that of the critic Carini who represents Guido's conscience and whose vague pseudo-intellectual aspirations Guido is always ready to deride. Carini is played by the Frenchman Rougeoul and rather obviously resembles, both in appearance and surname, Luigi Chiarini (now director of the Venice Film Festival). He suggests others too, especially figures of the literary world such as Moravia, Calvino, Fortini.

Shooting on the set began in May and ended in October and immediately aroused enormous interest and curiosity, destined to remain unsatisfied as the order of silence was very strictly maintained. Neither the actors nor technicians in the team knew the whole plot, and journalists bombarded them with questions in vain. At one point it was rumoured that Fellini could not go through with it, and intended to suspend the film (there was some truth in this story as we shall see, so much so that Fellini said with some pride: 'It will be my Unfinished'). The most extravagant rumours were spread about the plot, and it was even said that Fellini was making a science-fiction film, in the firm belief that the costly space ship the director had ordered to be constructed had a real and not just a symbolical meaning. In fact, the doubts had been more in the preparatory stages than in the making of the film. It had only just been mounted when Fellini decided to grant me an interview ('Fellini reveals the back-stage story of the most eagerly-awaited film of the year' in *Oggi* 1963, No. 7), which clarified many things and the article was widely reproduced because some of the director's statements undoubtedly rang true amongst less convincing ones.

'When I said that I didn't even know what the plot was', Fellini declared, 'journalists thought that I was telling one of my habitual lies. Instead, for me, it was the truth. I was looking for the Juno-like woman, I was busy, I appeared to have it all worked out in my head, but it was not like that. For three months I continued working on the basis of a complete production, in the hope that meanwhile my ideas would sort themselves out. Fifty times I was on the point of taking Fracassi, the production-director, by the arm and saying, "I can't remember the story any more, I can't go on making it." In short, the preparation was torture. Afterwards, everything was easy.'

'And no one suspected anything?'

'They had faith in me, they thought I knew what I was doing, that keeping the plot a secret from the actors was a great publicity stunt. In fact, all this became the film itself, or rather gave it unity. Two days before filming I was about to go to the producer and tell him the truth outright, begging him to stop the machinery of organization. But how do you tell a man of integrity: "I can't make a film that I can't remember, please excuse me, it was all a joke." Even he wouldn't have believed me.'

The reason for making the hero a film director instead of a writer or theatrical impresario, as had been planned earlier, does not embarrass Fellini:

'You must choose a profession you know well, and I had thought of an art director, someone whose job resembles mine. At the beginning it seemed too bold to depict a film director. I knew that everyone would identity the character with Federico Fellini himself, that they would have talked about autobiography. Now it is true that inevitably all the episodes in *8½* refer to my life, but some of them gradually became distorted, while others took shape during the shooting. The result was the story of a director who must begin a film but cannot remember the plot and continues to oscillate between two planes; reality and imagination.'

Without doubt *8½* is not a film which should be narrated, but seen. One senses it from the beginning when a man in a car caught in a traffic jam makes desperate attempts to get out. He is a prisoner in a motionless petrified world, with no way of escape, while all along the horizon very tall buildings form an insurmountable wall, encircling and suffocating the great stream of cars which cover the road as far as the eye can see. Admist a deafening chorus of klaxons from all sides, the man has a frantic desire to escape. At last his body rises, magically freed, into the air above the cars, and the nightmare vanishes. It is a contrived opening, like that of *La dolce vita*, but it is restricted to the hero's own psychic sphere and therefore all the more agonizing, even if the outcome promises the hope of freedom by supernatural means.

Shortly afterwards we meet the mysterious symbolic character again and find that he has a face and an identity. Doctors prescribe a rest cure for Guido at a spa, where there are thermal baths, and he goes away. But even there a thousand doubts assail him. He must prepare a film and the ideas will not come; he must reassure the producer, engage the actors and technicians and ward off demanding critics. When Carla, his mistress (a married woman who still loves her husband), joins him, her presence creates new difficulties. While Guido is lying with her, he has a vision of a country graveyard, in which his mother is frantically cleaning one of the chapels and his melancholy, restless father complains about his tomb.

'Look how low the roof is, they could have made it higher . . . it's terrible, Guido, terrible . . . couldn't you do anything about it?'

As his parents vanish his wife Luisa appears; 'Poor Guido, you must be tired, let's go home now.'

The next evening, during the entertainment at the hotel near the baths, an illusionist who is performing for the guests reads in the hero's mind just one very strange thought: '*Asa Nisi Masa.*' It is a cabalistic phrase which recalls his childhood to Guido and enables him to escape from the real world and enter the world of magic once more. This time his grandmother and aunts appear in the country house at Gambéttola, of which he has often dreamed nostalgically. But reality is stronger than the dream. Guido is compelled to look into himself and finds a chaos of doubt there. Now he fears that he is nothing more than 'A liar with no imagination or talent, unable to finish the film.' He hopes for guidance in his perplexities when he meets the Cardinal, who is also a guest at the Spa. But at the same time he remembers his youth in the Jesuit seminary where he was educated, and the day when he had his first revelation of Woman in the monstrous form of Saraghina. He was discovered and punished, and Guido can still hear the menacing words of the priest:

'But don't you know that Saraghina is the devil?'

Now, not even the meeting with the senile Cardinal is decisive. When his wife Luisa arrives there is a fresh crisis. As he realizes that he has ruined everything and is no longer able to make the film that he intended to make, ('A simple, honest film . . . but now my head is full of confusion. . . .'), he must also solve the practical problem of the simultaneous presence of the two women, Carla and Luisa. He has the first quarrel with Luisa when the whole company, led by the producer, visits the fantastic space ship which is to be used in Guido's film, but that doubtless will never appear on the screen. Amidst the geometrical scaffolding Rossella, a friend of Luisa's, expounds the nature of the rift to the man:

'She wants you to be different.'

'But why can't she accept me as I am?'

'Because she loves you. . . .'

Again Guido thinks that he can resolve the situation by taking refuge in his imagination: not only Carla and Luisa but all the women he has admired or desired are together in a large country house; they are all happy there and make a great fuss of him. The older ones, now middle-aged, are confined to an upper floor, the younger ones join the company below. Guido makes a speech to his concubines before he sits down at table:

'Happiness is being able to tell the truth without hurting anyone. . . .'

But even in his dreams he cannot make this axiom work; the notes of 'The Ride of the Valkyries' break the enchantment of this amazing harem and incite the women to revolt. Guido can only subdue them with the aid of a whip, like a circus animal trainer, and the dream vanishes.

Now Guido must hold a press conference at the foot of the huge launching site of the space ship. The producer insists on his making an explanatory speech. Guido has no ideas and can find nothing to say; he is tempted to flee ignominiously, to confess that the film will not be made; he sees suicide as the only answer, but even suicide cannot resolve anything. While the fortress of lies collapses around Guido, all the characters find themselves at the foot of the disquieting symbol of the airship, as the sun goes down. Guido has his first really sincere and compassionate exchange of words with Luisa; 'Life is to be enjoyed, let's live it together. Accept me as I am.'

'I can try, if you will help me.'

At a sign from the illusionist, everyone links hands and dances gaily over a narrow bridge, as if it were the finale of a revue. Guido joins the circle with Luisa. The lights gradually fade as the last of the company, a clown, disappears. In the middle of the deserted meadow, there remains only the figure of Guido the child, the last image of a purity that had been lost, yet perhaps found again.

In substance, the story of *8½* explains why the film was made and what inspired Fellini in the creation of the different themes. The director comments himself as the film unfolds, replying (through the mouthpiece of the critic Carini) to the possible objections from the public and critics. This trick unites the novelty of invention with the skill of a great professional entertainer. The only moment in which the 'fictional film' departs from the 'real film' is at the end when hope of a reconciliation with himself and with his wife is restored to Guido.

Fellini had previously made another ending in which Guido was sitting with his wife in the restaurant car of the train which was taking them home. They were talking about a separation; then the train went into a tunnel, Guido felt slightly sick, and the carriage lit up and was filled with the people he had known in his life, but they were all happy, just as in the space ship scene. Even in this ending, discarded because it was less effective, Guido realized that he had to start again with Luisa.

'I realize that *8½* is such a shameless and brazen confession,' Fellini said to me, 'that it is futile to try and make people forget that it is about my own life. But I try to make a film that pleases me, first of all, and then the public. In *8½* the boundary line between what I did for myself and what I created for the public is very subtle.'

In fact *8½* is Fellini's complete autobiography to the extent that one of those inevitable matrimonial quarrels with Giulietta Masina have come to light, to the actress' dismay. But she, like Luisa in the film, understood and forgave Federico in the end, showing real courage in the unexpected revelations of this artistic and literary daydream.

'What I should like most', Fellini confesses even today, 'is that *8½* should help banish the neurotic complexes that obsess people who want to change others. I think people should be taken as they are. If the film restored this sense of freedom, then it succeeded. So *8½* is a film of liberation —nothing more. Unfortunately I know that intellectuals will go and dig up James Joyce (whom I have never read) and everything will run the risk of becoming confused. But I still maintain that it is a positive work, more positive than *La dolce vita* and that it has no negative characters. Take the critic who consistently and bitterly derides Guido's efforts to escape from the moral abyss into which he has fallen (and at one point Guido sees him hanged, in his daydream). Well, even he is a positive character, because he is right to quarrel with the hero. In fact, everyone in the film is right; Guido with his faults, his wife, the priests in their seminary who say that Saraghina is the devil (and to a certain extent she is and does represent the devil), and even Saraghina herself.'

This kind of psychological catharsis, in which everyone confesses himself unreservedly, finds an ideal visual background in the baths, which are like the Valley of Jeosophat with its race of white phantoms, in which time is measured in fixed hours; an evanescent Limbo where everyone meets again and the images and faces of the past are recognized. The Cardinal acquires a precise meaning and character; from the beginning Fellini wanted him to be one of the key figures in the film, a mysterious being outside time, whom Guido carries in his heart from his distant childhood, a messianic omen of some miraculous power which restores peace and faith to the spirit. He is the image of Fellini's primitive religious faith, a mixture of catholicism and superstition, to which he has always remained attached in his films, with almost childish insistence. But reason tells him that this remedy alone is not sufficient, that it is an over-simplification and that his problems can find their solution only in himself. ('Who told you that you were born to be happy?' the Cardinal replies to an anxious question.)

In *8½* the Cardinal is played by Tito Masini, once an employee in the tax department, an old man of eighty-six, who was discovered by chance as he was leaving a library. While shooting was in progress Fellini treated him with the respectful consideration he would really have accorded to an eminent prelate, as if he wished to create the illusion of his character's identity and regretted the pretence imposed by the nature of the work.

When the film was shown to the Italian public in February '63 (at the exact time when the heroine, Sandra Milo, gave birth to a little girl), it had an immediate success, though not to the same extent as *La dolce vita.* It was most popular with women, the members of the audience Fellini had feared above all, probably because he thought he had treated them badly in the film. On the contrary, feminine imagination was caught by the incredible mixture of reality and dream in *8½*, in which they recognized thoughts and visions which had been secretly hidden in their subconscious. Perhaps not all understood the intellectual aspects of the film, thus proving the director right when he had been careful to explain that while the film spoke the language of sincerity, it was less intellectual than might appear.

'If you have the courage to confess that which is buried within you,' Federico said, 'if you can bear, as I can, to judge yourself, then I don't think you can call yourself an intellectual in the derogatory sense used in the cinema.'

The critics were disconcerted and divided at first, because of the difficulty of defining clearly, after *La dolce vita*, a work even broader in scope and the universality of its motives and themes which attempted to understand all things and all people from a personal and autobiographical standpoint. Some hailed *8½* as the director's masterpiece, admiring the novelty of its style, and others found the self-confession reticent and insincere, condemning its nebulous conception and the confusion of the underlying themes. Besides the current of left-wing criticism which, as had been foreseen, spoke of 'decadent agnosticism', 'excessive individualism', and 'recurrent delirium', were some who accepted in principle the 'anti-novel' idea, expounded and carried out by the director, but questioned its originality, citing Resnais and Bergman and, outside the cinema, Pirandello in *Sei personaggi* (*Six Characters in Search of an Author*) and *Questa sera si recita a soggetto* (*To-night we improvise*).

From Le tentazioni del dottor Antonio *to* 8½ *(1960-62)*

I see *8½* as the culmination of a theme begun by Fellini in *I vitelloni*, continued in *La strada*, *Cabiria*, and *La dolce vita*. *8½* contains Fellini's strongest and weakest qualities, but they are no longer hidden behind the traditional means of expression in the cinema, but have been presented in their purest form. Consequently, whatever there is of geniality, intoxication, defects and doubts contained in the director's art has come to the surface with extraordinary clearness. If *La dolce vita* was a courageous film, *8½* is even more so; in it Fellini is propelled by an irresistible desire to achieve a moral clarification at any cost to himself, as an example to others. He has overcome the danger of becoming the mouthpiece of a philosophy which is increasingly subjective and egocentric, leading only to isolation; he has done this through the strength of the poetry and the sureness and clarity of the images, even in the dream sequence.

Through that clarity, *8½* is presented as a genial work, which only Fellini could have conceived and made without allowing the disorganization of the motifs and the different planes on which the story is told to force his hand. For the sake of analysis a distinction should be made between the theories and the form of expression, even though they are closely linked in *8½*. Let it suffice to observe that one of the director's greatest qualities is the ability to adapt his ideas to the images.

With regard to the theme it should be noted that the confession of a crisis which is, fundamentally, the basis of *8½*, is not as consistently sincere as the director would have wished it to be. The best scenes in the film are those recording childhood and youthful memories, in which the director has described himself more frankly. They are superior to the others in which Guido expresses his dissatisfaction and uncertainty as an adult. ('It is time to have finished with symbols,' Guido murmurs at one point. 'And what if I have made a mess of everything?') The poetical evocations of the past revive an atmosphere of purity and simple emotions, often bordering on perfection. One of the most suggestive sequences is that in the cemetery—a desolate tract—in which Guido meets his father for the last time. Guido has never understood him or talked to him enough. Here the sense of an inability to communicate, of cold abstraction, is transmuted into sadly positive terms; the symbol becomes poetic reality.

The same may be said of Guido as a child in his grandmother's house and in the seminary, with the confession of his first sin in desiring a woman. The geometrical composition of the black confessionals against the bare white background of a room that has no well-defined limits exactly conveys a sense of guilt that identifies us all with the young boy. Sometimes the rejection of reality, instead of heightening the hero's crisis, reveals his intimate weakness, the arrogant vanity of the superman who thinks that he can do anything, as in the long harem sequence which combines in embarrassing promiscuity elements of his childhood (the doting aunts) with the adult's desires and facts of sexual life.

The ending, in which Guido is reconciled with his wife on the basis of a compromise, contains the most striking theme of *8½*: that we cannot change other people and that every attempt to do so is fruitless.

'Accept me for what I am,' Guido seems to say (and with him, Fellini). 'Accept me with my faults, my complexes, my genuine qualities, but don't try to change me. In exchange, I will give you the best of myself.' It is certainly an interesting point of view, though very one-sided and egoistic, so much so that one begins to wonder how long the momentary harmony between Guido and his wife will last on this slender presumption. Thus the freedom which Guido finally appears to grasp melts away into the satisfaction of being understood, rather than in the desire to understand another. In other words, the resolution of the crisis adds up to the materialistic concept: 'Let me do as I please, without asking me to account for anything. I will repay you by continuing to entertain you, telling you the truth, but my own version of it.'

Fortunately Fellini's artistic integrity touches upon more noble and demanding ideals, and often coincides with the common need for a universal truth, for the fulfilment of certain vague, unexpressed desires which lie within us, upon which *8½* acts as a catalyst. If the anguish and insecurity of our condition are assuaged by the discovery of a similar insecurity in others, then in this sense *8½* has achieved its purpose.

The whole film is enclosed within a framework which presents a new aspect of reality. Guido's profession as a director allows more than a superficial glance at a multicoloured, agitated, unstable, fascinating tinsel world which Fellini knows so well, the world of the cinema. This behind-the-scenes description of the making of a film shows us unforgettable many-sided characters, from the great producer to actors in search of work, from odd-job men to pseudo-intellectuals, in an atmosphere of gossip, improvisation, idleness, frantic action—all typical of film-making.

What I find least convincing about *8½*, placing it beneath *La dolce vita* on the aesthetic level, is the insufficient fusion of all its various elements, a harmony which would have avoided their dispersion. Where Fellini succeeded miraculously in *La dolce vita*, he only partially succeeded in this film; consequently there is not just one rhythm but several, corresponding to odd moments. And if we are often amazed by the lyrical fluency of the picture and are able to abandon ourselves as the author suggests to the rise and fall of emotion without thinking of anything else, this hypnotic state of grace does not last, and we shake ourselves and ask the meaning of this or that character, and the illusion is broken.

The old *viveur* Mezzabotta, the Cardinal, the mysterious woman, the sarcastic critic, the alluring girl whom Fellini introduced into the film, are individually alive and unconstrained artistically, but when they appear together, fleetingly, in unexpected corners, they do not always form a unified whole. The presence of this motley and bizarre crowd and the virtuosity of the continual changes in dimension makes one think of an ingenious game of Chinese puzzle-boxes, in which truth and reality and yet more dreams and transfigurations of every kind follow endlessly, one upon the other. The exercise was exhausting and sometimes Fellini has shown that he asked too much of his own skill, as in the nightmarish sequence of the screen tests, *a film within the film described by another film.*

An excess of symbolism might have been another weakness of *8½* if the author's poetic intuition and his strong sense of performance had not restricted the symbols to an aesthetically acceptable sphere and prevented the film from slipping into the type of work called 'literary' which is extraneous to Fellini's interests. Once more Fellini has found his most successful vein in the world of fantasy, or rather in the skill with which he is able to mould the fantasy to suit the needs of a reality transformed by his inventiveness. No one in the world rivals him in these gifts, which he has used to enrich the narrative and stylistic themes of *8½*, to endow it with an atmosphere of enchantment.

It is almost superfluous to comment upon the elegant photography, which is probably superior to that of any other of Fellini's films, thanks to Gianni di Venanzo's skill and the way in which the director has yet again been able to induce the actors to extemporize. Besides Mastroianni, who tried to imitate Fellini in every physical detail (including the hat rammed on the back of his head), the best performance was given by Sandra Milo who played the part of Guido's rich friend with intelligence. Anouk Aimée, Annibale Ninchi and Giuditta Rissone (the father and mother in the graveyard scene) were also excellent, but Claudia Cardinale remained in the shadows, due to the lack of depth in the character she played.

Two months after the première, *8½* was shown at the Cannes Film Festival, but there it was 'barred' by the previous triumph of *La dolce vita*, and Visconti's *Gattopardo* (*The Leopard*), which won first prize. At the beginning of summer '63, the film had a noisy comeback when it was victorious in the Moscow Festival, in the heart of the most conservative and traditional stronghold of the cinema. The young poet Yevtuschenko met Fellini in the Soviet capital and expressed his enthusiasm.

'What can we do after your film? You have said everything, you have shown in masterly terms how difficult and thorny is the search for truth. Your film is our film!'

Soviet bureaucrats vainly tried to contradict this declaration by stating that the film was 'far from the lives of the people, and on seeing it one is overcome with sadness and pessimism'.

More prizes were showered upon *8½* in April, 1964, when it was awarded an Oscar (the third awarded to Fellini, who went to California in person to receive it) for the best foreign film, while another Oscar was awarded to Gherardi for his costumes in a black and white film. A few days previously the film had obtained seven silver ribbons, an absolute record for what are considered to be the 'Italian Oscars'. These enjoy considerable prestige because they are awarded by the direct secret vote of all the Italian critics, without any foreign influence whatsoever. The greatest number previously awarded had been the six of fifteen years before given to De Sica's *Ladri di biciclette* (*Bicycle Thieves*). The 1964 ribbons recognized in some way all the collaborators of *8½*, and not just Fellini the director; Rizzoli, the producer, the art-directors, Sandro Milo as the best non-leading actress, Rota for the music, de Venanzo for the black and white photography.

Once again in *8½* Fellini's inventiveness puts the work of his partners (Pirelli, Flajano, Rondi) in the shade, and of the two 'rough scripts' which were said to have been amalgamated into the film, little remains in the final version, so that the provisional screenplay (published by Camilla Cederna in her book on *8½*) differs greatly from that made *a posteriori* from the film copy circulated for public viewing.

One last observation should be made on the black and white photography for which that magician of the camera, de Venanzo, was justly awarded a 'ribbon'. Fellini experimented with colour in the *Boccaccio '70* episode, but has not felt inclined to use it again, because his creations are better expressed by the grey, muted, rather mysterious tones of black and white. ('Dreams are never in colour,' he says.)

Statuettes, shields, prizes (someone has counted sixty for *8½* alone), recognition, success, have not, however, unduly affected the director, who merely comments somewhat sceptically: 'Now when I go by you can hear the tinkling of medals—I'm like an old retired general.' For him *8½* is now a closed chapter and he is preparing to open another, which will perhaps involve him more deeply, entitled '*Giulietta e gli spiriti*' (*Giulietta and the Spirits*). This film has been stimulated by the long period of inactivity of Giulietta Masina as an actress and by the subtle but deep remorse which Fellini has felt for having discarded the faithful companion of *La strada* and *Cabiria*. There was also the question of moral compensation to be offered Giulietta for having so openly alluded to their intimate conjugal relations in *8½*, compensation which both wife and actress richly deserve. And so in spring 1963, Fellini found himself involved with seers, magicians, little tables and 'chains' of spiritual séances, in which Giulietta is a convinced participant. He began to work out the plot for *Giulietta e gli spiriti*, the story of a madwoman (or rather, one subject to hallucinations) who has continual visions which are a mixture of the most absurd fantasies, from grandfather's ascent in balloons to Martians landing on the earth. Once again there are clear affinities with the grotesque elements of *8½*, with an echo of *La strada* in the figure of the heroine. But no one until he has seen the film (still in preparation in spring 1964) can tell what surprises the new plot, so bizarre yet so congenial to Fellini's temperament, holds in store for us.

But it will be a very demanding film (amongst the actors we shall see Totò and Valentina Cortese, besides some big Hollywood name), and the director is conscious of his responsibility towards audiences and critics the world over. Like one of the illusionists he has so often portrayed, he realizes that his task is becoming more and more difficult every year, and that everyone continually expects more of him.

With the spotlights in position and at the roll of drums, Fellini is ready to begin his new 'turn'. But he is not an easily frightened man; of course he is not the thoughtless *vitellone* of his youth in Rimini. In his deep-set eyes there lies the dark shadow of a maturity which has been gained through hard, tenacious fighting. Some of his friends even say that Fellini is becoming melancholy. 'It is the artist's fate always to move forward, never to turn round and contemplate the past or rest on his laurels,' he says. And indeed the director has never, quite literally, favoured the three or four hundred prizes of every description, plaques, cups, medals and diplomas which fill a whole room in his apartment in Rome, with more than an abstracted glance.

Fellini's real strength, his motivating force, lies in his innate curiosity: as long as he is able and inclined to observe the passionate reality which surrounds him, eternally changing and renewing, we can expect new masterpieces from him. But only time will tell us the direction in which he will move, the paths he intends to follow and the objectives which will inspire him. Will he continue along his path of 'poetical investigation', will he try to give new dimensions to neo-realism, or will he penetrate deeper into the magical, occult world which has always fascinated him so much? We can certainly say that Fellini will remain true to himself, and to his public, because of a moral obligation which is part of his character.

At a recent conference of Czechoslovakian cinema personalities (reported in an interview in *Europa*), one of them said, with reference to *La dolce vita*, that Fellini's films are like atoms. This is a definition which is entirely fitting and conclusive for all Fellini's work, and at the same time it is a synthesis of his art. Each one of his films is a perfect atom, consisting of a simple nucleus with more complicated particles that revolve around it. Nothing can be added or taken away without spoiling the mathematical regularity of its construction. This creator of cinematic atoms is preparing to make another link for the chain. He really is a symbol of modern man, who is projected by the thrust of progress ever onwards into the future, towards the farthest edge of experience vital to the whole of humanity.

Bibliography and Films

BIBLIOGRAPHY

Agel, Geneviève: 'Les chemins de Fellini' suivi du 'Journal d'un bidioniste', par Dominique Delouche, Préface de Roberto Rossellini. '7e Art', Les éditions du Cerf, Paris 1956.

Aristarco, Guido, in *Cinema nuovo*, no. 143, January–February, 1960, pp. 39–44. (*La dolce vita.*)

Aristarco, Guido, in *Cinema* (nuova serie) no. 55, 1 February, 1951, pp. 49–50. (*Luci del varietà.*)

Baragli, Enrico S. J. in *La civiltà cattolica*, vol. iii, 17 September, 1960, no. 2646, pp. 602–617. ('Dopo *La dolce vita* ' I: 'Tra realtà, arte e religione').

Baragli, Enrico S. J. in *La civiltà cattolica*, vol. iv, 15 October 1960, no. 2648, pp. 159–176. ('Dopo *La dolce vita* ' II: Critici, registi e pubblico.')

Bianchi, Pietro, *L'occhio del cinema*, Garzanti, Milano, 1957, pp. 57–62. ('Federico Fellini: *Il bidone.*')

Carpi, Fabio, *Cinema italiano del dopoguerra*, Schwarz, Milano, 1958, pp. 45–50 (ch. vii).

Castello, G. C., *Il cinema neorealistico italiano*, Edizioni RAI, Milano, 1956 pp. 54–61, and 71–76. (ch. x. 'Fellini', and app. i, *Il bidone.*)

Castello, G. C., in *Cinema* (nuova serie) nos. 99–100, 15–31 December, 1952, pp. 335–337. (*Lo Sceicco bianco.*)

Castello , G. C., in *Cinema* (nuova serie), no. 116, 31 August, 1953, pp. 109. ('Troppi "leoni" al Lido.')

Castello, G. C., in *Cinema* (nuova serie) no. 123, 15 December, 1953, pp. 339–342. (*L'amore in città.*)

Cavicchioli, Luigi, in *Oggi*, no. 30, 1954, pp. 26–28.

Cederna, Camilla, in *Espresso-mese*, July, 1960, pp. 54–63 and 108–109. ('Confesso Fellini.')

Chiarini, Luigi, *Panorama del cinema contemporaneo (1954–57)*, Edizioni di Bianco e Nero, Roma, 1957, pp. 139–148. (ch. 'Federico Fellini.')

Del Fra Lino, *Le notti di Cabiria di Federico Fellini.* 'Dal soggetto al film', collane cinematografica divetta da Renzo Renzi, Cappelli, Bologna, 1957.

Fellini, Federico, in *La table ronde*, no. 149, May, 1960, Librarie Plon, Paris, pp. 47–51.

Cederna, Camilla, *8½ di Federico Fellini*, Bologna, 1963.

Fellini, Federico, *La strada*, Aux éditions du Seuil, Paris, 1955 (plot and staging).

Fellini, Federico, in *Bianco e Nero*, Year XIX, no. 7, July, 1958, pp. 3–4. ('Crusi e neorealismo.')

Fellini-Flajano-Pinelli, in *Cinema* (nuova serie), no. 99–100, 15–31 December, 1952, pp. 289–293. (*I Vitelloni.*)

Ferrara, Giuseppe, *Il nuovo cinema italiano*, Le Monnier, Firenze, 1957, pp. 304–309, 344 and following.

Gromo, Mario, *Film visiti*, Edizioni di Bianco e Nero, Roma, 1957, pp. 376–377, 470–472, 522–524, 537–539.

Kezich, Tullio, "*La dolce vita*" *di Federico Fellini*. 'Dal soggetto al film', collana cinematografica diretta da Renzo Renzi, Cappelli, Bologna, 1959.

Mangini, Cecilia, in *Cinema nuovo*, no. 66, 10 September, 1955, pp. 174–175. ('I due bidoni.')

Mida, Massimo, in *Cinema* (nuova serie), no. 47, 1 October, 1950, p. 171. ('Fellini fra le luci del varietà.')

Mida, Massimo, in *Cinema* (nuova serie), no. 95, 1 October, 1952, pp. 163–165. ('Fellini, Diogene del cinema.')

Redi, Riccardo, in *Cinema* (nuova serie), no. 130, 31 March, 1954, pp. 163–165. (*La strada.*)

Renzi, Renzo, *Federico Fellini*, 'Piccola bibliotoca del cinema', Guanda, Parma, 1956.

Solmi, Angelo, in *Oggi*, no. 15, 1952 (*Lo Sceicco bianco*); no. 40, 1953 (*I vitelloni*); no. 39, 1954 (*La strada*); no. 43, 1957 (*Le notti di Cabiria*); no. 48, 1959 and no. 7, 1960 (*La dolce vita*); no. 33, 1961 (*Lo Sceicco bianco*). Nos. 7 and 9, 1963.

Spinazzola, Vittorio, *Film 1961*, Feltrinelli, Milano, 1961, pp. 63–72 ('Devo essere sincero per forza': interview by Gideon Bachmann with Fellini, taken from 'Film: Book I, The Audience and the Film-maker', ed. by Robert Hughes, Grove Press Inc., New York).

Various authors in *Cinema* (nuova serie), no. 139, 10 August, 1954. The issue is mainly dedicated to *La strada*, with articles by Stefano Ubezio, Fausto Montesanti, Federico Fellini, Tullio Pinelli, Ennio Flajano,

Giulietta Masina, Brunello Rondi, Moraldo Rossi, Luigi Giacosi, pp. 443–458.

The plot of *Moraldo in città* was published in *Cinema* (nuova serie), no. 139, 10 August, 1954; no. 142, 10 October, 1954; no. 144, 10 November, 1954; no. 145, 25 November, 1954; nos. 146–147, 10–25 December, 1954.

The staging of *La strada* was published in *Bianco e Nero*, Year XV, nos. 9–10, September–October, 1954.

The staging of *La dolce vita*, compiled after the film was made, was published in English by Hollis Alpert in the 'Ballantine Books' series (101 Fifth Avenue, New York, 1961).

FILMS

1. *Luci del varietà*, 1950

Production: 'Capitolium Film'. Direction: Alberto Lattuada and Federico Fellini. Script: Fellini. Staging: Fellini, Lattuada, Pinelli and Flajano. Photography: Otello Martelli. Art Direction: Aldo Buzzi. Music: Felice Lattuada.

Cast: Peppino De Filippo (Checco Dalmonte), Carla Del Poggio (Liliana), Giulietta Masina (Melina), John Kitzmiller, Folco Lulli, Franca Valeri, Carlo Romano, Silvio Bagolini, Dante Maggio, Gina Mascetti, Caprioli and Bonucci.

2. *Lo Sceicco bianco*, 1952

Production: 'P.D.C.' (producer Luigi Rovere). Direction: Federico Fellini. Script: Fellini, Antonioni and Pinelli. Staging: Fellini, Pinelli and Flajano. Photography: Arturo Gallea. Music: Rota.

Cast: Brunella Bovo (Wanda), Leopoldo Trieste (Ivan Cavalli), Alberto Sordi (lo Sceicco bianco—the white sheik), Giulietta Masina (Cabiria), Ernesto Almirante (the strip-comic director), Fanny Marchiò (Marilena Velardi), Enzo Maggio, Lilia Landi, Gina Mascetti.

3. *I vitelloni*, 1953

Production: 'Peg Film'—'Cité Films'. Direction: Federico Fellini. Script and staging: Fellini, Flajano, Pinelli. Photography: Trasatti, Martelli and Carlini. Art Direction: Mario Chiari. Music: Rota.

Cast: Franco Interlenghi (Moraldo), Alberto Sordi (Alberto), Franco Fabrizi (Fausto), Leopoldo Trieste (Leopoldo), Riccardo Fellini (Riccardo), Leonora Ruffo (Sandra), Carlo Romano, Enrico Viarisio, Paola Borboni, Lyda Baarova, Vira Silenti, Achille Majeroni, Silvio Bagolini, Franca Gandolfi.

FEDERICO FELLINI

**Un' agencia matrimoniale*, 1953

Production: 'Faro Film'. An episode of *Amore in città*, the first film-investigation of the *Spectator*, directed by Cesare Zavattini. Direction: Federico Fellini. Script and Staging: Fellini and Pinelli. Photography: Di Venanzo. Art Direction: G. Polidoro. Music: Nascimbene.

Cast: real-life characters with some actors from the Experimental Cinema Centre.

4. *La strada*, 1954

Production: 'Ponti-De Laurentiis'. Direction: Federico Fellini. Script: Fellini and Pinelli. Staging: Fellini, Flajano, Pinelli. Photography: Martelli. Art Direction: Ravasco (costumes by M. Marinari). Music: Rota. General organization: Giacosi.

Cast: Giulietta Masina (Gelsomina), Anthony Quinn (Zampanò), Richard Basehart (the 'Madman'), Aldo Silvani, Marcella Rovena, Lidia Venturini.

5. *Il bidone*, 1955

Production: 'Titanus'. Direction: Federico Fellini. Script and staging: Fellini, Pinelli, Flajano. Photography: Martelli. Art Direction: Cecchi. Music: Rota. Editor: Serandrei.

Cast: Broderick Crawford (Augusto), Richard Basehart ('Picasso'), Franco Fabrizi (Roberto), Giulietta Masina (Iris), Xenia Valderi, Alberto De Amicis, Lorella De Luca, Sue Ellen Blake.

6. *Le notti di Cabiria*, 1956

Production: 'Dino de Laurentiis' (distribution: 'Paramount'). Direction: Federico Fellini. Script and staging: Fellini, Flajano, Pinelli (adaptation of Roman dialogue: Pier Paolo Pasolini). Photography: Tonti and Martelli. Art direction: Gherardi. Music: Rota. Editor: Cattozzo.

Cast: Giulietta Masina (Cabiria), Amedeo Nazzari (the actor), François Périer (the accountant D'Onofrio), Aldo Silvani (the illusionist), Franca Marzi (Wanda), Dorian Gray (Jessy), Mario Passante, Ennio Girolami, Christian Tassou.

7. *La dolce vita*, 1959

Production: 'Riama Film'—'Pathé Consortium Cinema'. (Producer: Giuseppe Amato.) Distribution: 'Cineriz'. Direction: Federico Fellini. Script: Fellini, Pinelli, Flajano. Staging: Fellini, Pinelli, Flajano, Rondi. Photography: Martelli. Art Direction: Gherardi. Music: Rota. Editor: Cattozzo.

Cast: Marcello Mastroianni (Marcello Rubini), Walter Santesso (Paparazzo), Anouk Aimée (Maddalena), Anita Ekberg (Sylvia), Yvonne Fourneaux (Emma), Lex Barker (Robert), Alan Dijon (Frankie), Alain

Cuny (Steiner), Valeria Ciangottini (Paola), Renée Longarini (Mrs. Steiner), Annibale Ninchi (Marcello's father), Polidor (Clown), Magali Noël (Fanny), Giulio Questi (don Giulio), Nadia Gray (Nadia), Mino Doro, Jacques Sernas, Laura Betti, Daniela Calvino, Riccardo Garrone, Enrico Glori, Franca Pasutt.

8. *Le tentazioni del dottor Antonio*, 1961
Production: 'Carlo Ponti' (distribution 'Cineriz'). Episode of *Boccaccio '70*, 'a joke' in four acts from an idea by Cesare Zavattini. Direction: Federico Fellini. Script and staging: Fellini, Flajano, Pinelli (Collaborators: Brunello Rondi and Goffredo Parise). Photography: Martelli. Art Direction: Piero Zuffi. Music: Rota. Editor: Cattozzo.
Cast: Peppino De Filippo (dottor Antonio Mazzuolo), Anita Ekberg (Anita), Antonio Acqua (commendator La Pappa), Donatella Della Nora (Mazzuolo's sister), Monique Berger.

8½ Otto e mezzo, 1962
Production: Angelo Rizzoli (distribution 'Cineriz'). Direction: Federico Fellini. Script: Federico Fellini, Ennio Flajano. Staging: Fellini, Pinelli, Flajano, Rondi. Photography: Gianni di Venanzo. Settings: Gherardi. Music: Rota. Editing: Cattozzo.
Cast: Marcello Mastroianni (Guido), Sandra Milo (Carla, the mistress), Anouk Aimée (Luisa, the wife), Claudia Cardinale (Claudia, the girl at the baths), Rossella Falk (Rossella, friend of Luisa), Guido Alberti (the producer), Barbara Steele (Gloria, Mezzabotta's friend), Mezzabotta (Mario Pisu), Jean Rougeul (Carini, the critic), Marco Gemini (Guido, the child).

Note. In fact the question of the numbering, according to Fellini whilst he was making *8½*, is as follows: seven of the films count as one each, and three (*Luci del varietà*, *Un'agenzia matrimoniale*, and *Le tentazioni del dottor Antonio*) each count as a half, a total of one and a half. Thus $7+1\frac{1}{2}=8\frac{1}{2}$. This is the correct order which should satisfy both the producer and the mathematicians:

½. *Luci del varietà* (in partnership with Lattuada)
1½. *Lo Sceicco bianco*
2½. *I vitelloni*
3. *Un'agenzia matrimoniale* (episode)
4. *La strada*
5. *Il bidone*
6. *Le notti di Cabiria*
7. *La dolce vita*
7½. *Le tentazioni del dottor Antonio* (episode)
8½. *Otto e mezzo*